BRAVE
NEW
KNITS

BRAVE NEW KNITS

26 PROJECTS AND PERSONALITIES FROM **THE KNITTING BLOGOSPHERE**

JULIE TURJOMAN

Foreword by Jessica Marshall Forbes, Cofounder of Ravelry.com

Photography by Jared Flood of Brooklyn Tweed

RODALE

Rodale books may be purchased for business or promotional use or for special sales. For information, please write to: Special Markets Department, Rodale Inc., 733 Third Avenue, New York, NY 10017

Printed in the United States of America
Rodale Inc. makes every effort to use acid-free ♾, recycled paper ♺.

Book design by Christina Gaugler

Library of Congress Cataloging-in-Publication Data

Turjoman, Julie.
     Brave new knits : 26 projects and personalities from the knitting blogosphere / Julie Turjoman, foreword by Jessica Marshall Forbes.
          p.   cm.
     Includes index.
     ISBN-13: 978–1–60529–590–9   paperback
     ISBN-10: 1–60529–590–6   paperback
     1. Knitting—Patterns.   I. Title.
TT820.T86 2010
746.43'2—dc22   2010017169

Distributed to the trade by Macmillan

     4   6   8   10   9   7   5   paperback

We inspire and enable people to improve their lives and the world around them.

CONTENTS

PART 1: Garments (or Sweater Designers Tackle the Infinite Universe)

PART 2: Accessories (or A Little Luxury Goes a Long Way)

FOREWORD

The book you're about to enjoy explores a topic that's near and dear to me: the mingling of knitters and the Internet. When my husband, Casey, and I started Ravelry more than three years ago, I was just one of thousands of knit bloggers, trying to keep up with all the crafty things happening online. I had no idea our little site would blossom into the community it has become. But I couldn't be more thrilled that this is where we ended up.

I guess you could say Ravelry started with my need for a hobby. I taught myself to knit in 2004 with a little help from my local yarn shop and—I admit it—*Knitting for Dummies*. I was quickly hooked, despite making a tragic hat that would fit no living human. Naturally, I wanted to find other people who knit, too. One day Casey happened upon a knitting blog, which led him to another, and then another. We were amazed at how many knitters were blogging! I began following many of these blogs, and I even made friends from around the world along the way. Soon I wanted a blog, too, so Casey and I teamed up to make frecklegirl. com, where I started writing in May 2004.

There was just one problem with my newfound knitting community: The amount of inspiration and information available through it was staggering—and completely scattered. The only way to keep up was with an overloaded RSS reader and many, many bookmarks.

After a while I became frustrated with this inadequate system of organization, and who got to hear about it more than Casey? He started talking casually about how it could be neat to have an online database of pattern and yarn information that linked blogs and Web sites together. It would have to be easy to search, simple for users to make contributions, and, of course, pretty, with photos of projects and yarn. I really liked the idea, so we started playing around with it. We posted a mock-up of what the site would look like on my blog, and the positive feedback it received encouraged us to keep going.

When we first opened Ravelry to test among my knitting and blogging friends, it was far from finished. Fortunately, this didn't affect their ability to understand where we were headed. Timing was everything; a lot of them were comfortable with collaborative and social Web sites, so we didn't really have to explain things, like why we put so much emphasis on public sharing or connecting things like patterns and people.

Ravelry, like many grassroots organizations, evolved through the contributions of the community it was designed to serve. Our early test group helped us see the site's potential and motivated us to quickly make improvements and open it up to a broader audience. Before we knew it, we had more users than we ever dreamed of, functions we might never have thought up on our own, and just the right place for me to satisfy my urge to meticulously organize all my yarn, needles, projects, patterns . . . well, you get the picture.

One of the things that makes us so proud of Ravelry is how it has helped independent designers bring their creations to a large, concentrated audience. It's astounding how many patterns exist in the world. Really, with online self-publishing, nearly anyone, from casual dabbler to professional, can put a pattern out there. But on Ravelry, designers can promote their work and build a community around it. In essence, they can create a name for themselves without a magazine, book publisher, or yarn company backing up their work. That said, this isn't an issue of traditional publishing versus shiny, new, electronic publishing. Books and magazines haven't become irrelevant; they just have to bend a little to the new, ever-changing publishing landscape.

Considering how the yarn-loving community has embraced Ravelry, it might seem as if we have a secret code for what works for knitters online and why. We don't. While there is something a little magical about how the social Internet and old-school yarn crafts made such a strong connection, the phenomenon is also somewhat ordinary. Today, creative types from every discipline use the Internet to create their personal brands, self-publish their work, and communicate directly with their fans—just like designers do on Ravelry. People seem to crave real, personal connections with the businesses and artists they support. And knitters and crocheters, I am proud to say, seem to be at the front of this new wave, with young and old joining the online ranks every day.

As far as craft and the Internet and Ravelry and where it's all headed—honestly, I don't know for sure. But if Ravelry has revealed anything, it's that our community is full of creative and passionate people who are ready to contribute and try new things. Any of them could be the next breakout designer, blogger, and yarn-dyer . . . and we can't wait to see what they do next.

—*Jessica Marshall Forbes*
Cofounder of Ravelry.com

INTRODUCTION

When I discovered the blogosphere in general and knitting blogs in particular in 2005, the wonders of this brave new online world seemed overwhelming. Although I was elated to find a passionate, like-minded community that shared my obsession with all things knitting-related, it was also a shock to realize that I was so late to the party. As I tumbled excitedly down the rabbit hole of knitting blogs—because each new discovery led to yet another, equally captivating one—this universe expanded to include online patterns, amazingly comprehensive YouTube technique tutorials, and, of course, fiber shopping opportunities to supplement the offerings at my local yarn shop.

But best of all were the personalities I encountered on these blogs—the dozens of knitters who share everything from their latest stash enhancements to swatching conundrums, from works in progress to finished projects, from personal triumphs and tragedies to political and philosophical musings. Whether a blogger writes from Boston or San Francisco, New York or New Mexico, Canada or Finland, each invites me into the world—and the life—he or she inhabits. I meet his pets, her children; I discover her favorite yarns and patterns, his latest how-did-I-ever-survive-without-it tools—all with a click of the mouse.

I became a devoted lurker on my favorite blogs, bookmarking them so I could check in weekly (and sometimes, I confess, daily) on what these bloggers were making and what was happening in their lives. I began to feel as if I knew them; their words seemed as familiar as those of old friends, even though most details of their personal lives unfolded tantalizingly off the page.

Many of my favorite bloggers were also designers, and much of what fascinated me about their blogs had to do with their latest creations. Their styles and design preferences were as diverse as their blog personalities. Reading the details of their projects, I sympathized with their creative challenges and marveled at their sources of inspiration (nature! architecture! science!). It was fascinating to read their impressions of the yarns they chose for their projects and why. Their exacting standards and technical expertise both impressed and inspired me, and the humor with which they described their not-always-successful knitting experiments made them and their commentary seem all the more grounded and human.

When they posted photos from trips to the meccas of TNNA (The National NeedleArts Association) or Rhinebeck, from the nationwide Stitches conventions to local sheep-to-shawl festivals and county fairs, I felt almost as if I'd been there, too. But most of all, I appreciated the sense of community these designers fostered—their open acknowledgment that we're all in this together, to learn from one another, to share our wealth of knitting knowledge, and to create garments and accessories of lasting practicality, warmth, and beauty.

Then, in the late spring of 2007, Ravelry.com was born, starting a revolution of seismic force in the online knitting community. The creation of Boston couple Jessica Marshall Forbes and Casey Forbes, Ravelry offers knitters the same social networking opportunities as Facebook, the photo-sharing joys of Flickr, and the encyclopedic information of Wikipedia, but with a laser focus on knitting (and the big-tent inclusion of corollary craft crochet adds an extra dimension). Each registered user—and at press time that number is more than 700,000 with more than 2,000 new members joining every week—can document her yarn stash or his knitting book library; can queue up the next dozen projects as well as share the details of each one as it rolls off the needles; can seek or offer technical support and tutorials; and can quickly and easily find interest groups who are fans of individual designers, specific yarns, or even preferred types of knitting projects.

Clearly, blogging has changed knitting, yet knitting has influenced its little corner of the blogosphere in equally potent ways. The knitting community is one of the most fortunate subcultures to benefit from the rise of social networking sites on the Internet. I wondered why no one had assembled the staggering talents of this group in book form. It struck me that the most successful designer-bloggers have compelling personal stories, and that the larger knitting community would love to learn more about them.

Some of the designers featured in *Brave New Knits* are supernovas in the knitting universe, and others are bright new stars just beginning to make their presence known. Yet they share common ground—a combination of remarkable creative skill, irresistible blog identity, and generosity in sharing their designs with our community. The occasional podcast and magazine profile notwithstanding, until now there has been no single resource in which to share the success stories that are so closely linked to their blogs.

And what better way for the new technology to connect with knitters than with traditional print media? After all, the knitters among us who log on daily love our treasured knitting books as much as we do our favorite online resources. It is no coincidence that Ravelry offers its members a place to catalog their knitting books, just as it is no coincidence that many book publishers link individual projects from Ravelry to printed knitting books. Each enhances the other in ways none of us imagined even a decade ago.

While knitting blogs, Ravelry, and the online knitting community offer a special immediacy—instant knitting gratification for the twenty-first century—we return time and again to our libraries of knitting books for both inspiration and information. Holding these volumes in our hands, turning each page to compare the temptingly photographed projects, and then deciding which to make first; these are the most basic of many pleasures we take from our dog-eared books. For knitters, this fusion of old-school handcraft and modern technology represents an unlikely—yet wildly successful—synthesis of old and new, captured here for the first time in *Brave New Knits*.

Julie

PART 1

Garments
(or Sweater Designers Tackle the Infinite Universe)

When knitwear designers create a new garment, they are truly limited only by the scope of their imaginations. And it must be acknowledged that knitwear designers are an especially imaginative bunch. When designers are also bloggers, they give their readers the opportunity to participate vicariously in their design process. They may post swatch photos representing potential stitch combinations or construction techniques. Their readers probably learn about the inspiration that first led to the creation of each new garment. And it's likely they also bear witness to the various challenges and iterations that go along with the creation of a new project.

An original sweater pattern is a huge creative undertaking for any designer, no matter how experienced. The blogger-designers whose stories follow have been generous enough to share some of that process with the readers of *Brave New Knits*.

Connie Chang Chinchio, Physicsknits

Needing a respite from her PhD classes in condensed matter physics, Connie learned to knit in her second year of graduate school. Mostly, she wanted to make a personal gift for the boyfriend who is now her husband. "I thought, why not knit him a scarf?" Undeterred by the fact that she had not picked up needles and yarn since her grandmother had taught her to knit at age 6, she was pleasantly surprised to find that muscle memory took over, and she swiftly relearned the basics.

A garment struck her as the ideal second project, despite never having knit one before. Fortuitously, a friend had recently opened a yarn shop near the university and asked Connie to knit up several of the store samples, offering to pay her in yarn credit. The arrangement was a success, and it wasn't long before her stash grew to "obscene" proportions. Her only complaint is that the yarn is confined to available space in the home she shares with her husband, although "available space" can be defined in any number of creative, suspiciously open-ended ways. Like many knitters, she shares the conviction that knitting and yarn collecting is relatively benign as vices go. And thus the addiction was born.

Preferring classic styles and traditional yarns, she avoids anything that strikes her as "too ornate or fussy." Although at first she knit sweaters from existing patterns, soon she felt the urge to create her own designs based on what she prefers to wear. "I'm a real cardigan person—I find them so versatile and easy to wear. Whenever I reach for a sweater, it's almost always a cardigan." She had already begun to modify other designers' patterns to suit herself when she realized it wouldn't be such a leap to try her hand at designing from scratch. And while her physics background is not a direct source of inspiration, her math and spatial perception skills definitely help with designing and pattern-writing. As an unemployed physicist during the economic downturn, Connie found that knitting kept her busy, creatively stimulated, and intellectually challenged. A quick survey of her projects suggests that physics's loss is knitting's gain.

Her regular submissions to mainstream print magazines eventually paid off in a big way: fans of her patterns know that new ones appear reliably in the pages of *Interweave Knits* as well as *Knitter's*, *KnitScene*, and online magazine *Twist Collective*. She was *KnitScene*'s Featured Designer in its Spring 2010 issue, which included three of her original patterns. In fact, in just 4 years she has become one of the designers whose work we anticipate eagerly with the arrival of each new issue of our favorite knitting magazines. In addition, yarn distributor One Planet Yarn and Fiber sells kits assembled for her patterns.

She credits Ravelry for facilitating her success. "I was very lucky that my designing career began at around the same time Ravelry started taking off; so where previously designers had to search the blogs or random Internet craft forums to find people making their projects, now with Ravelry everything is in one easily accessible place."

Even more important, Ravelry gives this independent designer the means to promote her original designs. She has a small fan group on the site, but the popularity of her patterns reaches well beyond its membership into the broader community that frequents Ravelry. With more than two dozen of her patterns being knit by members at any one time, "It's great to see all the different iterations." She cites the direct access knitters have to designers through Ravelry as one of the most valuable features of her fan group and of the site itself. "As designers, the best we can do is try to be as responsive as possible, and correct errors as soon as we find them."

Her style, for all its classic inspirations and graceful wearability, is distinctive and pleasingly consistent; even new design elements have a way of blending happily into her body of work. She has a clear preference for set-in sleeves and shaped necklines. Most of her garments can be identified by the clever use of lace details or texture that melds organically with the broader concept, but reveals a subtle restraint at work in their application. While her sweaters almost always have a delicate, feminine quality, none could be described as precious. The Après Surf Hoodie (*Interweave Knits*, Summer 2008) is one example of her signature classic-with-a-twist style. She takes a wardrobe staple—the rough-and-tumble hooded sweatshirt—and gives it a fitted, feminine makeover using an unexpectedly light-gauge yarn and featuring an airy allover lace motif on the bodice and sleeves.

With her preference for lightweight yarns that drape well, Connie's portfolio has grown to include a number of body-skimming, empire-waist garments that flatter a wide variety of body types. Acknowledging the practical popularity of this style, she maintains, "I'll never design something for the sake of making an artistic statement. I want everything I design to be wearable." Her Printed Silk Cardigan published in *Interweave Knits* (Spring 2008) is just one example among many; the hip-length flyaway waist and delicately patterned bodice reveal a fine eye for choosing stitches and textures that amplify all the best qualities of the project's silk yarn. A review of members' project photos on Ravelry demonstrates its versatility and flattering proportions.

While many designers are known for top-down, seamless garment construction, Connie is committed to knitting her sweaters in pieces, with seams. "Personally, I love seams; they give more stability to garments. And from a practical point of view, I love knitting garments in pieces because knitting in the round can make it harder to check gauge consistency."

In 2006, she started her blog, Physicsknits, for two reasons: to document her projects and yarn stash, and to join a New York City–based knitting group known as the Spiders. Having a blog was a requirement both to become a Spider and to participate in certain "destash" groups she had found online. But as the Physicsknits blog evolved, she discovered the wider community of knitting bloggers as well as the ease with which it allowed her to promote her own design work. "Now that I'm designing, I can announce new patterns when they come out in magazines."

In addition to patterns that appear in mainstream publications, Connie launched her eponymous pattern collection, *PhysicsKnits: Designs by Connie Chang Chinchio*, in 2008. She is also a member of the Independent Knitwear Designers Web Ring, which exists to promote the work of indie designers.

Although she knits almost constantly, she acknowledges it can be challenging for an active designer to have enough material to blog about when so many of her commissioned projects have to be protected until the magazine previews or publications are available. Indeed, there are times when the photo of a tantalizing "spoken-for" skein of yarn or the blurred edge of a secret project is the only hint to make its appearance on her blog, suggesting wonderful things to come.

TULIP PEASANT BLOUSE

by Connie Chang Chinchio

Rustic in look but luxurious in feel, Classic Silk is the perfect yarn for a simple peasant blouse trimmed in a tulip lace stitch. A notched neckline adorned with a leaf motif complements the tulip edgings. Wide dolman sleeves add a bit of whimsy, and gentle princess-line shaping flatters the figure, nipping in the oversized silhouette by just the right amount.

Difficulty: Intermediate
Skills Used: Basic increasing and decreasing, three-needle bind-off, following lace charts, single crochet edging, and short-row shaping.

SIZE

XXS (XS, S, M, L, 1X, 2X)

Finished Measurements
Bust circumference: 31½ (34½, 38, 41½, 45½, 48½, 52½)"
Length: 24 (24, 24¼, 24½, 24½, 24¾, 25)"

MATERIALS

- Classic Elite Yarns Silk Classic Silk (50% cotton, 30% silk, 20% nylon; 135yd per 50g); Color: #6985, South Seas Coral; 6 (7, 8, 8, 9, 10, 10) skeins

- 29" US 6 (4mm) circular needle, or size needed to obtain gauge

- US 6 (4mm) double-pointed needles or short circular needle for sleeve edging

- 4 stitch holders

- Stitch markers

- Tapestry needle

- Size F/5 (3.75mm) crochet hook

GAUGE

20 sts and 28 rows = 4" in St st

PATTERN NOTES

The Sleeve Lace Chart and Body Lace Chart only show the odd-numbered rows. On the even-numbered rounds and rows, work stitches as they appear: knit the knits and purl the purls, treating yarnovers as knit sts.

For the Neckline Lace Chart, both even- and odd-numbered rows are included.

w&t: Wrap next stitch and turn work. Bring yarn to front and slip next stitch, bring yarn to back and return st to left-hand needle. Turn work, bring yarn to the back, and knit to the end of the row.

DIRECTIONS

Body

CO 162 (180, 198, 216, 234, 252, 270) sts and join in the rnd.

BEGIN LACE PATTERN:

Next rnd: Pm to indicate beg of rnd, rep the 18 sts of the Body Lace Chart around, beg with Row 1.

Cont to work the Body Lace Chart through Row 41.

Switch to St st and inc 4 sts as follows: *k1, M1, k79 (88, 97, 106, 115, 124, 133), M1, k1, place seam marker, repeat from * to end of round—166 (184, 202, 220, 238, 256, 274) sts.

SHAPE WAIST:

Dart set-up rnd: *Slip seam marker, p1, k20 (22, 24, 26, 28, 31, 33), place dart marker, k42 (47, 52, 57, 62, 65, 70), place dart marker, k20 (22, 24, 26, 28, 31, 33), rep from *.

Next rnd (Dec rnd): Slip seam marker, p1, k to 1st dart marker, slip marker, ssk, k to 2 sts before 2nd dart marker, k2tog, slip marker, k to 2nd seam marker, slip marker, p1, k to 3rd dart marker, slip marker, ssk, k to 2 sts before 4th dart marker, k2tog, slip marker, k to end.

Rep Dec rnd every 5th rnd 5 times more—142 (160, 178, 196, 214, 232, 250) sts.

Work 10 rnds even in St st.

SHAPE BUST:

Next rnd (Inc rnd): Slip seam marker, p1, k to 1st dart marker, slip marker, M1, k to 2nd dart marker, M1, slip marker, k to 2nd seam marker, slip marker, p1, k to 3rd dart marker, slip marker, M1, k to 4th dart marker, M1, slip marker, k to end.

Rep Inc rnd every 7th rnd 3 (2, 2, 2, 2, 2, 2) times more—158 (172, 190, 208, 226, 244, 262) sts.

Work even in St st until piece measures 14½" from CO edge.

SEPARATE FRONT AND BACK:

You will work on the back first, working back and forth in rows rather than in the round.

Next row (RS): K80 (87, 96, 105, 114, 123, 132). Turn.

Next row: P1, M1, p to last st, M1, p1.

Next row: K1, M1, k to last st, M1, k1.

Next row: CO 3 sts at beg of row, p to end.

Next row: CO 3 sts at beg of row, k to end.

Rep last 2 rows once more.

Next row: CO 5 sts at beg of row, p to end.

Next row: CO 5 sts at beg of row, k to end—106 (113, 122, 131, 140, 149, 158) sts.

Work even in St st until piece measures 6½ (6¾, 7, 7¼, 7½, 7¾, 8)" from division of front and back, ending with a WS row.

NECK SHAPING:

Next row: K38 (41, 45, 49, 53, 57, 61), BO 30 (31, 32, 33, 34, 35, 36) sts, k38 (41, 45, 49, 53, 57, 61).

Cont on left side only.

Next row: Work even.

Next row (Dec row): K1, ssk, k to end.

Rep Dec row on next RS row.

Work even in St st until armhole depth measures 8¼ (8¼, 8½, 8¾, 8¾, 9, 9½)", ending with a WS row.

LEFT SHOULDER:

Next row (RS): Work to last 10 (10, 11, 12, 13, 14, 14) sts, wrap and turn (w&t); purl back.

Next row (RS): Work to last 20 (20, 22, 24, 26, 28, 28) sts, w&t; purl back.

Next row (RS): Work to last 30 (30, 33, 36, 39, 42, 42) sts, w&t; purl back.

Next row (RS): Work across all sts, picking up and working wraps as you go.

Place the 38 (41, 45, 49, 53, 57, 61) sts on holder.

RIGHT SHOULDER:

With WS facing, attach yarn to neck edge of the left back piece.

Next row (WS): Work to last 10 (10, 11, 12, 13, 14, 14) sts, w&t; knit back.

Next row (WS): Work to last 20 (20, 22, 24, 26, 28, 28) sts, w&t; knit back.

Next row (WS): Work to last 30 (30, 33, 36, 39, 42, 42) sts, w&t; knit back.

Next row (WS): Work across all sts, picking up and working wraps as you go.

Place the 38 (41, 45, 49, 53, 57, 61) sts on holder.

Front

With RS facing, attach yarn to left armhole edge of the front piece.

Next row (Inc row) (RS): K1, M1, work to last st, M1, k1.

Next row (Inc row) (WS): P1, M1, work to last st, M1, p1.

Rep RS Inc row once more.

Next row (WS): CO 3 sts at beg of row, p to end.

Next row (RS): CO 3 sts at beg of row, k to end.

Rep last 2 rows 1 time more.

Next row (WS): CO 5 sts at beg of row, p to end.

Next row (RS): CO 5 sts at beg of row, k to end—106 (113, 122, 131, 140, 149, 158) sts.

Work even until piece measures 2" from division of front and back, ending with a WS row.

SHAPE NECK:

Next row (RS): K52 (56, 60, 65, 69, 74, 78), BO 2 (1, 2, 1, 2, 1, 2) sts, k52 (56, 60, 65, 69, 74, 78).

Cont on right side of neck only.

Next row (WS): Purl.

Next row (RS): K1, work Row 3 of Neckline Lace Chart over next 12 sts, k to end.

Cont to work even, working lace chart as est, until armhole depth measures 6½ (6½, 6¾, 7, 7, 7¼, 7¾)", ending with a WS row.

Next row (RS): BO 6 sts at beg of row, k to end.

Next row (WS): Work even.

Next row (RS): BO 4 sts at beg of row, k to end.

Next row (WS): Work even.

Next row (RS): BO 3 sts at beg of row, k to end.

Next row (WS): Work even.

Next row (Dec row) (RS): K1, ssk, k to end.

Rep Dec row on following RS rows 0 (1, 1, 2, 2, 3, 3) times more.

Work even in St st until armhole depth measures 8¼ (8¼, 8½, 8¾, 8¾, 9, 9½)", ending with a WS row.

SHAPE SHOULDER:

Next row (RS): Work to last 10 (10, 11, 12, 13, 14, 14) sts, W&T; purl back.

Next row (RS): Work to last 20 (20, 22, 24, 26, 28, 28) sts, W&T; purl back.

Next row (RS): Work to last 30 (30, 33, 36, 39, 42, 42) sts, W&T; purl back.

Next row (RS): Work across all sts, picking up wraps as you go.

Place these 38 (41, 45, 49, 53, 57, 61) sts on holder.

Left Front

With WS facing, attach yarn to neck edge of the left front piece.

Next row (WS): Work even.

Next row (RS): K to last 13 sts, work Row 9 of Front Lace Chart over next 12 sts, k1.

Cont to work even, working lace chart as est, until armhole depth measures 6½ (6½, 6¾, 7, 7, 7¼, 7¾)", ending with a RS row.

Work as for right front piece, reversing shaping. Place 38 (41, 45, 49, 53, 57, 61) sts on holder.

Sleeve Edging

CO 37 (37, 39, 41, 41, 43, 45) sts. Join in the rnd.

Next rnd: K0 (0, 2, 4, 4, 6, 8), work Sleeve Lace Chart to end of rnd.

Cont to work lace chart as est, maintaining any extra sts in St st (this will be the underarm).

Work through row 27.

BO all sts.

FINISHING

Block pieces. With right sides together and wrong sides facing out, use three-needle bind-off to create shoulder seams. Sew the underarm seams. Sew the sleeve edgings to the dolman sleeves. With crochet hook, sc around neck opening.

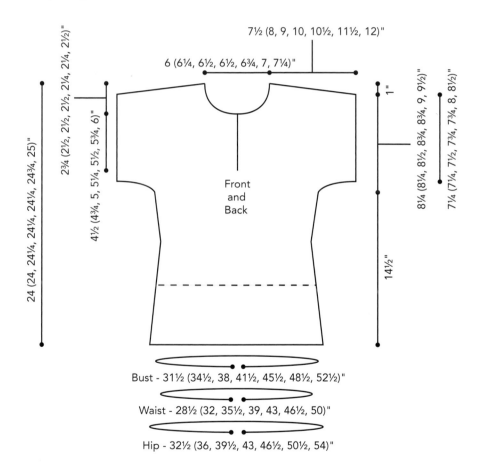

7½ (8, 9, 10, 10½, 11½, 12)"

6 (6¼, 6½, 6½, 6¾, 7, 7¼)"

2¾ (2½, 2½, 2½, 2¼, 2¼, 2½)"

1"

8¼ (8¼, 8½, 8¾, 8¾, 9, 9½)"

4½ (4¾, 5, 5¼, 5½, 5¾, 6)"

7¼ (7¼, 7½, 7¾, 7¾, 8, 8½)"

24 (24, 24¼, 24¼, 24¾, 25)"

Front and Back

14½"

Bust - 31½ (34½, 38, 41½, 45½, 48½, 52½)"

Waist - 28½ (32, 35½, 39, 43, 46½, 50)"

Hip - 32½ (36, 39½, 43, 46½, 50½, 54)"

Knitters' Guide to Essential Blogging Terminology

Blogiversary—noun: the annual recognition of another completed year of blog posts.

Stitch Key

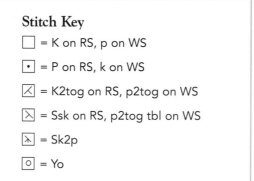

☐ = K on RS, p on WS

⚫ = P on RS, k on WS

╱ = K2tog on RS, p2tog on WS

╲ = Ssk on RS, p2tog tbl on WS

⋏ = Sk2p

○ = Yo

Body Lace Chart

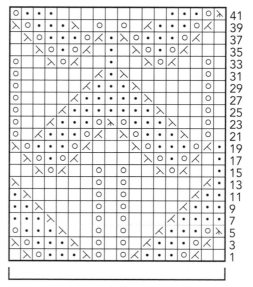

18-Stitch Repeat

Neckline Lace Chart

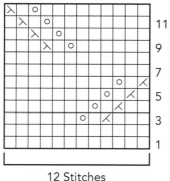

12 Stitches

Sleeve Lace Chart

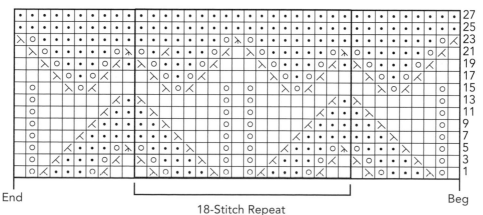

End

18-Stitch Repeat

Beg

Teresa Gregorio, CanaryKnits

Teresa Gregorio's weekly "Indie Designer Day" posts put this Canadian blogger in a class by herself. When she turns her reportorial attention to the scores of independent designers in the blogosphere, no one escapes her quest to bring new talent to light. When introducing her readers to new designers, she focuses on the attributes of the designer's knitwear and provides a link to the designer's Ravelry profile or blog so that interested readers can learn more. These profiles evolved from her continual discovery of wonderful new—but obscure—patterns on the Internet. "But they were designed by people I'd never heard of—they weren't in *Vogue Knitting*, perhaps, but they were hidden gems. I wanted to share them with others. [It's important to let designers know] when their work is being recognized. It's a way to say, 'You're doing really good stuff. Someone out there is noticing it.'"

The ever-widening pool of new talent suggests that this feature could go on indefinitely, to the delight and edification of CanaryKnits's readers. Such generosity is a typical characteristic of Teresa's blog: She also shares most of her own original designs for free on the site and on Ravelry, and she provides thorough project details in her posts.

Equally fascinating is her blog series on the Elements and Principles of Art in Knitting, which she confesses is "an attempt to marry my profession with my passion." In addition to her day job as a museum information officer, she has found an ingenious way to make her art history degree relevant to her leisure pursuits. This is her scholarly-but-accessible exploration of the relationships among modern knitting, fashion history, and visual elements such as balance, proportion, and texture. Haunting her local library to find examples that illustrate each principle was, for her, "the harmony of the universe coming together." She had been applying these principles subconsciously, almost intuitively, to her own knitting until she was struck by their connections and began to think deliberately about them.

Teresa's project for this book is just one example of that analytic process. Historical references abound in this former art history major's designs, which are often inspired by centuries-old works of art such as *The Milkmaiden* by Lucas Van Leyden. The subject's fitted lace-up bodice led Teresa to create a sexy modern interpretation of that garment, with ribbing across the bust and lace edging embellishment.

Largely a self-taught knitter, Teresa picked up the hobby in 2002, but by 2006 (when she started blogging) it had become a passion, to the extent that she now "shuns every other craft I was ever interested in. I'm not sure exactly what the magic is, but it's partly the intellectual challenge of [being able to] create something so functional, to feel that I've accomplished something, that makes it so attractive." Aside from the powerful appeal of luscious fibers and colors, Teresa finds inspiration everywhere she goes. "I do a lot of my shopping just by watching people go by and seeing what they are wearing. I'll think, 'Oh, that's an awesome sweater, and I want to make it for myself.'"

The evolution of her design process started with routine modifications. "That's what drove me to design in the first place. Either the sizes weren't in the range I wanted, or there were several elements I wanted to change, or I wanted to use yarn I already had so I'd have to regauge—and fiddle with the design." But what began as simple modification soon became a creative mantra: "Let's See What I Can Do Now."

Her style is distinctive for the curvaceous fit as well as a preference for short sleeves and deep necklines. From her perspective, the overriding connection among her designs is that she always designs things she'd wear herself. Feminine shaping and those judiciously applied lace details are hallmarks of her work. Her designs almost always hug the body closely, and she puts a great deal of attention into getting this shaping right. This self-described "lazy" knitter nonetheless turns a perpetually critical eye to her own results, constantly seeking to improve her skills—and to make garments that will appeal to a wide range of knitters with varying experience.

"Knitters have to make decisions for themselves about what they feel good in. Looking good is one thing; but as long as you feel good and you've had fun making it, that's what's most important. People hopefully have enough self-awareness to know what will look good on them and what won't."

Teresa has no shortage of design ideas—for every design she completes, there are another ten in her design notebook that she might never get to. For this former art historian, the inspiration for many of those back-burnered designs is found in historical sources, including period fashion from literary idol Jane Austen. One of her favorite patterns, the Eliot Spencer, is named after an Austen character. Sometimes ideas spring from a need to challenge herself. For example, following an anti-sock rant on her blog, she cast on for a pair of socks just to be able to say she had made them.

As long as her skill set is a work in progress, she's never so committed to a particular technique or piece of equipment that she won't consider alternatives. "I was absolutely adamant that I hated circular needles and DPNs and would never convert—but now all I do is knit on circs. All these different ideas on whether you need seams in garments or not challenged me to design a shrug that is knit in pieces."

Knitting and the online knitters' community have been linked in her mind since she started learning the craft in 2002. "The first time I came across a knit blog was the Yarn Harlot's. My first thought was, 'What the hell is this?'" But Teresa scrolled through the site for a while and quickly realized it was "an amazing and convenient resource. The fact that you can actually ask someone if you have a question, rather than having to navigate those waters all on your own, was fantastic."

"Hand knitting is a skill traditionally passed on from person to person, but the technology acts as the intermediary rather than, say, your mother teaching you by hand. The technology facilitates the communal aspect and the sharing."

Twenty-first-century knitting offers an instantly accessible community—when a knitter "belongs" to Ravelry, blogs, and participates in knit-alongs or swap groups, those are as much a form of community as the stitch-and-bitch meetings held in private homes or coffee shops.

"Instant accessibility" has a lot to do with that; from yarn and pattern purchases to video tutorials, she fulfills her knitting needs online. "At this point, I'm thoroughly satisfied with the free license, creativity, and satisfaction that comes with knitting." Tongue in cheek, she calls herself a selfish knitter, and she expresses what many other knitters think but won't say out loud: "I knit 99 percent of what I make for myself. I've never really understood why people feel the need to knit for others, or feel guilty about knitting for themselves." That said, Teresa's generosity is revealed in her ongoing efforts to shine the CanaryKnits spotlight on new and indie designers for the pure enjoyment of the online community.

MILK MAIDEN PULLOVER

by Teresa Gregorio aka CanaryKnits

As a museum worker, I'm constantly surrounded by wonderful art. This sexy sweater gets its inspiration from an engraving by sixteenth-century Dutch artist Lucas van Leyden. With a few modernizing modifications, van Leyden's *Milk Maiden* makes for a luscious knit!

Difficulty: Intermediate
Skills Used: Basic increasing and decreasing, lace knitting, following multiple sets of instructions at the same time

SIZE

XS (S, M, L, 1X, 2X, 3X)

Finished Measurements
Chest circumference: 26 (28, 30½, 34, 39, 45, 47)"
Length: 23 (24, 26, 27, 28, 28, 30)"

This top is designed with negative ease. Choose the size approximately 5" smaller than your chest circumference.

MATERIALS

- Blue Sky Alpacas Melange (100% baby alpaca; 110 yd per 50g); color: Salsa; 7 (7, 9, 10, 12, 13, 15) skeins

- 24" US 3 (3.25mm) circular needle, or size needed to match gauge

- 24" US 2 (2.75mm) circular needle

- 1 set US 2 (2.75mm) double-pointed needles

- 1 set US 3 (3.25mm) double-pointed needles

- Stitch markers

- Scrap yarn

- Tapestry needle

GAUGE

22 sts and 32 rows = 4" in St st, unblocked

DIRECTIONS

Body

CO 154 (164, 180, 200, 226, 258, 270) sts using smaller circular needles.

Being careful not to twist sts, pm for beg of rnd, and join.

Work 77 (82, 90, 100, 113, 129, 135) sts in k1, p1 rib, pm, work to end of rnd in rib.

Continue in 1x1 rib for 1".

Switch to larger circular needle and work in St st for 2"; the piece now measures 3" from the CO edge.

SHAPE WAIST:

Next rnd (Dec rnd): *Sm, k1, ssk, k to 3 sts before next marker, k2tog, k1, rep from * once more.

Work 3 rnds even.

Rep these 4 rnds 9 more times—114 (124, 140, 160, 186, 218, 230) sts. Work measures 8" from CO.

Work even until piece measures 10 (10, 10, 11, 11, 11, 11)" from CO edge.

SHAPE BUST:

Next rnd (Inc rnd): *Sm, k1, kfb, k to 2 sts before marker, kfb, k1, rep from * once more.

Work 3 rnds even.

Rep these 4 rnds 2 more times—126 (136, 152, 172, 198, 230, 242) sts. Piece measures 11½ (11½, 11½, 12½, 12½, 12½, 12½)".

BEGIN BUST RIBBING:

Set-up rnd: Sm, k6, pm, k 0 (0, 4, 2, 2, 3, 6), *k1, kfb, k2 (2, 3, 4, 5, 6, 7), rep from * until 6 (5, 9, 7, 7, 8, 11) sts before next marker, **for sizes S, M, and L only, work 1 extra increase, - (kfb, kfb, kfb, -, -, -)** k 0 (0, 4, 2, 1, 2, 5), pm, k6, sm, k1, kfb, k to 2 sts before last marker, kfb, k1. There are 142 (153, 169, 189, 214, 246, 258) sts total, 77 (83, 91, 101, 113, 129, 135) sts for the front and 65 (70, 78, 88, 101, 117, 123) sts for the back.

You will be shaping the back as you work in rib across the front.

Next rnd: Sm, k6, sm, *p1, k1, rep from * to 1 st before marker, p1, sm, k6, sm, k1, kfb, k to last 2 sts, kfb, k1.

Work 3 rnds even, maintaining rib as set over front.

Rep these 4 rnds 5 more times. Back now has 77 (82, 90, 100, 113, 129, 135) sts.

Work even until ribbing section measures 4 (4, 5, 5, 5, 5, 6)".

Work now measures 15½ (15½, 16½, 17½, 17½, 17½, 18½)" from CO edge.

SHAPE NECK:

Next rnd: Sm, k to marker before ribbing, sm, k11 (12, 14, 16, 19, 22, 24), BO 43 (46, 50, 56, 63, 73, 75) sts in patt, k11 (12, 14, 16, 19, 22, 24) to end of ribbing, sm, k to end of rnd.

Next rnd: Sm, k to marker, sm, k11 (12, 14, 16, 19, 22, 24), turn work.

You will now work back and forth in rows.

Next row (WS): K11 (12, 14, 16, 19, 22, 24), sm, p to last 11 (12, 14, 16, 19, 22, 24) sts, k11 (12, 14, 16, 19, 22, 24).

Next row (RS): Knit.

Rep these 2 rows until piece measures 1" from rib BO, ending with a WS row.

You have 111 (118, 130, 144, 163, 185, 195) sts. Do not BO. Set aside.

Sleeves (Make 2)

Using smaller dpns, CO 48 (48, 54, 60, 66, 72, 78) sts.

Pm and join in the rnd, being careful not to twist sts.

Work in k1, p1 rib for 1".

Switch to larger dpns and cont ribbing as est for 3".

Piece now measures 4" from CO edge.

BEGIN SLEEVE INCREASES:

Next rnd: *K7 (7, 8, 9, 10, 11, 12), kfb, rep from * to end of rnd—54 (54, 60, 66, 72, 78, 84) sts.

K 2 rnds.

Next rnd: *K8 (8, 9, 10, 11, 12, 13), kfb, rep from * to end of rnd—60 (60, 66, 72, 78, 84, 90) sts.

K 2 rnds.

Next rnd: *K9 (9, 10, 11, 12, 13, 14), kfb, rep from * to end of rnd—66 (66, 72, 78, 84, 90, 96) sts.

Work even in St st until sleeve measures 7 (7, 8, 8, 9, 9, 10)" from CO edge.

Cut yarn.

Place 4 sts from beg of rnd and 4 sts from end of rnd on holder (8 sts total) for underarm.

Place rem 58 (58, 64, 70, 76, 82, 88) sts on a separate piece of scrap yarn.

ATTACH SLEEVES TO BODY:

Return to Body with RS facing, and k11 (12, 14, 16, 19, 22, 24), sm, *k to 4 sts before next marker, put 4 sts before and 4 sts after marker (8 sts total) on scrap yarn, pm, continuing with the same yarn, pick up and k58 (58, 64, 70, 76, 82, 88) sts of first sleeve, pm, rep from *, then k to end of row—211 (218, 242, 268, 299, 333, 355) sts.

BEGIN RAGLAN SHAPING:

Row 1 (WS): K11 (12, 14, 16, 19, 22, 24), p to last 11 (12, 14, 16, 19, 22, 24), sm, k to end of row.

Row 2 (RS): K11 (12, 14, 16, 19, 22, 24), sm, k to first sleeve marker, **sm, k1, ssk, k to 3 sts before next sleeve marker, k2tog, k1, sm,** k across back to next sleeve marker, rep from ** to **, k to end of row.

Rep these 2 rows 20 (20, 23, 26, 29, 32, 42) more times.

Piece measures 6 (7, 7½, 8, 9, 9, 10)" from sleeve join and you have 123 (130, 142, 156, 175, 197, 207) sts.

FINISHING THE NECKLINE:

Next row (WS): K11 (12, 14, 16, 19, 22, 24), sm, p to next marker, sm, p across sleeve sts, sm, p3, (k1, p1) across back to 3 sts before next marker, p3, sm, p across sleeve sts, sm, p across front sts, sm, k11 (12, 14, 16, 19, 22, 24).

Next row (RS): K11 (12, 14, 16, 19, 22, 24), sm, k across front sts, sm, *k1, sl 1—ssk—psso, k across sleeve to 4 sts before marker, sk2p, k1, sm*, work across back in est pattern, rep from * to *, k across front sts, sm, k11 (12, 14, 16, 19, 22, 24).

Rep these 2 rows once more.

Next row (WS): Work in patt as est.

Next row (RS): K11 (12, 14, 16, 19, 22, 24), sm, k3, *sm, sl 1—ssk—psso, sk2p, sm*, work in est patt across back, rep from * to * k3, sm, k11 (12, 14, 16, 19, 22, 24).

Next row (WS): Work in patt as est.

Next row (RS): K11 (12, 14, 16, 19, 22, 24), sm, k across front, *sm, k2tog, sm*, work across back as est, rep from * to *, k across front sts, k11 (12, 14, 16, 19, 22, 24) sts.

Cut yarn, leaving a 12" tail for seaming.

GRAFT SHOULDER SEAMS:

Put first 15 (15, 17, 19, 22, 25, 27) sts on a dpn.

Put next 15 (15, 17, 19, 22, 25, 27) sts on a second dpn.

Graft these two sets of sts tog.

Rep these instructions for other shoulder seam.

FINISHING

Rejoin yarn for back, and BO ribbing in pattern.

LACE EDGING:

The lace is worked separately and sewn in place.

With larger needles, CO 8 sts.

Purl 1 row. Begin lace pattern with Row 1 of Lace Edging Chart.

Rep rows 1–18 until lace piece measures 8 (8, 10, 10, 12, 12, 14)". BO.

Stitch lace to top of bust ribbing. Graft underarm sts tog. Sew seams. Lightly block, if desired.

Knitters' Guide to Essential Blogging Terminology

Knitterly—adjective: pertaining to one's passion for knitting. Often applied to gorgeous fiber, i.e., "Never before have I touched such knitterly goodness."

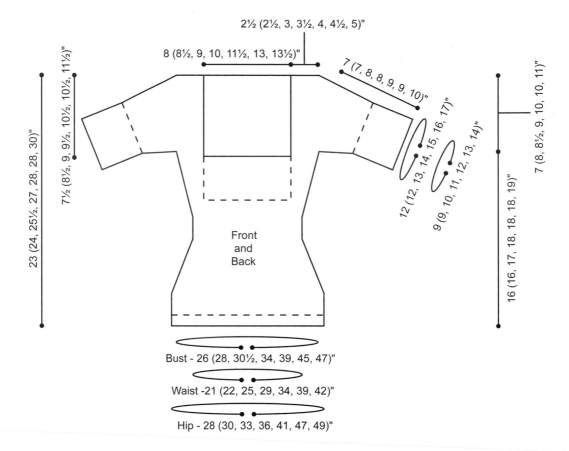

2½ (2½, 3, 3½, 4, 4½, 5)"

8 (8½, 9, 10, 11½, 13, 13½)"

7 (7, 8, 8, 9, 9, 10)"

7½ (8½, 9, 9½, 10½, 10½, 11½)"

23 (24, 25½, 27, 28, 28, 30)"

Front
and
Back

12 (12, 13, 14, 15, 16, 17)"

9 (9, 10, 11, 12, 13, 14)"

16 (16, 17, 18, 18, 18, 19)"

7 (8, 8½, 9, 10, 10, 11)"

Bust - 26 (28, 30½, 34, 39, 45, 47)"

Waist -21 (22, 25, 29, 34, 39, 42)"

Hip - 28 (30, 33, 36, 41, 47, 49)"

Stitch Key

□ = K on RS, p on WS

• = P on RS, k on WS

◿ = K2tog

◮ = P2tog and bind off

◺ = Ssk

⅄ = Sk2p

∨ = Kfb

○ = Yo

Milk Maiden Lace Edging

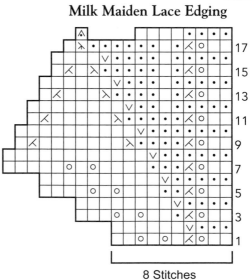

8 Stitches

Jennifer Hagan, Figknits

Gentle Southern cadences reveal Jennifer Hagan's small-town Alabama roots, although she has lived in the Pacific Northwest for many years. This lifelong knitter, Celtic culture connoisseur, and former high school English teacher launched Figheadh (pronounced "fee-yugh"), her pattern design business, in 2005. She nearly quit in frustration 2 years later when it failed to take off as planned, yet her designs are now—to her continuing amazement—sold by more than 300 yarn shops in 42 states. And her blog, Figknits, is an integral part of her business plan.

Taught to knit by her grandmother, Jennifer sewed, needlepointed, and knit her way through high school and college. An early marriage was quickly followed by three daughters, and it was the gift of a hand-knit baby cardigan that really catalyzed her knitting. That tiny garment made a deep impression on her: "It was a beautiful buttery color wool, with a simple lace finish around the buttonhole band. The minute I saw it I thought: I need to learn to knit like that!" That's when she began making Aran sweaters, building on her fascination with Celtic culture. Self-taught from that point forward, she embraced the challenge of mapping out complex cable combinations until life, teaching, and family commitments became too demanding and her creativity dropped off.

Several years later, a second marriage resulted in a cross-country move to Washington state and gave Jennifer an opportunity to re-evaluate her career choices. She knew only that she didn't want to go back to teaching high school full-time. "I wanted to be doing something I loved, something that would make me get up in the morning and not be able to wait to get to it. Teaching was making me old and angry. While I was figuring all that out, I picked up my knitting again for the first time in years. My husband watched me at it for a while, and finally said, 'That's what you should be doing!' But it took a while to figure out how to make a business out of it."

In 2002, just as knitting began to resurface as a trendy handcraft but before it gained serious traction as "the new yoga," Jennifer did some market research and decided she could generate the most income by writing up her patterns. "In complete ignorance, I just plunged in and started learning how to do it. It was the audacity of the naïve—not only was I really, really bad at math, but writing knitting patterns is totally different than anything else I'd ever done."

She poured all her energy into developing a solid foundation of patterns with which to launch the business. But for the first couple of years, Figheadh struggled to break even. Nobody had ever heard of Jennifer Hagan, and with no understanding of her love for Irish and Celtic influences, the company name was off-putting. Would-be buyers wondered, "What the heck is a Figheadh?"

Jennifer started reading knitting blogs just as her own business was taking off. "How inspiring to see other people's projects and be able to watch their progress. I looked at all the pictures—it was so much fun, it inspired me to start my own. When I started mine in 2005, it was not so much with business in mind but because I wanted to be part of that whole community. It was: 'Look what I did!' It was like a new toy."

At first, she just had fun with it. She likens its creation to "furnishing a room," putting all the links and photos into it. But her pattern business still lagged well behind projected earnings. She decided to make one last attempt to turn it around—failure of that effort would mean a return to teaching.

She obtained a list of local yarn shops and began visiting them one by one. The owner of a new yarn shop in town became an instant fan. "She immediately 'got' what I do; she jumped on my patterns, and she's now one of my best friends. She introduced me to other yarn shop owners, some of whom are now my biggest supporters."

Knitters' Guide to Essential Blogging Terminology

Swap—verb: a round-robin yarn trade, often sponsored by members of Ravelry groups or a blogger, when each participant assembles a package containing the swap item and usually an assortment of little goodies, and ships these off to a "swap partner," who is preparing a similar package for someone else.

Those early introductions led to a yarn manufacturer's sales representative wanting to carry the Figheadh pattern line, which in turn brought her a connection to Cascade Yarns. The ongoing relationship with Cascade resulted in introductions to several other yarn company sales representatives, and now her patterns are carried nationwide.

Suddenly swamped with pattern orders, questions, and fan mail from knitters, Jennifer realized what a business tool her blog could be and what it offered in terms of promotional opportunities. Figknits quickly became the place to announce trunk shows, teaching engagements, and new pattern launches. Finding the time to post regularly has been her latest challenge.

"I'm amazed every day that I get to keep doing this, that it's becoming a success, and all because I walked into that one particular yarn shop. It has shown me that it doesn't matter what you do—you need people." Jennifer now works with two tech editors as well as multiple test knitters and sample knitters. She runs the business end of Figheadh, developing patterns, keeping the books, and managing publicity, and she has a part-time office assistant to help keep her organized and free her up to create new designs. "I am very fortunate, and I remind myself of that every day. Last year, I couldn't even breathe I was so busy." With success has come certain sacrifices; for instance, now she has to schedule time for blogging and catching up on others' blogs, which eliminates some of the spontaneity but makes it easier to post regularly.

Her Figheadh Yarnworks line includes 78 patterns that are wholesale only. An additional twenty of her designs were published in magazines and books, including Debbie Stoller's *Son of Stitch 'n Bitch* (Workman Publishing Company, 2007), and Clara Parkes's *The Knitter's Book of Yarn* (Potter Craft, 2007). In 2010, intent on freeing herself to some extent from the cycle of printing, packing, and shipping those wholesale patterns, she launched a new online pattern collection called Mirth which is available directly to the knitting consumer. These new knitting and crochet designs are available as PDF downloads only. Committed to bringing crocheters into the fold, Jennifer designed several patterns for them as well.

In addition, she has been working with a local cashmere farmer (Delia Rasmussen of Ravenwood Cashmere and Soaps) to design projects for the yarn produced by North American cashmere goats. This joint venture promotes not just the production of a luxury fiber that rivals any imported cashmere for softness and beauty, but a pioneering farmer in the U.S. cashmere-producing industry. With such a variety of ongoing projects, Jen consistently improves, innovates, and builds on the foundations of her business model.

And what about the Celtic theme of the Figknits blog? "I've always loved Celtic culture, focused on the Irish part of it." But "knitting" in Irish was hard to pronounce, so she researched the British Isles further. Her persistence paid off when she eventually discovered that "figheadh" means "knitting" in Gaelic. The patterns themselves are rich with cables and other Aran elements. Influenced by garment details in sources that range from the *Lord of the Rings* movies to vintage 1940s fashions to the designs of Alice Starmore, Jennifer is never at a loss for inspiration.

Ravelry has added levels of both accountability and measurable market research to Jennifer's design work. "I put all my designs on there—it's one of the best things I ever did. I have a Ravelry fan group, Figheadh Fans, that I check every day to see if there are any comments or questions on my designs. I look at the activity on my designer page; all I have to do is pop on there to see who hearts my designs, queues them, makes them."

The greatest satisfaction for Jennifer is the ways in which the new technology supports the practice of an ancient art. Blogging has been as much a means to share her passion for knitting as it has been a marketing tool. "I'm very proud to be involved in such an old craft; it's very important that we keep these things alive." When she first started knitting again, it seemed like a dying craft, but one that she felt a personal responsibility to preserve. In fact, ". . . this downturn in the economy has been really good for knitting. It's wonderful that people are buying good yarns and supporting independent dyers and spinners. That's why I decided to sell wholesale only, and sell my patterns through yarn shops; it's a way of getting people to go to their local yarn shops, buy the pattern and the yarn. I make an effort to support both small yarn producers and larger manufacturers. Peoples' lives are stressful enough, and when they sit down to knit with one of my patterns in hand, I want them to have fun with it. The best part of this is people expressing their creativity. That's what it's all about."

Knitters' Guide to Essential Blogging Terminology

Meet-Up—noun: a pre-arranged meeting of knitters who share a specific common interest but who have previously "met" only as part of an online community. Members of Ravelry groups often arrange meet-ups at knitting conventions such as Stitches, TNNA, or Sock Summit.

GLOBAL CABLE COAT

by Jennifer Hagan

Three different knitting traditions were drawn on for this design inspiration: Aran cables, a Cowichan-style collar, and the structure of a Mandarin jacket, with generous sleeves and a toggled front closure. Put it all together and you have the Global Cable Coat! With only two short seams to work, you'll love knitting this cozy coat for yourself. The body is worked in one piece, and the sleeves and collar are knitted onto the body. Handmade wooden buttons from Jay Beesmer of Wooden Treasures (etsy.com/shop/WoodenTreasures) give the coat just the right handcrafted finishing touch.

Difficulty: Intermediate
Skills Used: Basic increasing and decreasing, decreasing in patt, cable knitting, knitting in the round, following multiple sets of instructions at the same time, picking up sts to knit pieces attached to the garment, three-needle bind-off

SIZE

XS (S, M, L, 1X, XL)

Finished Measurements
Bust circumference: 36 (38, 40, 42, 44)"
Length: 28¾ (29½, 30½, 31½, 33)"

MATERIALS

- Beaverslide Dry Goods McTaggart Tweed 3-Ply (100% Beaverslide Merino; 160yd per 113g); color: Fringed Sagewort; 11 (12, 13, 14, 15) skeins
- 30" US 9 (5.5mm) circular needle, or size needed to obtain gauge
- 2 16" US 9 (5.5mm) circular needles
- 1 set US 9 (5.5mm) double-pointed needles
- US 9 (5.5mm) needles
- Stitch markers
- Scrap yarn or stitch holders
- 6 buttons, 1¼" diameter
- Tapestry needle

GAUGE

15 sts and 23 rows = 4" in St st

16 sts and 24 rows = 4" in cable pattern stitch

PATTERN NOTES

This design features an allover cable pattern. Take care to stay in pattern as you also work decreases for garment shaping. Decrease at least 1 st in from the edge to create a tidier finish. Do not work a cable or decrease at the very edge of the fabric unless you absolutely must do so to preserve the flow of the stitch pattern.

This coat has an unshaped sleeve; the structure of the cable stitch pattern lends itself to creating a closer fit at the upper arm and for blocking the lower arm and cuff to produce a bell shape. Blocking is very important in any cable project, and especially so in this one.

The Cowichan-style collar is worked in three sections: each lapel is worked onto the neck edge and increased to shape. Then stitches are picked up at the back of the neck and joined by short rows and decreased to form a collar stand. The remaining lapel stitches are added to the back of the collar by short rows.

The coat body is worked in one piece to the armholes, then divided to work the two front sections and the back separately.

A Cable Chart is included at the end of the pattern. The information is identical to the written cable directions included in the Special Stitch section below, and is provided simply as a helpful tool for readers, depending on their preference.

SPECIAL STITCHES

C2F (2-st left cable): Sl next st onto cn and hold to front. K1 from LH needle, k1 from cn.

C3F (3-st left cable): Sl 2 onto cn and hold to front. K1 from LH needle, k2 from cn.

C3B (3-st right cable): Sl next st onto cn and hold to back. K2 from LH needle, k1 from cn.

T3F (3-st left twist): Sl 2 onto cn and hold to front. P1 from LH needle, k2 from cn.

T3B (3-st right twist): Slip next st onto cn and hold to back. K2 from LH needle, p1 from cn.

C4F (4-st left cable): Sl 2 onto cn and hold to front. K2 from LH needle, k2 from cn.

M1L: Make a left-leaning increase by picking up the horizontal thread between sts front to back and knitting into the back of the picked-up stitch.

M1R: Make a right-leaning increase by picking up the horizontal thread between sts from back to front, and knitting into the front of the picked-up st.

STITCH PATTERN
Cable Repeat:

The pattern repeat is 12 stitches.

Row 1 (RS): C2F, p1, k8, p1.

Row 2: K1, p2, k4, p2, k1, p2.

Row 3: C2F, p1, T3F, k2, T3B, p1.

Row 4: (K2, p2) 3 times.

Row 5: C2F, p2, T3F, T3B, p2.

Row 6: K3, p4, k3, p2.

Row 7: C2F, p3, C4F, p3.

Row 8: As Row 6.

Row 9: C2F, p2, C3B, C3F, p2.

Row 10: As Row 4.

Row 11: C2F, p1, C3B, k2, C3F, p1.

Row 12: As Row 2.

DIRECTIONS
Lower Body

With longer circular needle, CO 160 (168, 176, 184, 192) sts. Do not join. Work in garter stitch (knit every row) for 12 rows.

Follow the Set-Up Row for your size below and follow the Cable Chart for the cable pattern as described. For all sizes, work the first and last 8 sts in garter stitch to form the button bands (place markers to set off the button bands from the body of the coat). C2F cables are crossed on RS rows. On WS rows, work all sts outside the chart as they appear except for sections that are labeled as garter stitch, which should be knit on all rows.

Side panels will be set off with markers where indicated for each size below; you will make decreases within these panels.

Size XS: K8, p1, work 12-st cable patt twice, C2F, pm, work sts 4–11 of cable patt, pm, work 12-st cable patt 6 times, C2F, pm, work sts 4–11 of cable patt, pm, work 12-st cable patt twice, C2F, p1, k8.

Size S: K8, p1, work 12-st cable patt twice, C2F, pm, p1, work sts 3–12 of cable patt, p1, pm, work 12-st cable patt 6 times, C2F, pm, p1, work sts 3–12 of cable patt, p1, pm, work 12-st cable patt twice, C2F, p1, k8.

Size M: K8, p1, work 12-st cable patt twice, C2F, pm, p3, work sts 3–12 of cable patt, p3, pm, work 12-st cable patt 6 times, C2F, pm, p3, work sts 3–12 of cable patt, p3, pm, work 12-st cable patt twice, C2F, p1, k8.

Size L: K8, work 12-st cable patt twice, work sts 1–11 of cable patt, pm, p1, C2F, work 3 sts in garter st, C2F, pm, work sts 3–12 of cable patt, work 12-st cable patt 6 times, pm, C2F, work 3 sts in garter st, C2F, p1, pm, work sts 4–12 of cable patt, work 12-st cable patt twice, C2F, k8.

Size XL: K8, p1, work 12-st cable patt 3 times, pm, C2F, work 6 sts in garter st, pm, work 12-st cable patt 7 times, C2F, pm, work 6 sts in garter st, C2F, pm, work sts 3–12 of cable patt, work 12-st cable patt 2 times, C2F, p1, k8.

All sizes: Work in patt as est until piece measures 11½ (12, 12½, 13, 13½)" from CO edge, ending with a WS row.

WAIST SHAPING:

Maintaining patt as set, dec 2 sts between first and second markers, and another 2 sts between third and fourth markers. Work this dec every 4 rows 4 times. Work the dec as foll:

Size XS: Reduce the cable until you have a repeating C4F cable rem (i.e., turn the cable every fourth row), and then only a C2F cable rem, and then decrease 2 sts at once by

working to one st before marker, sl st to RH needle without working it, remove marker, move sl st back to LH needle, k3tog, replace marker, remove next marker, and cont in patt.

Size S: Reduce the p sts to either side of the center cable and then reduce the sts just after and just before the C2F cables, three times until you have only repeating C2F, C4F, C2F cables rem (i.e., turn the cables in patt as established).

Size M: Reduce the p sts to either side of the cable by working p2tog until only the C4F cable rem.

Size L: Dec all sts between the markers, beg with the p st, then the garter sts between the C2F sts, and then the C2F cable. Dec the last 2 sts by working to one st before marker, sl st to RH needle, remove marker, sl st back to LH needle, p3tog, replace marker, remove next marker, and cont in patt.

Size XL: Dec all sts between the markers, beg with the garter sts by working p2tog or k2tog, whichever side is facing, and then reduce the C2F cable (rem 2 sts) by working to one st before marker, sl the st to the RH needle, remove marker, sl st back to LH needle, p3tog, replace marker, remove next marker, and cont in patt.

When waist shaping is complete, there are 144 (152, 160, 168, 176) sts on the needle and the piece should measure 14 (14½, 15, 15½, 16)". Work in patt until piece measures 21 (21½, 22¼, 23, 24)" from CO edge, ending with a WS row.

Upper Back

Next row (RS): Work in patt to last 36 (38, 40, 42, 44) sts, removing markers. Place the last 36 (38, 40, 42, 44) sts on scrap yarn for left front. *Take note of where in the patt you have stopped so you can resume the pattern properly on the left front.* Turn the work.

Next row (WS): BO 6 sts for underarm, work in patt to last 36 (38, 40, 42, 44) sts and place them on scrap yarn for right front. Turn the work.

Next row (RS): BO 6 sts for underarm and work in patt across rem 60 (64, 68, 72, 76) sts.

Cont in patt as established on the back sts only until piece measures 27¾ (28½, 29½, 30½, 32)" from CO edge, ending with a WS row.

Next row (RS): Work 22 (22, 23, 23, 24) sts, BO center 18 (20, 22, 24, 26) sts, and work across rem 22 (22, 23, 23, 24) sts.

Turn and work WS row in patt up to BO. Join a second ball of yarn in order to work sides separately.

Dec 1 st at each neck edge on RS rows 2 times. Cont in patt as established until entire piece measures 28¾ (29½, 30½, 31½, 33)" from CO edge, then place each set of 20 (20, 21, 21, 22) shoulder sts on scrap yarn.

Right Front

Return 36 (38, 40, 42, 44) sts held for left front to working needle. Join yarn with RS facing and work across all sts in patt.

Next row (WS): BO 6 sts for armhole shaping, work to end of row in patt.

Work in patt for 1 (1¼, 1¼, 1¼, 1½)" more on rem 30 (32, 34, 36, 38) sts.

SHAPE NECK:

Dec 1 st at neck edge every RS row 5 (6, 7, 8, 9) times, then every *other* RS row (every 4th row) 5 (6, 6, 7, 7) times. When piece measures 28¾ (29½, 30½, 31½, 33)" from CO edge, place rem 20 (20, 21, 21, 22) shoulder sts on scrap yarn.

Left Front

Return 36 (38, 40, 42, 44) sts held for right front to working needles. Join yarn with RS facing. BO 6 sts, work to end of row in patt.

Work in patt for 1 (1¼, 1¼, 1¼, 1½)" more on rem 30 (32, 34, 36, 38) sts.

SHAPE NECK:

Dec 1 st at neck edge every RS row 5 (6, 7, 8, 9) times, then every *other* RS row (every 4th row) 5 (6, 6, 7, 7) times. When entire piece measures 28¾ (29½, 30½, 31½, 33)" from CO edge, place rem 20 (20, 21, 21, 22) shoulder sts on scrap yarn.

Shoulder Seams

Move the sts for the right back shoulder and right front shoulder to working needles. Hold the needles parallel in the left hand with right sides of fabric together, and join with the three-needle bind-off. Rep for the left shoulder.

Sleeves

Note: Pick up 1 st in each bound-off st and 3 sts for every 4 rows along the edges.

Beg at lower armhole, with RS facing, pick up and knit 6 sts across BO edge, pick up 31 (32, 33, 34, 36) sts before shoulder seam, another 31 (32, 33, 34, 36) sts after shoulder seam, and 6 sts from BO edge. Pm and join the 74 (76, 78, 80, 84) sts in the rnd and work as follows:

Size XS: Work 12-st patt 6 times, C2F.

Size S: P1, work 12-st patt 6 times, C2F, p1.

Size M: P2, work 12-st patt 3 times, C2F, p2.

Size L: C2F, p1, work 12-st patt 6 times, C2F, p1.

Size XL: P2, C2F, p1, work 12-st patt 6 times, C2F, p1, C2F.

Work sleeves in patt as established with no shaping until sleeve measures 17 (17½, 18, 18½, 19)", ending with rnd 1, 11, or 13 to avoid puckering.

CUFF:

Work garter st for 12 rnds (p 1 rnd, k 1 rnd). BO loosely knitwise.

Collar

The collar is worked in garter st (knit every row). When picking up sts along the edge of the neck, pick up sts at a rate of 3 sts per 4 rows.

To work left lapel, join yarn on WS edge of lowest point of V-neck shaping with 16" circular, and pick up and knit 1 st.

Next row (RS): Kfb (2 sts).

Next row (WS): K1, pick up st from edge and p2tog with rem st.

Next row (RS): Sl 1 pwise wyib, M1L, k1—3 sts.

Next row (WS): K to last st, sl 1 pwise, pick up 1 st from edge and p2tog with slipped st.

Rep these last 2 rows, always working the M1L on RS rows just before the last st. Cont to inc until there are 20 (20, 21, 21, 22) sts on the needle. Leave the sts on the needle, break yarn, leaving 8" tail to weave in, and work right lapel.

On right lower neck edge with second 16" circular, attach yarn on RS edge and pick up and knit 1 st.

Next row (WS): Kfb—2 sts

Next row (RS): Kfb, pick up st from edge and k2tog with rem st—3 sts.

Next row (WS): Sl 1 pwise wyif, move yarn to back, k2.

Next row (RS): K to last st, M1R, k1, pick up 1 st from edge and k2tog with slipped st.

Rep these last 2 rows, always working the M1R after the first st on RS rows. Cont to inc until there are 20 (20, 21, 21, 22) sts on the needle. Leave the sts on the needle, break yarn, leaving 8" tail to weave in, and work collar back.

Work the collar back. With 29" circular needle and with RS facing, pick up and k32 (34, 36, 38, 40) sts across back.

Next row (WS): K to last st, k last st tog with first st from right lapel.

Next row (RS): K to last st, k last st tog with next st on left lapel.

Rep these last 2 rows 3 times more until there are 16 (16, 17, 17, 18) sts left on each lapel needle.

Next row (WS): K across back neck needle, k1 from right lapel needle. Turn.

Next row (RS): K across back neck needle, k1 from left lapel needle. Turn.

Rep these last 2 rows until all lapel sts have been worked onto back neck needle. BO all sts loosely and evenly.

FINISHING

Weave in ends. Block to finished measurements. After blocking, attach buttons along front opening, three on each side, as shown.

Make toggles: Work three I-cords, each 7" long. Be sure to leave 6" tail at both ends. Weave end through live sts and attach ends of each cord to make a ring. Give the ring one half turn to form a figure eight, hiding the join behind the overlapping cord. With ends, secure the shape by making a few hidden sts at the middle twist of the figure eight. Weave in the ends by running them up into the cord, and cut the ends so that they will not show. Slip a button from each side of the closure into one loop of the figure eight. The toggles may be removed entirely, or they may be further secured and sewn to the garment on one side to attach permanently.

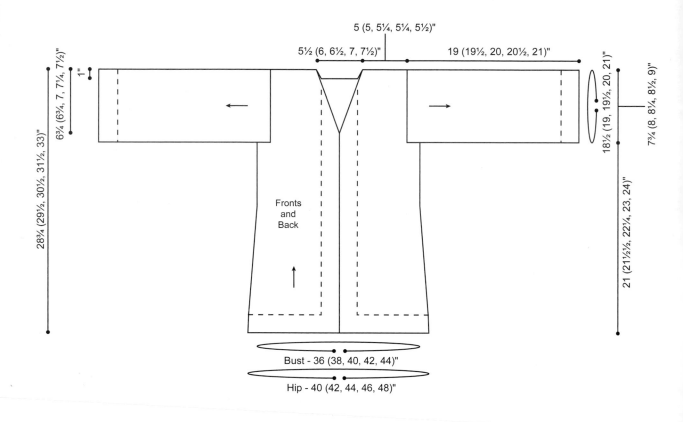

Fronts
and
Back

5 (5, 5¼, 5¼, 5½)"

5½ (6, 6½, 7, 7½)"

19 (19½, 20, 20½, 21)"

1"

6¾ (6¾, 7, 7¼, 7½)"

28¾ (29½, 30½, 31½, 33)"

18½ (19, 19½, 20, 21)"

7¾ (8, 8¼, 8½, 9)"

21 (21½, 22½, 22¼, 23, 24)"

Bust - 36 (38, 40, 42, 44)"

Hip - 40 (42, 44, 46, 48)"

Stitch Key

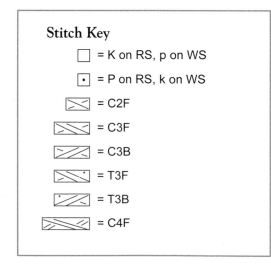

☐ = K on RS, p on WS

⊡ = P on RS, k on WS

▧ = C2F

▧ = C3F

▧ = C3B

▧ = T3F

▧ = T3B

▧ = C4F

Cable Pattern Stitch

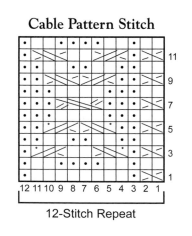

12-Stitch Repeat

Angela Hahn, Knititude

How does a Boston veterinarian wind up living the life of an independent knitwear designer in a charming village in Italy? For Angela Hahn, the opportunity to shift gears so completely came in early 2006 when her husband relocated his business to a town near Lake Como. It proved the perfect impetus to set aside her veterinary career and embark on a new venture. A few months prior to the move, she started her blog, Knititude, as a way to build design credentials and to market her original patterns.

Newly transplanted to Italy, she discovered to her surprise that hand-knitting is not nearly as popular a hobby there as it is in other European countries and in the United States. And in an unanticipated tragic twist, very few of the gorgeous yarns that are milled in Italy for the American market ever find their way into Italian yarn shops. Residents stared at her as an oddity when she knit in public, and it took many months even to locate a yarn shop near her new home.

After enrolling her two young sons in the local Italian elementary school, Angela set about reviving the knitting and design skills that had lain dormant since a frustrating sweater project was tossed unfinished into a closet 10 years earlier.

The blog Knititude was integral to that process. In addition to photos of the beautiful town in which she lived with her family, one of the blog's charming features is its bilingual posts in English and Italian (although she insists that her proficiency is far from fluent). Although she makes a conscious decision to keep most personal information out of her blog, details about her life have a tendency to creep in because "a blog takes on a life of its own."

"At first I had no traffic, because nobody knew who I was. I hadn't really *done* anything. So I started submitting patterns to online magazines." *MagKnits* accepted several of her designs right off the bat, and *Knitty.com* soon followed suit. "Without the online magazines that are willing to give new designers a chance, it would have been much harder [to establish myself]." Those initial successes led to her regular publication in print magazine *Interweave Knits* as well as the online publication *Twist Collective*. "Luckily for me, most magazines now accept online submissions . . . which made things a lot easier, because I didn't have to worry about putting actual swatches into the mail." The themed story boards from these magazines never fail to inspire her, helping her narrow down the potentially infinite possibilities when she begins to develop a new project.

In the fall of 2009, Angela and her family returned to the United States to live, but they return to their beloved Italy during the summer months. While the full-time Italian adventure may be over, Angela's knitting adventures continue to enthrall and engage us. Although her designs began to gain recognition while she lived in Italy, her record of pattern publication gathered steam once she was back home in the United States.

For example, Lisa Shroyer, senior editor at *Interweave Knits*, says of Angela, "Her work has consistently been strong; the designs are traditional but contemporary in silhouette, highly wearable, and, because of her intriguing stitch pattern choices, fun to knit. The iconic Hahn design for me is the Wakame Lace Tunic from the summer 2008 issue of *IK*—allover, large-motif lace patterning laid on a dolman-style garment that has amazing drape and movement in a silk blend; it's strikingly feminine and modern."

Angela also sources most of her yarn online. Despite the scarcity of interesting yarns in Italy, the fashion industry's strong presence there provided her with an endless visual feast. Shop window displays are whimsical and creative, and the fashions themselves are at least a year ahead of whatever trend is current in the United States. Photos of these displays pop up from time to time on Angela's blog, often accompanied by tongue-in-cheek commentary on the weirder examples she spotted.

While lace motifs feature prominently in Angela's patterns, experimentation is integral to her process-oriented approach; she modifies the motifs, turning them on their heads until they are sometimes unrecognizable from the original source material. One example of the way she reworks existing stitch patterns to force them into a different design is in her use of structured decreases, working decreases into a standard lace repeat until it forms, for example, the crown of a hat. These modifications are necessary because as much as she is drawn to traditional lace, "frankly, there is no place in my house for a doily, but the designs are so beautiful I like to find other places and ways to use them."

One of the most engaging aspects of the Knititude blog is Angela's transparency about her work. When she posts about her design process, she is as likely to discuss her most egregious mistakes as she is her successes, and she generously takes the reader along for the ride as she frogs, makes corrections, and modifies her designs. This is part of what makes her patterns a joy to make; they are clear, concise, and on the rare occasion that there are errata, she posts the fixes quickly and in detail.

"The knitting community is so vocal; I definitely look at what people write about my patterns and read the comments on my blog, so I can make my patterns as easy as possible to read and follow. [Reader comments] definitely influenced me to write patterns in a wider range of sizes, because that's important, too." When designing, Angela thinks about her own pet peeves in clothing and works to make her designs both practical and wearable. While she focuses on fairly simple shapes, her work demonstrates a preference for all-over texture rather than panels of stockinette—one reason she is so inspired by Japanese stitch and pattern books. She only creates garments that she would enjoy wearing and that are adaptable to different body types. A review of her body of work reveals a penchant for versatile vests and sleeveless tops that function as year-round layering pieces. These pieces reflect her commitment to offering projects that require both a shorter time commitment and an affordable financial investment from the knitter.

Her own experiences as a knitter make her even more appreciative that designers are so accessible through the Internet, and that so many participate in the online community. "Even very well-known designers get right back to you if you have questions."

Abundant photographs document her design process, and her 5-year-old son is a willing photographer. "The angle is sometimes a bit odd because he's short, but he's getting pretty good!" It doesn't hurt that both the Italian and the New England landscapes are utterly gorgeous, and the backdrops in her photos are usually as luscious as her finished garments.

Knitting is a source of endless fascination for Angela. With so many possible design variations and regional knitting histories that influence the way styles evolve, she constantly challenges herself to try new ideas and to apply different, and unfamiliar, techniques. It does not surprise her that even during the recent economic downturn, yarn shops continued to experience slow but steady growth and that the Internet has played such an important role in that success. "Everybody enjoys making things with their own hands—personal things that have emotional value. The current knitting trend has more legs than anybody anticipated because it's a way for people to connect on a more personal level, both in person and online."

SEAWEED VEST
by Angela Hahn

This simple vest is worked in the round to the armholes, then back and forth for the straps. The neck and armholes are finished in a narrow applied I-cord for a clean finish. The resilience of the unusual undulating "seaweed" rib gives the vest a body-skimming silhouette; no waist shaping decreases or increases are used. The chosen yarn, a slightly variegated silk/wool combination, complements the diagonal and vertical movement of the stitch pattern with its muted color changes and subtle sheen. The wool content in the yarn gives added stretch to the rib and helps the vest to hold its shape. This vest is designed to be worn with the deep scoop neck in front or in back, and in a nod to knitwear's versatility it can also be worn comfortably as a tank in warm weather.

Difficulty: Easy
Skills Used: Reading a simple chart, working in the round, decreasing, three-needle bind off, attached I-cord

SIZE

XXS (XS, S, M, L, 1X, 2X)

Finished Measurements
Chest: 30½ (34½, 38½, 42½, 46, 50, 53½)"
Length: 21½ (22, 22½, 22½, 22½, 23, 23)"

MATERIALS

- Handmaiden Fine Yarns Lady Godiva (50% silk, 50% wool; 273yd per 100g); color: Cedar; 3 (3, 4, 4, 4, 5, 5) skeins

- 24"–40" US 6 (4mm) circular needle (choose length based on chosen garment size), or size needed to obtain gauge

- 16" US 6 (4mm) circular needle

- Stitch markers

- 4 stitch holders, 3 small and 1 large

- Tapestry needle

GAUGE

20 sts and 32 rows = 4" in St st

25 sts and 32 rows = 4" in pattern stitch, lightly blocked

SPECIAL STITCHES

Ssp: Sl 2 sts as if to knit with yarn in front, then purl these 2 sts tog through back loops

DIRECTIONS
Body

Using longer circular needle, CO 192 (216, 240, 264, 288, 312, 336) sts. Pm to indicate beg of rnd and left side seam, and join for working in the rnd, taking care not to twist sts.

BEGIN SEAWEED PATTERN:

Beg with row 1 of 6-st Seaweed Pattern chart, work 16 (18, 20, 22, 24, 26, 28) reps of patt; pm for right side seam; work Seaweed Pattern to end of rnd.

Continue Seaweed Pattern as est through rnd 120 (120, 118, 116, 114, 112, 108), **stopping 5 (6, 7, 8, 9, 10, 11) sts before the end of the last**

rnd—10 (10, 9, 9, 9, 9, 9) complete patt reps plus another 0 (0, 10, 8, 6, 4, 0) rnds.

DIVIDE FRONTS AND BACK:

Next rnd: BO 5 (6, 7, 8, 9, 10, 11) sts, remove marker, BO 6 (7, 8, 9, 10, 11, 12) sts; work 34 (38, 42, 46, 50, 55, 60) sts in patt; BO 17 (19, 21, 23, 25, 25, 25) sts for Front Neck; work 34 (38, 42, 46, 50, 55, 60) sts in patt; BO 11 (13, 15, 17, 19, 21, 23) sts, remove marker; work 85 (95, 105, 115, 125, 135, 145) sts for back in patt. Turn to work Back sts only, leaving Front sts on needle or on holder.

Back

Note: *On all WS rows, work the sts as they appear (knit the knits and purl the purls).*

As you continue on the Back and Front, work edge sts as St st selvage sts (k on RS, p on WS), and work shaping in patt with the 2 sts just inside the edge sts. Keep track of row numbers as you work.

WORK DECREASES AS FOLLOWS:

RS rows: If 3rd st from edge will be purled, p2tog to decrease. If 3rd st will be knit, k2tog. If 3rd-to-last will be knit, ssk. If 3rd-to-last st will be purled, ssp.

WS rows: If 3rd st from edge will be knit, ssk to decrease. If 3rd st will be purled, ssp. If 3rd-to-last st will be purled, p2tog. If 3rd-to-last st will be knit, k2tog.

ARMHOLE SHAPING:

SIZES S, M, L, 1X, 2X, ONLY

Next row (WS): P1, dec 1, work in patt to last 3 sts, dec 1, p1.

Next row (RS): K1, dec 1, work in patt to last 3 sts, dec 1, k1.

Rep these 2 rows - - (-, 0 1, 2, 3, 5) times—85 (95, 101, 107, 113, 119, 121) sts.

ALL SIZES CONTINUE:

Next row (WS): P1, work in patt to last st, p1.

Next row (RS): K1, dec 1, work in patt to last 3 sts, dec 1, k1.

Rep these 2 rows 2 (4, 4, 4, 5, 6, 7) times—79 (85, 91, 97, 101, 105, 105) sts.

Work even through WS Row 148 (152, 154, 156, 158, 160, 160)—12 (12, 12, 13, 13, 13, 13) complete patt reps plus another 4 (8, 10, 0, 2, 4, 4) rows.

SHAPE BACK NECK:

Next Row (RS): Work 31 (33, 35, 37, 38, 40, 40) sts in patt; BO next 17 (19, 21, 23, 25, 25, 25) sts; work last 31 (33, 35, 37, 38, 40, 40) sts in patt.

LEFT NECK AND SHOULDER:

Next and following WS rows: Work in patt to end.

Next 2 RS rows: BO 4 sts, work in patt to end.

Next 1 (1, 1, 2, 2, 3, 3) RS row(s): BO 3 sts, work in patt to end.

At the beg of the next 5 (6, 7, 5, 5, 4, 4) RS rows, dec 1 st as directed above—15 (16, 17, 18, 19, 19, 19) sts.

Work even through WS row 172 (176, 178, 180, 182, 184, 184)—14 (14, 14, 15, 15, 15, 15) complete patt reps plus another 4 (8, 10, 0, 2, 4, 4) rows. Break yarn and place sts on holder for Left Shoulder.

RIGHT NECK AND SHOULDER:

With WS facing, join yarn. Continue in patt, shaping neck and shoulder as follows.

Next 2 WS rows: BO 4 sts, work in patt to end.

Next 1 (1, 1, 2, 2, 3, 3) WS row(s): BO 3 sts, work in patt to end of row.

At the end of the next 5 (6, 7, 5, 5, 4, 4) RS rows, dec 1 st as directed above—15 (16, 17, 18, 19, 19, 19) sts.

Work even through WS row 172 (176, 178, 180, 182, 184, 184—14 (14, 14, 15, 15, 15, 15) complete patt reps plus another 4 (8, 10, 0, 2, 4, 4) rows. Break yarn, leaving yard-long tail for three-needle bind-off, and place sts on holder for Right Shoulder.

Left Front

You will shape armhole and neck *at the same time;* read through all directions in this section before beginning to knit. Remember to work selvage st and decreases as directed for Back, and keep track of row count.

ARMHOLE SHAPING:

With RS facing, join yarn.

Dec 1 st at armhole edge every row 0 (0, 2, 4, 6, 8, 12) times, then every RS row 3 (5, 5, 5, 6, 7, 8) times. *At the same time,* shape neck as follows:

NECK SHAPING:

Next WS row: BO 3 at neck edge.

Dec 1 st at neck edge every RS row 5 times, then every 4 rows 8 (9, 10, 11, 11, 13, 13) times—15 (16, 17, 18, 19, 19, 19) sts.

Work even through WS row 172 (176, 178, 180, 182, 184, 184)—14 (14, 14, 15, 15, 15, 15)

complete patt reps plus another 4 (8, 10, 0, 2, 4, 4) rows. Break yarn, leaving yard-long tail for three-needle bind-off, and place sts on holder for Left Shoulder.

Right Front

You will shape armhole and neck *at the same time;* read through all directions in this section before beginning to knit. Remember to work selvage st and decs as directed above, and keep track of row count.

ARMHOLE SHAPING:

With RS facing, join yarn.

Dec 1 at armhole edge every row 0 (0, 2, 4, 6, 8, 12) times, then every RS row 3 (5, 5, 5, 6, 7, 8) times.

NECK SHAPING:

Next RS row: BO 3 at neck edge.

Dec 1 st at neck edge every RS row 5 times, then every 4 rows 8 (9, 10, 11, 11, 13, 13) times—15 (16, 17, 18, 19, 19, 19) sts.

Work even through WS row 172 (176, 178, 180, 182, 184, 184)—14 (14, 14, 15, 15, 15, 15) complete patt reps plus another 4 (8, 10, 0, 2, 4, 4) rows. Leave sts on needle and do not break yarn.

FINISHING

SHOULDER SEAMS:

Turn tank inside out. Place back right shoulder sts on extra needle, hold this and the needle with the right front shoulder sts parallel with RS together; use long tail (not working yarn) and free end of circular needle to attach the shoulder using the three-needle bind-off.

Place left shoulder sts from back and front onto separate needles, RS together, and attach shoulder with the three-needle bind-off.

NECK EDGING:

With RS facing, using longer circular needle and working yarn, start at right shoulder seam and pick up and k56 (60, 64, 68, 72, 76, 80) sts evenly spaced along back neck edge and 84 (90, 96, 102, 108, 114, 120) sts evenly spaced along front neck edge—140 (150, 160, 170, 180, 190, 200) sts.

WORK ATTACHED I-CORD:

Turn work to WS and CO 2 sts using knitted cast-on. *K1, ssk, place the 2 sts now on right-hand needle back on left-hand needle. Rep from * until all neck sts have been worked, with 2 sts rem on right-hand needle. Break yarn and use tapestry needle to graft these 2 sts to beg of I-cord.

ARMHOLE EDGING:

With RS facing and 16" circular needle, starting at center underarm, pick up and k80 (86, 92, 98, 104, 110, 116) sts evenly spaced around armhole edge. Work Attached I-cord as directed for neck edging. Repeat for second armhole.

Weave in all ends and block to measurements, taking care to reshape ribs so they retain some resilience.

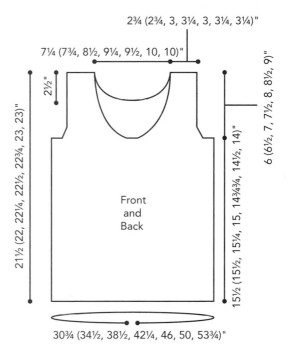

2¾ (2¾, 3, 3¼, 3, 3¼, 3¼)"

7¼ (7¾, 8½, 9¼, 9½, 10, 10)"

2½"

6 (6½, 7, 7½, 8, 8½, 9)"

21½ (22, 22¼, 22½, 22¾, 23, 23)"

Front and Back

15½ (15½, 15¼, 15, 14¾, 14½, 14)"

30¾ (34½, 38½, 42¼, 46, 50, 53¾)"

Stitch Key

☐ = K on RS, p on WS

⊡ = P on RS, k on WS

Pattern Chart

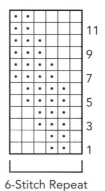

11
9
7
5
3
1

6-Stitch Repeat

Stefanie Japel, Glampyre Knits

With the publication of her first two books, *Fitted Knits* (North Light Books, 2007) and *Glam Knits* (North Light Books, 2008), Stefanie Japel (pronounced like "apple") has established herself as a sought-after expert in top-down sweater design. But she also has the distinction of being one of the knitting world's earliest bloggers, having begun Glampyre Knits in 1999. At the time she was working on her PhD in interplanetary science, and she often found herself with too much downtime in the lab. An on-again, off-again knitter since childhood, Stefanie picked up her needles in grad school and discovered that the craft provided her with a welcome respite from the demands of her studies. In fact, that was when she first succumbed to the "total addiction" of applying her mind to the creation of original designs.

A friend helped her create the knitting blog, but what began as a simple online gallery to showcase her various crafts projects (in addition to knitting, she is an accomplished quilter) soon evolved into much more. During any lull in her doctoral program requirements, she took advantage of the free time to design and publish free knitting patterns on her site. As one of the few knit blogs in existence in those days, Glampyre Knits quickly attracted a following. "I enjoyed the feedback and comments; so even though it started by accident, once it was there I was really glad to have it."

She admits to being shy about submitting her early design ideas to knitting magazines, a lucky break came when *Knitty.com* published her Postmodern Legwarmer pattern in the Spring 2003 issue. That exposure brought a big jump in traffic to her blog and led to a mentoring relationship with *Knitty*'s editor, Amy Singer. "Amy was the first person who encouraged me to submit to other knitting magazines and to stop giving away all my designs free on my Web site." Her relationship with *Knitty* is ongoing, and in the ensuing years the magazine has published several more of her designs.

A corollary benefit of the exposure she gained from *Knitty* is that Stefanie found her niche: "I am really a garment knitter; I love to make clothes." The editors of other publications agreed with *Knitty*: Her designs have also been featured in *MagKnits* and in books including *Stitch 'n Bitch Nation* (Workman, 2004), *Not Another Teen Knitting Book* (Sterling, 2006), *KnitGrrl* (Watson-Guptill, 2005) and *Big Girl Knits* (Potter Craft, 2006). At least a half-dozen of her patterns have been knit-along projects, and her feminine, shapely sweaters were clearly a hit with the knitting public; but at that point, she still considered her design work a hobby.

Although Glampyre Knits had attracted a passionate fan base (with often as many as 14,000 hits in a day—an achievement that most of us only dream about) and Stefanie had developed a significant collection of original designs, she was nonetheless astonished when knit-blogger and trend-spotter extraordinaire Shannon Okey (aka "Knitgrrl") approached her to suggest she write a top-down knitting book. This turn of events led to the ensuing 180-degree shift in her professional focus. "I never would have thought about doing a book. I was serious about my science career and still pretty shy [even after her success with *Knitty.com*] about submitting to magazines." Okey then introduced her to the publisher that developed her book *Fitted Knits*.

In 2006, she and her equally creative husband moved to New Mexico, where she planned to do post-doctoral research and teach astronomy at New Mexico State University. Her teaching schedule and the demands of research grew infinitely more complicated with the arrival of daughter Mazie in 2008. But with a perennially popular blog, an ever-growing collection of self-published patterns, and soon not one, but two, successful books under her belt, a new path gradually revealed itself.

At first, acclimating to the desert southwest climate was a challenge after living on the east coast and abroad in Germany. "The light is so intense in New Mexico. In Germany, the light was always filtered—misty and ethereal. Here it is so bright it can be unforgiving; I have to wait and go outside in the evening to take photos [of my knitted projects]."

But the new climate also lent an immediacy to Stefanie's knitting challenges, as well as the determination to make the transition into a full-time knitting career. She began to teach more workshops on custom-fitting knitted garments; her books act as calling cards to local yarn shop owners who vie for her teaching skills. And the brick-and-mortar yarn shop is a critical component in her success. "You can't touch the yarns through your computer screen; there's no replacing that immediacy. The yarn shop with a business model that meshes an online presence with a physical store, that offers an enticing space for shopping and classes, will ensure [its] success in this environment."

Today, Stefanie credits her blog and the knitters' online community with launching her onto her present course, however innocently it began. Once she left academia for the life of a freelance knitting book author and independent designer, it nonetheless took a while to find a comfortable balance. Now, in addition to her design work, she coordinates all the knitting patterns for the Mission Falls yarn company on a freelance basis. She evaluates their design submissions and determines which ones to feature in each of the yarn company's seasonal pattern books.

The Internet makes all this possible, and the rise of social media is a phenomenon of which Stefanie is keenly aware. "The sheer numbers of people we bloggers are able to reach is overwhelming—and wonderful. One blogger with influence can work up a new project, and suddenly *thousands* of knitters discover it, and 'need' to make it—that's amazing! The knit-along concept didn't even exist when my grandmother taught me to knit. And she'd be overwhelmed by all the yarn choices we have now."

Ravelry has, of course, been a boon to the Glampyre. Her Ravelry fan group has more than 1,900 members making her projects at any one time, and she was one of the earliest volunteer editors on the site. She credits Ravelry not only for promoting her designs and those of other independent designers, but for providing an unparalleled forum for indie yarn dyers and spinners. "We're able to get so many new and different fibers to play with, and we can be so much more experimental with our yarn choices," at least partly because Ravelry makes it possible to identify all the yarns being used in projects that are documented on the site.

In 2009, Stefanie added a variety of online classes to her teaching schedule, and they have been hugely successful. Following the birth of her second child in early 2010, she planned for more online classes. "They have been a fabulous way to reach out to the knitting community and interact with more knitters than I'd ever be able to in real life. I love the online classes, and over the next year I hope to expand, including offering classes from guest teachers." The classes range from simple shawl tutorials to sharing her methods for achieving the shaping and custom fit for which her designs are known.

(IT COMES IN) WAVES PULLOVER

by Stefanie Japel

Top-down raglan short-sleeved pullover with cables at front, back, and sleeves to add both shaping that flatters and texture that makes it interesting to work.

Difficulty: Intermediate
Skills used: Cabling, knitting in the round

SIZE

S (M, L, 1X, 2X)

Finished Measurements
Bust circumference: 34 (38, 42, 46, 50)"
Length from underarm: 15½ (16, 17½, 17½, 17½)"

MATERIALS

- Lorna's Laces Green Line DK (100% organic Merino; 145yd per 56g); Color: Mirth; 7 (8, 8, 9, 10) skeins
- 24" US 6 (4mm) circular needle, or size needed to obtain gauge
- 8 stitch markers; 4 of one color, 4 of another
- Tapestry needle

GAUGE

24 sts and 32 rows = 4" in St st

PATTERN NOTES

Use one color marker during CO to mark raglan increase points. Use the second set of markers to indicate beginning and end of ribbed sections later in the pattern.

The cables are worked on a background of garter stitch on the Front and Back. Every other row will be knit all the way across the cable sections to maintain garter stitch in the round. The sleeves are worked in rib, so each row will have knits and purls.

SPECIAL STITCHES

RLI: Knit into right leg of stitch below the next stitch on the needle

LLI: Knit into left leg of stitch below the stitch just worked

RLIp: Purl into right leg of stitch below the next stitch on the needle

LLIp: Purl into left leg of stitch below the stitch just worked

---

Knitters' Guide to Essential Blogging Terminology

Noise—noun: on a blog or Ravelry, noise is the visual clutter that makes it difficult for readers to focus on the blog's content or on specific targeted advertisements or patterns on Ravelry.

C4L: Place 2 sts on CN and hold in front, k2, k2 from CN

C4R: Place 2 sts on CN and hold in back, k2, k2 from CN

C4Lp: Place 2 sts on CN and hold in front; k1, p1; k2 from CN

C4Rp: Place 2 sts on CN and hold in back; k2; p1 k1 from CN

C3L: Place 2 sts on CN and hold in front, k1, k2 from CN.

C3R: Place 1 st on CN and hold in back, k2, k1 from CN

C3Lp: Place 1 st on CN and hold in front, k2, p1 from CN

C3Rp: Place 2 sts on CN and hold in back, p1, k2 from CN

DIRECTIONS

CO 13 (13, 13, 29, 29) sts, pm, CO 43 (43, 43, 59, 59) sts, pm, CO 13 (13, 13, 29, 29) sts, pm, CO 43 (43, 43, 59, 59), pm—112 (112, 112, 176, 176) sts. Join in the rnd.

Rnd 1: *RLI, k to next marker, LLI, sm, rep from * 3 more times.

Rnd 2: Purl.

Rep these 2 rounds 7 times—16 rounds total.

Rnd 17: Rep Rnd 1; you should have 184 (184, 184, 248, 248) sts total—31 (31, 31, 47, 47) sts for each sleeve and 61 (61, 61, 77, 77) sts each for front and back.

Cable Set-up (Size S, M & L Only)

Rnd 18: Sleeve: k4, p5, k4, p5, k4, p5, k4;

Front: K4, p2, k4, p7, k4, p2, k4, p7, k4, p2, k4, p7, k4, p2, k4;

Sleeve: K4, p5, k4, p5, k4, p5, k4;

Back: K4, p2, k4, p7, k4, p2, k4, p7, k4, p2, k4, p7, k4, p2, k4.

Rnd 19 (Inc Round): Work raglan incs in purl as follows: *sl raglan seam marker, RLIp, work next sts in k4, p4 rib as est in Rnd 18, sl cable marker, k sts in cable section, sl cable marker, work to raglan seam marker in k4, p4 rib as est in Rnd 18, LLIp, rep from * 3 more times.

Rnd 20: Sleeve: P1, place marker to denote beginning of cable section, k4, p5, k4, p5, k4, p5, k4, place marker, p1;

Front: P1, place marker to denote beginning of cable section, k4, p2, k4, p7, k4, p2, k4, p7, k4, p2, k4, place marker, p1;

Sleeve: P1, place marker to denote beginning of cable section, k4, p5, k4, p5, k4, p5, k4, place marker, p1;

Back: P1, place marker to denote beginning of cable section, k4, p2, k4, p7, k4, p2, k4, p7, k4, p2, k4, p7, k4, p2, k4, place marker, p1.

Rnds 22–27: Follow instructions on Body Cable Section chart as for rows 68–73. This will give your cables their "legs" before you need to cross them.

Continue at "All Sizes" below.

Cable Set-up (Sizes 1X & 2X Only)

Rnd 18: Sleeve: K4, p4, pm to denote beg of cable section, k4, p5, k4, p5, k4, p5, k4, pm, p4, k4;

Front: K4, p4, pm to denote beg of cable section, k4, p2, k4, p7, k4, p2, k4, p7, k4, p2, k4, p7, k4, p2, k4, pm, p4, k4;

Sleeve: K4, p4, pm to denote beg of cable section, k4, p5, k4, p5, k4, p5, k4, pm, p4, k4;

Back: K4, p4, pm to denote beg of cable section, k4, p2, k4, p7, k4, p2, k4, p7, k4, p2, k4, p7, k4 p2, k4, pm, p4, k4.

Rnd 19 (Inc Round): Work raglan incs in purl as follows: *sl raglan seam marker, RLIp, work next sts in k4, p4 rib as est in Rnd 18, sl cable marker, k sts in cable section, sl cable marker, work to raglan seam marker in k4, p4 rib as est in Rnd 18, LLIp, rep from * 3 more times.

Rnd 20: *P1, work in rib to cable marker, sl cable marker, work cable section as est in cable set-up round, keeping knit columns in knit and the purl stitches from the set-up rnd in garter stitch, sl cable marker, work to raglan inc marker in rib, rep from * 3 more times.

ALL SIZES CONTINUE:

Rnd 21: Rep Rnd 19.

Rnd 22: *Rib to cable marker, work section between markers following chart, rib to raglan inc marker, rep from * 3 more times.

Rep these 2 rounds twice more.

Rnd 27: Work as set but work raglan incs in k as follows: *LLI, rib to cable marker, work across cable section, rib to raglan marker, RLI, rep from * 3 more times.

Rnd 28: *Rib to cable marker, c4L, p5, c4L, p5, c4R, p5, c4R, rib to raglan marker, sm, rib to cable marker, c4L, p2, c4R, p7, c4L, p2, c4R, p7, c4R, p2, c4L, p7, c4R, p2, c4L, rib to raglan marker, sm, rep from * to end.

Rnd 29: Rep Rnd 27.

Rnd 30: *Rib to cable marker, k4, p5, k4, p5, k4, p5, k4, rib to raglan inc marker, sm, rib to cable marker, k3, c4L, k3, p7, k3, c4L, k3, p7, k3, c4R, k3, p7, k3, c4r, k3, rib to raglan inc marker, rep from * to end.

Rnd 31: Rep Rnd 27.

Rnd 32: *Rib to cable marker, k4, p5, k4, p5, k4, p5, k4, rib to raglan inc marker, sm, rib to cable marker k5, C4Lp, k1, p7, k5, C4Lp, k1, p7, k1, C4Rp, k5, p7, k1, C4Rp, k5, rib to raglan inc marker, rep from * to end.

Rnd 33: Rep Rnd 27.

Rnd 34: *Rib to cable marker, k4, p5, k4, p5, k4, p5, k4, rib to raglan inc marker, sm, rib to cable marker, k5, p2, c3L, p7, k5 p2 c3F, p7, c3R, p2, k5, p7, c3R, p2, k5 rib to raglan inc marker, rep from *.

Rnd 35 and all odd rnds: Cont incs in p4, k4 ribbing as est.

Rnds 36–42: Work even in patt as est, keeping knit columns in knit and garter st columns in garter st. Cont to cross sleeve cables every 10th rnd (rnds 38, 48, 58, etc.).

Rnd 44: *Work sleeve, sl raglan marker, work in ribbing as est to cable marker, k5, p2, c3R, p7, k5, p2, c3R, p7, c3L, p2, k5, p7, c3L, p2, k5, work in ribbing as est to raglan marker, rep from * to end.

Rnd 46: *Work sleeve, sl raglan marker, work in ribbing as est to cable marker, k5, p1, c3R, k1, p7, k5, p1, c3R, k1, p7, k1, c3L, p1, k5, p7, k1, c3L, p1, k5, work in ribbing as est to raglan marker, rep from * to end.

Rnd 48: *Work sleeve, sl raglan marker, work in ribbing as est to cable marker, k5, c3R, k2, p7, k5, c3R, k2, p7, k2, c3L, k5, p7, k2, c3L, k5, work in ribbing as est to raglan marker, rep from * to end.

Rnd 50: *Work sleeve, sl raglan marker, work in ribbing as est to cable marker, k3, c4Rp, k3, p7, k3, c4Rp, k3, p7, k3, c4Lp, k3, k3, c4Lp, k3, work in ribbing as est to raglan marker, rep from * to end.

Rnd 52: *Work sleeve, sl raglan marker, work in ribbing as est to cable marker, k2, c3Lp, p1, k4, p7, k2, c3Lp, p1, k4, k4, p1, c3Rp, k2, p7, k4, p1, c3Rp, k2, work in ribbing as est to raglan marker, rep from * to end.

Rnd 54: *Work sleeve, sl raglan marker, work in ribbing as est to cable marker, c4R, p4, c4L, p7, c4R, p4, c4L, p7, c4L, p4, c4R, p7, c4L, p4, c4R, work in ribbing as est to raglan marker, rep from * to end.

Rnd 56: Work even in patt as est.

Rnd 57: Work incs in p4, k4 ribbing as est.

SIZE S ONLY:

Cont with "Separate Sleeves from the Body."

SIZES M AND L ONLY:

Rnds 58–68: Work in patt as est, following boxed patt repeat for cables of chart.

Rnd 69: Work incs in p4, k4 ribbing as est.

Cont with "Separate Sleeves from the Body."

SIZES 1X AND 2X ONLY:

Rnds 58–74: Work in patt as est, following boxed patt repeat for cables.

Rnd 75: Work incs in p4, k4 ribbing as est.

Cont with "Separate Sleeves from the Body."

SEPARATE SLEEVES FROM THE BODY:

Place sleeve sts onto length of scrap yarn to be worked later, remove marker, work across front in patt, remove marker, place sleeve sts onto length of scrap yarn to be worked later, remove marker, work across back in patt, remove marker.

Body

CO 0 (0, 12, 0, 12) sts using the backward loop method. Work across front, CO 0 (0, 12, 0, 12) sts, work across back.

Incorporate CO sts into k4,p4 ribbing at sides.

Work back and front in the rnd, with no incs or decs for 32 (36, 40, 40, 40) rounds or 4 (4½, 5, 5, 5)" following boxed patt repeat for cables.

WAIST DECREASES:

Cont with cable patt as est, turning the cables every 12 rows as set.

Work dec rnd every 10th rnd 5 times as follows:

Dec rnd 1: *Work in ribbing to cable marker, work 10 sts in cable patt, work 5 sts in garter st, work 2 sts tog, work 10 sts in cable patt, work 7 sts in garter st, work 10 sts in cable patt, work 2 sts tog, work 5 sts in garter st, work 10 sts in cable patt, rep from * to end— 4 sts decreased.

Work 9 rnds even in patt as est.

Dec rnd 2: *Work in ribbing to cable marker, work 10 sts in cable patt, work 4 sts in garter st, work 2 sts tog, work 10 sts in cable patt, work 7 sts in garter st, work 10 sts in cable patt, work 2 sts tog, work 4 sts in garter st, work 10 sts in cable patt, rep from * to end—4 sts decreased.

Work 9 rnds even in patt as est.

Dec rnd 3: *Work in ribbing to cable marker, work 10 sts in cable patt, work 3 sts in garter st, work 2 sts tog, work 10 sts in cable patt, work 7 sts in garter st, work 10 sts in cable patt, work 2 sts tog, work 3 sts in garter st, work 10 sts in cable patt, rep from * to end—4 sts decreased.

Work 9 rnds even in patt as est.

Dec rnd 4: *Work in ribbing to cable marker, work 10 sts in cable patt, work 2 sts in garter st, work 2 sts tog, work 10 sts in cable patt, work 7 sts in garter st, work 10 sts in cable patt, work 2 sts tog, work 2 sts in garter st, work 10 sts in cable patt, rep from * to end—4 sts decreased.

Work 9 rnds even in patt as est.

Dec rnd 5: *Work in ribbing to cable marker, work 10 sts in cable patt, work 1 st in garter st, work 2 sts tog, work 10 sts in cable patt, work 7 sts in garter st, work 10 sts in cable patt, work 2 sts tog, work 1 st in garter st, work 10 sts in cable patt, rep from * to end—4 sts decreased.

Work 9 rnds even in patt as est.

HIP INCREASES:

Work inc round every 5th rnd 5 times as follows:

Inc rnd 1: *Work in ribbing to cable marker, work 10 sts in cable patt, work 2 sts in garter st, m1, work 10 sts in cable patt, work 7 sts in garter st, work 10 sts in cable patt, m1, work 2 sts in garter st, work 10 sts in cable patt, rep from * to end—4 sts increased.

Work 4 rnds even in patt.

Inc rnd 2: *Work in ribbing to cable marker, work 10 sts in cable patt as est, work 3 sts in garter st, m1, work 10 sts in cable patt, work 7 sts in garter st, work 10 sts in cable patt, m1, work 3 sts in garter st, work 10 sts in cable patt, rep from * to end—4 sts increased.

Work 4 rnds even in patt.

Inc rnd 3: *Work in ribbing to cable marker, work 10 sts in cable patt as est, work 4 sts in garter st, m1, work 10 sts in cable patt, work 7 sts in garter st, work 10 sts in cable patt, m1, work 4 sts in garter st, work 10 sts in cable patt, rep from * to end—4 sts increased.

Work 4 rnds even in patt.

Inc rnd 4: *Work in ribbing to cable marker, work 10 sts in cable patt as est, work 5 sts in garter st, m1, work 10 sts in cable patt, work 7 sts in garter st, work 10 sts in cable patt, m1, work 5 sts in garter st, work 10 sts in cable patt, rep from * to end—4 sts increased.

Work 4 rnds even in patt.

Inc rnd 5: *Work in ribbing to cable marker, work 10 sts in cable patt as est, work 6 sts in garter st, m1, work 10 sts in cable patt, work 7 sts in garter st, work 10 sts in cable patt, m1, work 6 sts in garter st, work 10 sts in cable patt, rep from * to end—4 sts increased.

Work even in patt as est to 6 rows following the next cable.

HEM:

Work 18 rnds of garter stitch. BO.

Sleeves

Transfer sleeve sts to needle. Cast on 0 (0, 12, 0, 12) sts, and work back and forth in garter st (purl every row) for 9 rows, beginning with a P row. BO.

FINISHING

Seam sleeves. Weave in ends.

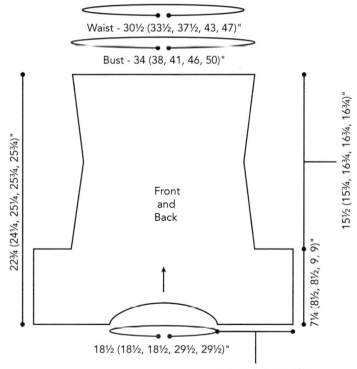

Waist - 30½ (33½, 37½, 43, 47)"

Bust - 34 (38, 41, 46, 50)"

22¾ (24¼, 25¼, 25¾, 25¾)"

15½ (15¾, 16¾, 16¾, 16¾)"

Front and Back

7¼ (8½, 8½, 9, 9)"

18½ (18½, 18½, 29½, 29½)"

7¼ (8½, 8½, 9¼, 9¼)"

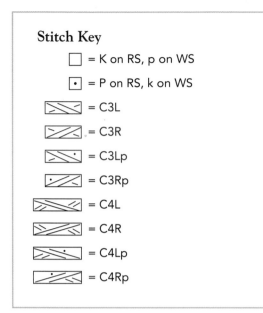

Stitch Key

☐ = K on RS, p on WS

· = P on RS, k on WS

= C3L

= C3R

= C3Lp

= C3Rp

= C4L

= C4R

= C4Lp

= C4Rp

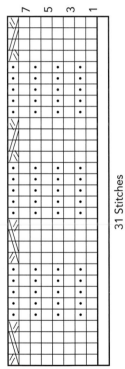

Sleeve Cable Section

31 Stitches

24-Row Repeat

Body Cable Section

61 Stitches

Joan McGowan-Michael, White Lies Designs

J oan McGowan-Michael's lacy, ultra-feminine knitwear designs bring to mind the words "romantic" and "pulchritude." And let's not forget "unabashedly sexy." Fashion-obsessed from childhood, she soaked up the lessons imparted by her stylish mother, who inspired Joan's ongoing appreciation of 1940s vintage clothing and custom shaping details. The creator of Internet-based pattern business White Lies Designs and author of the successful volume *Knitting Lingerie Style* knew from adolescence that fashion would be her career. "There's never been anything else I wanted to do. There were no other options for me."

No sooner had she graduated from fashion school in southern California than she was able to begin applying the dressmaking skills she had acquired there. In the early years of her career, her style ran the gamut from racy (she cut her design teeth creating risqué lingerie for Frederick's of Hollywood) to luxe (before "Bridezilla" made it into reality TV's public domain, she ran a custom bridal shop where referrals from satisfied newlyweds kept her booked solid as much as a year in advance). In both, she adopted a range of "little visual tricks" to create designs known for their flattering fit on the body.

Her segue into knitwear design was a happy accident, when soon after relocating to northern California she joined the local knitting guild as a way to meet new people. A lifelong hobby knitter, she soon began designing patterns for another guild member who had just launched a knit kit business. With the success of those patterns, she tried her hand at knitting magazine submissions. Her first two submissions made the cover of *Interweave Knits* (Summer and Winter, 1998), and that early recognition was followed by several additional published designs. Most recent was her lacy babydoll sweater on the cover of British knitting magazine *YARN Forward* (April, 2009).

Purchase of the domain name WhiteLiesDesigns.com was a well-timed Christmas gift from her husband. Although it had been the name of her bridalwear business, this time she had no idea how she would use it—although even then she suspected that the name had followed her throughout her career for a reason. After all, "white lies are flattering little lies that make everybody feel good."

In 2001, when four of her plus-size designs for a pattern company were dropped because the company decided they were too "shapely" for larger women, she put them up on her new website on a whim. Even with line drawings standing in for photos, the group of patterns was an immediate success. Realizing quickly that she was on to something, White Lies Designs was officially reborn. The site is a lush reflection of her design philosophy, visually romantic in rosy pinks and reds and embellished with graceful floral motifs.

Her reputation was soon cemented as a plus-size-friendly designer (her garment sizing often includes up to a 56" bust), whose curve-flattering sweaters offer large women a refreshing departure from the usual "rectangular bags." Soon, she was teaching garment-fitting classes at yarn shops nationwide, and she and her husband became popular fixtures at knitting and fiber shows.

In fact, Joan and her husband manage White Lies Designs as a team. "We run the business together, and we are *always* together." Their close relationship inspired her business mantra that every woman should believe in her own beauty, because: "He makes me feel like a goddess, and that's something I want every woman to feel about herself. Every woman [no matter what her size] has a right to feel that she is beautiful. So many women don't knit for themselves; they give away everything they knit. I want them to love themselves enough to give to themselves."

She deployed all of her pattern-drafting skills as well as her bridalwear, lingerie, and swimsuit design experience in writing her first book, *Knitting Lingerie Style* (Stewart Tabori & Chang, 2007). Her deep understanding of the principles of fit results in supremely flattering clothing. This gives her a distinct advantage in the industry "because many knitwear designers do not sew and don't necessarily understand traditional garment construction." The unusual subject matter of her book—lingerie as a knitwear design influence—combined with the vintage '40s style and tailoring that had been her first love, made it a success.

The book's 32 projects are perfect distillations of her theories on garment design. Her mission was to ensure that knitters everywhere could benefit from her wealth of experience. After all, generations of pre-Spanx women wore severe undergarments that manipulated and shaped the body so that outer garments could simply sit, with deceptive comfort and ease, on top of those pieces. With a woman's body thus contained, even the most tailored clothing appeared "natural." Joan understood, however, that "there's some serious engineering that goes into designing bras with adequate support for a larger bust." To that end, she educates women on how to achieve a custom fit in their knitted garments because when they fit properly, none of those antiquated foundation garments are needed.

She is often hired as a consultant by savvy yarn shop owners who recognize consumer desire to make garments that fit; she trains shop staff to help customers achieve that happy ending through accurate measurements, pattern modifications, and gauge adjustments.

In addition, she teaches a fit workshop called "Whip Your Knits into Shape," which divides the body into front and back and then measures each separately, "because you don't have breasts in the back. When you're applying measurements to real life, there's always going to be a difference between front and back." Students graph out the stitches to create pattern-making building blocks for short rows, increases, and decreases. "Once you have those measurements . . . you have the clarity to see what you're really working with. Certain dressmaker techniques such as set-in sleeves, darts, and waist shaping had gone out of fashion among knitters because they are a little more challenging," but they improve fit so much that Joan is determined to restore them to the average knitter's skill set. She is among the designers responsible for renewed interest in vintage patterns because of, rather than in spite of, these details.

Finished projects from both White Lies Designs and *Knitting Lingerie Style* pop up regularly on Ravelry, and it's always a thrill when Joan sees that "people are getting it, that 'aha' moment"—when they understand how to create a wearable garment that really fits. From her perspective, it is a truth universally acknowledged that "everybody has to wear clothes, and most people care how they look in them."

The Internet and knitters' online communities are integral parts of her business. She reads dozens of knitting blogs and regularly surfs the forums on Ravelry to supplement her addiction to fashion magazines. Her own blog, White Lies Knits!, is a place to comment on fashion trends that interest her, talk about her business, and introduce new designs. White Lies Designs's 40-plus patterns reach knitters worldwide, and individuals in countries from Russia to Japan to Australia order her patterns from the Web site. In addition to downloadable PDFs that are available to customers exclusively through the site, she continues to supply hard-copy printed patterns to dozens of yarn shops around the United States.

Proud of her backward-looking fashion instincts, she believes that vintage knits are making a comeback; Joan's knitwear does for 1940s fashions what the cable TV series *Mad Men* does for the fashions of the early 1960s. While knitters don't necessarily look at their own grandmothers as fashion icons, reaching further back to their great-grandmothers' generation, she sees "gracious shaping details, unique finishing touches, and interesting fashion that's due for a revival."

Challenging herself to provide knitters with a wide range of feminine and flattering patterns, Joan works consistently to ramp up her design aesthetic. Aware of the proliferation of free patterns available online, she builds more shaping into her patterns, more lace, and more interesting construction techniques, intent on making them a good value. And through it all, she's grateful to have made a career of knitwear design. "It's very humbling. . . . I'm a classic 30-year overnight success."

KIMBERLY CARDIGAN
by Joan McGowan-Michael

This little cardigan is a great cover for a bare top or dress, or a sweet topping just by itself. Its shaped body and flattering vertical lace panels show off some feminine curves. Tiny front pockets provide a place to put that handsome gentleman's business card.

Difficulty: Intermediate
Skills Used: Lace, pockets, gathered sleeve shoulders, simple buttonholes

SIZE

S (M, L, 1X, 2X)

Finished Measurements
Bust circumference: 34 (37, 40, 43, 46)"
Length: 22 (22½, 23½, 24, 24½)"

MATERIALS

- Cascade Yarns Venezia Worsted (70% wool, 30% silk; 219yd per 100g); Color: 164 Shell Pink; 4 (4, 5, 5, 6) balls

- US 6 (4mm) needles, or size needed to obtain gauge

- US 5 (3.75mm) needles

- Tapestry needle

- ⅛ yd fine-gauge bridal tulle for pocket linings
- 6 half-dome pearl buttons, ½" diameter
- Sewing needle, thread, pins
- 8 stitch markers, 2 in contrasting color
- Stitch holders

GAUGE

20 sts and 28 rows = 4" in St st using larger needles

PATTERN NOTES

The cardigan is worked in one piece to the armholes and then divided. It's designed to have a close fit; choose a size that flatters your figure.

SPECIAL STITCHES

S2KP: Sl 2 sts as if to k2tog, k1, pass the 2 slipped sts over the st just knit

K tbl: K through the back loop.

M1R: (RS) Make 1 Right (increase) by inserting the left needle from back to front into the horizontal strand between the last stitch worked and the next stitch on the left needle. Knit the strand through the front loop (this twists the stitch). This results in a nearly invisible increase that slants to the right on the right side.

M1L: (RS) Make 1 Left (increase) by inserting the left needle from front to back into the horizontal strand between the last stitch worked and the next stitch on the left needle. Knit the strand through the back loop (which twists the stitch). This increase slants to the left on the right side.

STITCH PATTERN

Triple Leaf Pattern (worked over 15 sts)

Note: The stitch count increases by 2 on Rows 6 and 8; Rows 10 and 12 each decrease 2 stitches, returning you to the original stitch count at the end of the 12 rows.

Row 1 and all other WS rows: Purl.

Row 2: K1, yo, k2tog, k3tog, (yo, k1) 3 times, yo, k3tog tbl, ssk, yo, k1.

Row 4: K1, yo, k3tog, yo, k7, yo, k3tog tbl, yo, k1.

Row 6: K1, yo, k2tog, yo, k1, yo, k2, s2kp, k2, yo, k1, yo, ssk, yo, k1.

Row 8: K1, yo, k2tog, yo, k3, yo, k1, s2kp, k1, yo, k3, yo, ssk, yo, k1.

Row 10: K1, yo, (k2tog) 2 times, k3, yo, s2kp, yo, k3, (ssk) 2 times, yo, k1.

Row 12: K1, yo, (k2tog) 3 times, (k1, yo) 2 times, k1, (ssk) 3 times, yo, k1.

DIRECTIONS
Body

Using larger needles, CO 178 (193, 208, 223, 238) sts. Work 6 rows in garter st.

Begin St st and work 4 rows, starting with a k row.

Next row (RS): K1, (yo, k2tog) across; k last st if necessary.

Next row (WS): Purl.

Set-up row (RS): K11 (13, 14, 15, 15), pm, work 2nd row of Triple Leaf Pattern across 15 sts, pm, k18 (20, 23, 25, 29), pcm (place contrasting marker), k18 (21, 23, 25, 29), pm, k54 (55, 58, 63, 62), pm, k18 (21, 23, 25, 29), pcm, k18 (20, 23, 25, 29), pm, work 2nd row of Triple Leaf Pattern across 15 sts, pm, k11 (13, 14, 15, 15).

Continue in St st, working Triple Leaf Pattern between first and second and seventh and eighth markers until body measures 3½ (3½, 4, 4, 4½)", ending with a WS row.

SHAPE WAIST:

Note: *Throughout waist shaping, do not decrease or increase at the conrasting side seam markers.*

Next row (Dec row) (RS): Work in patt to second marker and slip it, ssk, *k to 2 sts before next marker, k2tog, sm, ssk, rep from * 3 times, k to 2 sts before 7th marker, k2tog, work in patt to end of row, 8 sts decreased.

Rep Dec Row every 4th row 4 more times—138 (153, 168, 183, 198) sts.

Work 4 rows in St st, discontinuing Triple Leaf Pattern.

Resume Triple Leaf Pattern and work even for 1½", ending with a WS row.

Next row (Inc Row) (RS): Work in patt to second marker and slip it, k1, M1R, *k to 1 st before next marker, M1L, k1, sm, k1, M1R, repeat from * 3 times, k to 1 st before 7th marker, k1, M1L, work in patt to end of row.

Rep Inc Row every 8th row 3 more times—170 (185, 200, 215, 230) sts.

Work even until garment measures 15½ (15½, 16½, 16½, 16½)" from CO edge, ending with a WS row.

SHAPE ARMHOLES:

Next row (RS): Work in patt to 4 (5, 6, 7, 8) sts before 3rd marker, BO 8 (10, 12, 14, 16) sts, knit to and remove 4th and 5th markers, work to 4 (5, 6, 7, 8) sts before 6th marker, BO 8 (10, 12, 14, 16) sts, work in patt to end.

Place sts for left and right front on stitch holders. Attach a second ball of yarn to WS of back and p across.

BO 4 (3, 6, 4, 4) sts at beg of next 2 rows.

Dec 1 st at each end of needle every RS row 2 (3, 3, 3, 3) times—66 (73, 70, 81, 86) sts.

Work even until back measures 6½ (7, 7, 7½, 8)".

SHAPE SHOULDERS:

BO 7 (7, 7, 8, 9) sts at beg of every row 6 times.

BO rem 24 (31, 28, 33, 32) sts.

Left Front

Return sts for Left Front to working needles. Yarn is attached, ready to work a WS row.

Next row (WS): Purl.

Next row (RS): BO 4 (3, 6, 4, 4) sts at armhole edge, work in patt across.

Dec 1 st at armhole edge every RS row 2 (3, 3, 3, 3) times.

Next row (WS): BO 11 (13, 14, 15, 15) sts at neck edge, work to end of row—21 (21, 21, 24, 27) sts. Work even until armhole measures same as back.

SHAPE SHOULDER:

BO 7 (7, 7, 8, 9) sts at the armhole edge of every RS row 3 times.

Right Front

Return sts for Right Front to working needles. Attach yarn with WS facing.

Next row (WS): BO 4 (3, 6, 4, 4) sts at armhole edge, work in patt across.

Dec 1 st at armhole edge every RS row 2 (3, 3, 3, 3) times.

Work 1 WS row.

Next row (RS): BO 11 (13, 14, 15, 15) sts at neck edge, work to end of row—21 (21, 21, 24, 27) sts. Work even until armhole measures same as back.

SHAPE SHOULDER:

BO 7 (7, 7, 8, 9) sts at the armhole edge of every WS row 3 times.

Sleeves

With larger needle, CO 71 (79, 79, 87, 87) sts.

Work 4 rows in St st, beginning with a k row.

Next row (RS): K1, (yo, k2tog) across.

Next row (WS): Purl.

Next row: K28 (32, 32, 36, 36), pm, work 2nd row of Triple Leaf Pattern over 15 sts, pm, k28 (32, 32, 36, 36).

Continue to work in patt as est until sleeve measures 1 (1, 1½, 1½, 2)" from beg.

BO 4 (5, 6, 7, 8) sts at beg of next 2 rows—55 (63, 55, 65, 63) sts.

Work even until sleeve measures 9 (9, 10, 10, 11)" from beg. BO.

FINISHING

Steam all pieces lightly to spread out lace and set stitches.

With smaller needle and RS facing, pick up and k 4 sts for every 5 rows along left front edge for button band.

Work in garter st (k every row) for 3 rows.

Next row: Make 7 buttonholes evenly spaced by using the k2tog, yo method.

Work 2 more rows in garter st, then BO.

Pick up sts for right front band as for left.

Work 6 rows in garter st (k every row), then BO.

Sew shoulder seams.

With smaller needle pick up and k in each stitch around neck.

K 1 row, then BO, taking care to BO loosely in lace areas.

Make small pleats in lower sleeve, 1 on either side of lace panel, and sew in place with sewing needle and thread.

With smaller needle, pick up and k54 (62, 62, 71, 71) sts along bottom edge of sleeve for band.

K 5 rows, then BO.

Sew sleeve seam. Gather top of sleeve, set in to armhole, and sew in place.

For pockets, snip the yarn in the center of 2nd stockinette row where Triple Leaf Pattern is interrupted. Carefully unravel 8 (8, 8, 9, 9) sts on each side of the center st and put top sts on holder.

Place bottom sts on smaller needle and work 6 rows in Garter st. BO all stitches.

Place upper sts on needle, attach yarn, and BO loosely. Weave in ends.

Cut pocket facings from tulle, with each facing measuring 7 x 4½".

Fold under top and bottom edges of tulle and press with cool iron. With sewing thread, hand-sew facings to backs of pocket areas invisibly to add stability.

Stitch Key

☐ = K on RS, p on WS

⟋ = K2tog

⟍ = Ssk

⟋ = K3tog

⟍ = K3tog tbl

⋀ = S2kp

○ = Yo

Triple Leaf Pattern

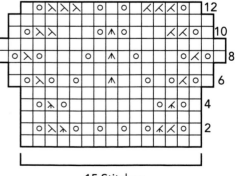

15 Stitches

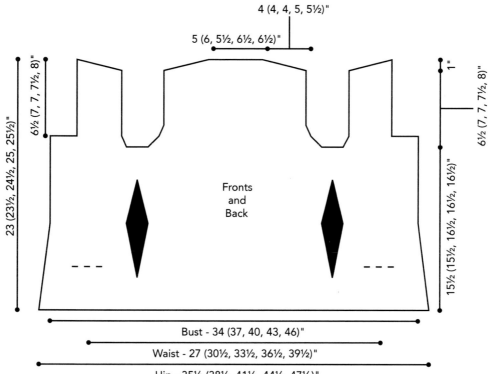

4 (4, 4, 5, 5½)"

5 (6, 5½, 6½, 6½)"

6½ (7, 7, 7½, 8)"

23 (23½, 24½, 25, 25½)"

1"

6½ (7, 7, 7½, 8)"

15½ (15½, 16½, 16½, 16½)"

Fronts
and
Back

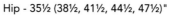

Bust - 34 (37, 40, 43, 46)"

Waist - 27 (30½, 33½, 36½, 39½)"

Hip - 35½ (38½, 41½, 44½, 47½)"

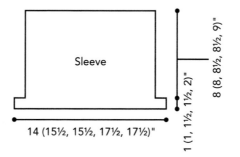

Sleeve

8 (8, 8½, 8½, 9)"

1 (1, 1½, 1½, 2)"

14 (15½, 15½, 17½, 17½)"

Mari Muinonen, Madebymyself

During the school year, Finland resident Mari Muinonen (pronounced MWEE-no-nen) is an elementary school teacher in a small village school (make that *really* small; altogether there are only 50 students), where she is responsible for two groups of children. The 8-year-olds do their lessons on one side of the classroom and the 11- and 12-year-olds do theirs on the other. But during school breaks and summers she assumes her other identity, that of a sought-after knitwear designer whose fascination with cables is matched only by her fearless design experiments. The common ground between her two occupations is blogging.

As is true for many knitters, 2005 was the year it struck her that a knitting blog could be a meaningful way to interact with other knitters—and that this could be especially important for knitters in a small country like Finland. Madebymyself has evolved dramatically since she began it; at first, its only purpose was to track new stitches and yarns and to document her projects, but now she writes it with her family and other readers in mind. She posts in both Finnish and in English because her international readers asked her to include the translations. "They comment sometimes when I write in Finnish only, 'What have you said?' so I have to include the English." And when she goes too long without providing those English translations, her fans are vocal with their dismay.

As a teacher, she also uses a blog as a learning tool in her class. "My students use it to post photos. It's new to use blogs in schools here, but because of my knit blog we were the first school in Finland to have one. Social media can be very helpful in a class setting, and my co-workers were thrilled to be part of it." Her eighteen students share a total of six computers and spend part of each day working (and playing) on them.

Her knitting blog has attracted an ever-growing international readership since the appearance of her first published patterns (the Green Gable Hoodie and Yellow Harvest

Mittens) in *Vogue Knitting*'s Fall 2008 issue. Since those first patterns reached the public domain, she has had original designs in every subsequent issue of *Vogue Knitting*. In addition, in its Winter 2008 issue, *Twist Collective* featured her spectacular Sylvi hooded cable coat. Worked in vibrant scarlet wool with exuberant undulating cables and boldly oversized flowers snaking down the back of the coat from hood to hem, Sylvi was an immediate sensation that brought even more readers to Madebymyself.

Having knit since she was 6, Mari started designing her own projects early on. "I've always made things my way." From the start, she posted photos of her original designs on the blog, and pretty soon readers were asking when the patterns would be available. The success of her knitwear projects has come as a surprise to this designer who still considers herself a teacher first. "I had no intention to become known as a knitter. I only do what I can, and I only do this when I have time, when ideas come into my head. I like to do different kinds of projects."

Although a glance through her Featured Projects section on Ravelry attests to her enduring love of cables, there are forays into other techniques as well—and all are beautifully rendered. In fact, despite her reputation as a designer of cabled projects, her knitting is quite versatile. "When I make cables, I have a particular design in my head; I know people like certain motifs and styles. Nowadays, I am making some lace and colorwork designs; I want to challenge myself. Sometimes I have huge technique problems to solve, but that's the most interesting thing about knitting and designing. I sketch out an idea, and [then I figure out how to] make it work."

She checks in on Ravelry "many times a day," admitting that she "loves it to the point of distraction. You can get every kind of information there, and speak with people from all over the world." It has also proven to be a good promotional tool for her; when *Vogue Knitting* editors first approached her about designing for the magazine, it was after seeing some of her project photos on the site. Today, her fan group has members that are making the Sylvi coat as well as several of her other designs; but for Mari one of Ravelry's most important features continues to be its ability to shrink the knitting community into an accessible, manageable size. "Knitting is truly international. You can speak with people in Australia or the United States. I can check out yarn on Rav and then order it from the other side of the world. There are no borders in the world of knitting anymore."

The face-to-face social component of knitting is not one in which she can often participate, so Ravelry fills that role for her as well. Although structured knitting groups are very popular in Finland, she has been too busy with both teaching and her commissioned design commitments to join one. Instead, she knits in the evenings, to keep her husband company in front of the TV, and on long car trips with her family on the way to their weekend cottage.

Of course, she has a lot of yarn, and she says there's a spinning mill dangerously close to her home. She recently acquired some yarn from that mill to make a big project for a Finnish crafts magazine. Fortunately, her mind is always filled with new design concepts. "Ideas come—they just pop—and I get them so quickly. I get inspired by everything around me. Architecture, from Alvar Aalto to romantic castles in middle Europe, has inspiring elements. The lines and shapes of plants; leaves are inspiring in many ways. Movies; their color schemes, costumes, details . . ."

Madebymyself often features photos of the Finnish countryside that inspires Mari, and she believes that her photography skills improved when she began blogging and sharing images of her world. Although she produces just a handful of original designs each year as her teaching career permits, she regularly adds new sketches to one of the several notebooks she keeps crammed with drawings, notes, and ideas. "When I have a deadline for a submission, I always review my sketchbooks to see if there's anything I can use." For example, the pronounced A-line shape of her Krookus ("Crocus" in Finnish) cardigan project had been on her mind for a long time, just waiting for the right opportunity. The placement of its dramatic diminishing cables, the banded neckline and cuffs, and the modest button band all evolved after much swatching and sketching.

When she gets together with family members, Mari is the only one with needles and yarn in hand despite the craft's long tradition in Finland and throughout northern Europe. "People knit when they need mittens or something else for the cold weather, but it's more for practical purposes. Here in Finland, people have always knit, but I had no idea how *many* people were knitting before I began to read blogs. It's my impression that there are many more knitters here now than there were even 5 years ago." This is supported by the fact that Ravelry's Nordic Knitters group boasts more than 2,700 members, some of whom are also surely members of the Finnish Knitters group, numbering more than 1,700.

Her alternative life as a knitwear designer is sometimes at odds with the assumptions people make about her when they know her only as a teacher. "Before I published in *Vogue Knitting*, no one but my husband even knew that I had a blog. Then I had to tell the rest of my family and friends, who took it surprisingly well. Even my father, once the *VK* came out, showed it to all his friends, telling them, 'This is my daughter!' He's not a knitter, but he understands more than I thought. Now he uses his own computer more than he used to so he can read my blog." The only downside of counting her relatives among her blog fans is that they don't phone her nearly as often as they used to. "Nowadays, they get all my news online."

KROOKUS CARDIGAN
by Mari Muinonen

Nature always inspires Mari: colors, forms, and shapes of the flowers and leaves. The vibrant color of the yarn suggested the cardigan's name, Krookus, which is the Finnish name for the flower *Crocus chrysanthus*. Architecture is also a source of inspiration; pure shapes and strong lines define this A-line style, and simple but powerful cables go through the garment and highlight the shape of the body.

Difficulty: Experienced
Skills Used: Cables, multiple increases and decreases, three-needle bind-off, following multiple sets of instructions at the same time, short-row shaping

SIZE

XS (S, M, L, 1X, 2X)

Finished Measurements
Chest: 32 (36, 40, 44, 48, 52)"
Length: 15¾ (15¾, 16, 16, 16½, 16½)"

MATERIALS

- Classic Elite Yarns Montera (50% llama, 50% wool; 127yd per 100g); color 3832, 6 (6, 7, 7, 8, 9) skeins

- 1 set US 8 (5mm) double-pointed needles, or a 16" US 8 (5mm) circular needle

- 32" US 8 (5 mm) circular needle, or size needed to obtain gauge

- Cable needle

- Stitch markers

- 6 buttons, ¾"–1" diameter

- Safety pins

- Scrap yarn

- Tapestry needle

GAUGE

16 sts and 21 rows = 4" in St st

PATTERN NOTES

The hem and sleeves have edgings, which are knit flat. Sleeves are knit in the round to the underarm, then joined to the body; all other pieces are knit back and forth and joined for seamless construction. Work the sleeves first, then add them to body and follow yoke instructions to join the pieces. By starting with the sleeves, you can use them to verify your gauge and size more accurately.

Work in St st unless instructed otherwise.

SPECIAL STITCHES

SSSK: slip 3 sts knitwise, one at a time, then knit them together (double decrease).

DIRECTIONS

Sleeves

CUFF BAND:

Using dpns, CO 8 sts.

Row 1 (RS): K4, p4.

Row 2 (WS): K4, p4.

Rep these 2 rows until cuff band measures 16 (16, 17, 18, 19, 20)". Join the CO edge to the 8 sts on the needle using Kitchener stitch.

Right Sleeve

With WS facing and beg from the seam, pick up 65 (65, 69, 73, 77, 81) sts around the band (k4 edge) using dpn needles or short circular needle, working into the back loop of the 2nd st from the edge. Join for working in the rnd. Place marker (pm) to indicate beg of rnd.

K2 (4, 6, 6, 8, 10) rnds.

Next rnd: K31(31, 33, 35, 37, 39), work Chart 1A starting with Row 1, k31 (31, 33, 35, 37, 39).

Cont with Chart 1A through Row 28, maintaining the rest of the sleeve in St st.

Work Row 29 to the last 5 sts of rnd. Move next 10 sts to scrap yarn for underarm. Move rem sts to holder or spare needle.

Left Sleeve

Work the left sleeve as the right sleeve but replace left twisting cable (shaded gray on Row 29) with the right twisting cable, as indicated in chart key.

Body

HEM BAND:

CO 8 using dpns.

Row 1 (RS): K4, p4.

Row 2 (WS): K4, p4.

Rep these 2 rows until band measures 40 (44, 48, 52, 56, 60)". BO all sts.

With WS facing, pick up 167 (185, 201, 215, 231, 247) sts from the band (on the k4 edge), using long circular needle, working into the back loop of the 2nd st from the edge.

Place stitch markers to indicate side seams with 42 (46, 50, 53, 37, 61) sts for right front, 85 (93, 101, 109, 117, 125) sts for back, and 42 (46, 50, 53, 37, 61) sts for left front.

Row 1 (RS): Sl 1, p3, k to last 4 sts, p4.

Row 2 (WS): Sl 1, k3, p to last 4 sts, k4.

Rep these 2 rows 1 (1, 2, 2, 3, 3) more times.

Set-up row (RS): Sl 1, p3, k to 2 sts before right stitch marker (rsm), begin Chart 1A with Row 1 for right side cable, k41 (45, 49, 53, 57, 61), work Chart 1A for back cable, k to 1 st before left stitch marker (lsm), begin Chart 1A with Row 1 for left side cable, k to last 4 sts, p4.

Note: *Work s2kp shown in blue on Row 27 of Chart 1A for back cable only. For all other cables, work these 3 sts as k3.*

Cont working through Row 66 of Chart 1A.

Work Rows 67–73 of Chart 1A for the right and left side cables then continue in St st through Row 79 (the side cables are now complete); for the back cable, work Rows 67–79 of Chart 1B.

YOKE:

The yoke has raglan shaping; stitch markers indicate the points where shaping is done. You will make the buttonholes as you knit the yoke. Continue the cables on the sleeves from Chart 1A beginning with Row 30 and continue the back cable from with Row 80 of Chart 1B through the ends of the charts as you work the raglan shaping. After the charts are complete

(Row 110 for the back and Row 74 for the sleeves), continue in St st.

Next row (RS): Sl 1, p1, BO 2 for buttonhole, work to 5 sts before rsm, pm, put the next 10 sts on holder for underarm removing rsm, work across the sts held for right sleeve, leaving 10 held sts for sleeve aligned with 10 held sts from body, pm, work across back to 5 sts before lsm, pm, place next 10 sts on holder removing lsm, work across the sts held for right sleeve, pm, work to end of row—217 (235, 259, 281, 305, 329) sts.

Next row (WS): Work to gap left by BO sts, CO 2, k2.

Rep buttonholes every 10 (10, 10, 12, 12, 14) rows 3 more times as you continue raglan shaping.

Next row (Dec row) (RS): Sl 1, p3, work to 2 sts before first marker, ssk, slip marker (smarker), k2tog, work to 2 sts before second marker, ssk, sm, k2tog, work to 2 sts before third marker, ssk, sm, k2tog, work to 2 sts before fourth marker, ssk, k2tog, work to end of row.

Next row (WS): Work across in patt.

Rep raglan decs every 4th row 9 (10, 10, 11, 10, 10) times and then every 2nd row 0 (1, 3, 3, 7, 10) times—101 (111, 111, 125, 125, 125) sts.

NECKLINE SHAPING:

Row 1 (WS): Work to last 12 sts, wrap and turn (w&t).

Row 2 (RS): Make raglan decs as before, work to last 12 sts, w&t.

Row 3: Work to last 16 sts, w&t.

Row 4: Make raglan decs only after second marker and before third marker, work to last 16 sts, w&t.

Row 5: Work to last 18 sts, w&t.

Row 6: Make raglan decs only after second marker and before third marker, work to last 18 sts, w&t.

Row 7: Work to last 22 sts, w&t.

Row 8: Make raglan decs only after second marker and before third marker, work to last 22 sts, w&t.

Row 9: Work to end of row, picking up wraps and working them together with the wrapped sts.

Row 10: Work to end of row, picking up wraps and working them together with the wrapped sts.

Row 11: Work to end of row, then CO 16 sts for the collar.

Collar

Row 1 (RS): P4, k4, p4, k3, ssk (1 st from collar and 1 st from neckline), turn.

Row 2 (WS): Sl 1, p3, k4, p4, k4, turn.

Rows 3 and 4: Rep Rows 1 and 2.

Row 5: P4, k1, BO 2, k1, p4, k1, BO 2, sssk, turn.

Row 6: Sl 1, CO 2, p1, k4, p1, CO 2, p1, k4, turn.

Rep Rows 1–6, replacing Rows 5 and 6 as follows until no yoke sts remain.

Row 5: P4, k4, p4, k3, sssk, turn.

Row 6: Sl 1, p3, k4, p4, k4, turn.

BO rem 16 sts.

FINISHING

Pick up sts from underarms and join them together using three-needle BO. Sew on buttons opposite buttonholes. Weave in ends. Wash and block the coat, opening cables, and allow to dry.

Chart 1A

Stitch Key

☐ = K on RS, p on WS

◺ = K2tog

◹ = Ssk

▲ = Central Double Dec on Back only; k3 on Fronts and Sleeves

△ = K7tog: Sl 4 sts knitwise to right-hand needle, k1, *sl 1 on right-hand needle, remove 1 to left-hand needle, sl 1 on left-hand needle over slipped sts, remove 1 to right-hand needle; repeat from * 2 more times

△ = K9tog: Sl 4 sts knitwise to right-hand needle, k1, *sl 1 on right-hand needle, remove 1 to left-hand needle, sl 1 on the left-hand needle over slipped sts, remove 1 to right-hand needle, repeat from * 3 more times

M = Make 1 by lifting strand in between st just worked and the next st, k into back of this thread

V = (K1, p1, k1) in same st

■ = No stitch

◿◺ = C4 over 1L: Place 4 sts on CN and hold in front, k1, k4 from CN

◿◺ = C4 over 1R: Place 1 st on CN and hold in back, k4, k1 from CN

◿◺ = C4 over 2L: Place 4 sts on CN and hold in front, k2, k4 from CN

◿◺ = C4 over 2R: Place 2 sts on CN and hold in back, k4, k2 from CN

◿◺ = C4 over 3L: Place 4 sts on CN and hold in front, k3, k4 from CN

◿◺ = C4 over 3R: Place 3 sts on CN and hold in back, k4, k3 from CN

◿◺ = C4 over 4R: Place 4 sts on CN and hold in back, k4, k4 from CN

▨ = C4 over 5L for Back, Right Side Cable and Right Sleeve; C4 over 5R for Left Side Cable and Left Sleeve

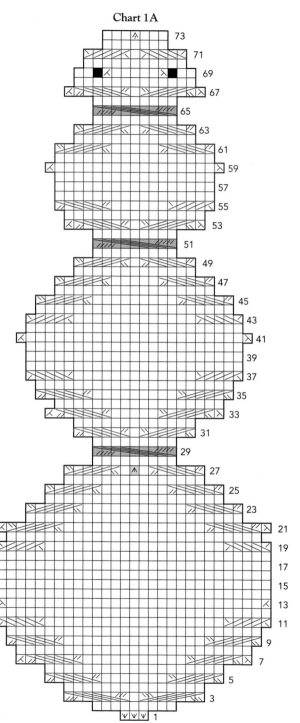

Chart 1B

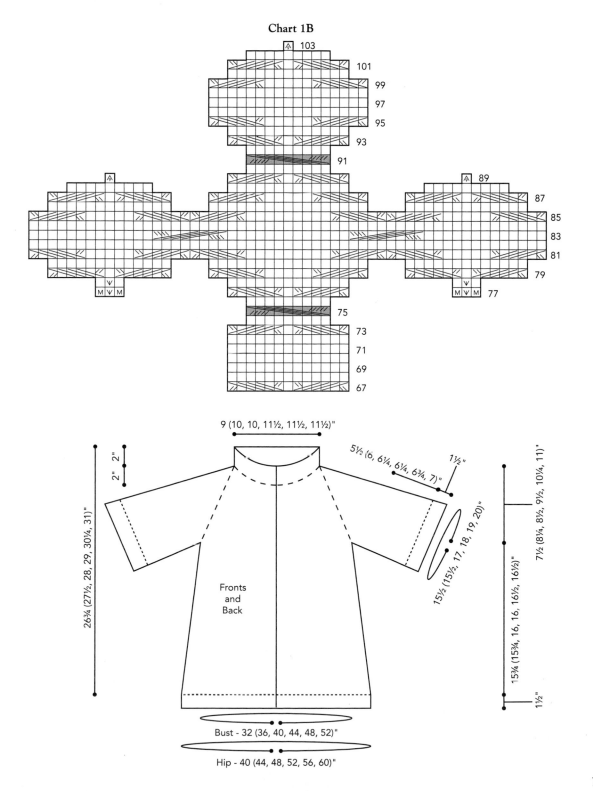

9 (10, 10, 11½, 11½, 11½)"

5½ (6, 6¼, 6¼, 6¾, 7)"

1½"

2" 2"

2"

26¾ (27½, 28, 29, 30¼, 31)"

Fronts
and
Back

15½ (15½, 17, 18, 19, 20)"

7½ (8¼, 8½, 9½, 10¼, 11)"

15¾ (15¾, 16, 16, 16½, 16½)"

1½"

Bust - 32 (36, 40, 44, 48, 52)"

Hip - 40 (44, 48, 52, 56, 60)"

Shannon Okey, Knitgrrl

In the summer of 2009, Shannon Okey moved into new studio space near her home on Cleveland's west side. It is a raw loft space carved out of a former factory, made bright and welcoming by the wall of windows and ample room for her knitting, spinning, and felting classes. A year later, it is a fully functioning hive of creativity. Yet from the age of 14, Shannon had dedicated herself to meeting the stringent requirements of an entirely different destiny—to join the Foreign Service. She picked up foreign languages the way some people acquire stray animals or new shoes, at one point studying German, Chinese, Latin, and French simultaneously. A government internship in Munich was followed by a fellowship in Prague, where her tech support skills were also put to good use.

Before knitting entered the picture, she worked in professions that were almost exclusively male dominated. But all that experience was turned on its head when she detoured into knitwear design and never looked back. This unforeseen deviation has proven entirely to the benefit of the knitting community. As someone who learned to knit in her twenties, her trajectory has been surprisingly swift and fearless. For the last 6 years she has kept her finger firmly on the pulse of pop culture, and her knitting persona harnessed securely to social media, applying her technical skills to develop one successful knitting-related venture after another.

Once she persuaded a favorite aunt to teach her to knit, beginner scarves did not hold her interest for long. Raised by parents who are both artists, she intuitively understood that knitting offered far more creative possibilities than those she found in a typical scarf's long rectangles. Soon afterward, a yarn shop owner taught her the basics of sweater construction, and within a few weeks she had made her first sweater. She has considered herself a garment knitter ever since. "All I want to wear are cardigans—classic styles that are not crazily trendy—and I design to reflect those desires. I like things that are interesting to knit, and that have enough challenges to keep me amused." An iconic example of her style is the Rivulet cardigan. Ingeniously placed cables on the garment back create waist shaping that seems to grow organically out of the ribbed peplum, while on the front, garter stitch borders give a pleasingly rustic impression. A newly sophisticated take on this style appears in the Silke Jacket project that follows.

A similar intuitive ability presented itself when she decided to learn to spin. The same yarn shop owner ordered her a wheel, gave her a quick lesson on how to use it, and then left her to her own devices. Subsequent fascination with felting and dyeing were learned with equal ease, coupling her seemingly innate understanding of fiber arts with unstoppable curiosity. A teacher of popular knitting workshops herself these days, she steadily reassures students who get nervous about making mistakes or who are fearful of not "getting it" right away. "I ask them, 'What nuclear explosion is going to come about because you have to rip back a few rows?' They freak out, but I help them realize everything will be all right."

She counts among her closest friends several other stars in the knitting firmament, such as *Knitty.com*'s Amy Singer and Glampyre Knits's Stefanie Japel (see page 42), and she maintains that the knitting world is "small but tight," a veritable "family tree of who knows who" in the business. Having quickly learned her way around the publishing industry when her first books came out, and now considered a go-to resource for new authors, she describes herself as the "underground railroad" for designers negotiating their first book contracts.

Among the earliest bloggers to create a site devoted to her fiber pursuits, Shannon started the Knitgrrl blog in 2002 and published the first *Knitgrrl* book in 2004. Her blog is, above all, an online testimonial to her wide-ranging activities and interests. A wealth of links direct readers to her patterns, books, and podcasts; to knitting-related events and workshops; to the charitable causes she supports; and more.

By the time the second book in the *Knitgrrl* series came out, she was already preparing to take on her next fiber-related endeavor. *AlterNation* (Watson-Guptill, 2007) is a sewing book about creating new clothes from thrift store items, and with the contractions that began in the U.S. economy around that time, the concept could not have been more timely. As the author or co-author of more than a dozen craft books that include *Spin to Knit: The Knitter's Guide to Making Yarn* (Interweave Press, 2006) and *Alt Fiber* (Ten Speed Press, 2008), it's mind-boggling that she also finds time to teach workshops and to organize her region's annual indie craft fair, the Bizarre Bazaar.

But it is her history with the Internet that really demonstrates her contributions to the knitting community. "There were not that many of us even 6 years ago . . . but then it exploded when the wider knitting community became aware of blogs. It was only natural that niche blogs would spring up and craft blogs would really take off." In her opinion, the Internet has had a two-fold effect on knitting. "Before Ravelry, knitters had to read the blogs to see who was making which projects, and how. Then they would hop back over to their own blogs to post about what they had found." For many, that exposure led to the decision to make the same project. It started what Shannon refers to as the "feedback loop" of project and comment sharing, whereas before blogs, "You bought your book; you went home; you knitted [a project], and maybe the people in your knitting group saw it finished. That was *it*. Now, *everyone* is seeing it oline, and you get comments. It spreads virally, rippling exponentially out, out, out to all the people who would not necessarily have seen it before."

Ravelry's appearance announced the beginning of a "virtual water cooler for all of us who are in this niche of a business. It brings together the best of social media, and its beauty is that it allows people to share their projects immediately. If a thousand people comment that they love something, even more people will click on over to check it out." But how to keep information overload at bay? "Ravelry is a good place to find a lot of concentrated information all at once . . . it's an efficient resource that is not going to supplant or replace blogs, but augment them." And that kind of additional resource is especially important for tracking trends, because "You can keep an eye on what's popular, what's new, what's coming out . . . and instead of searching through all those different blogs, you have all that information aggregated in one place. We're all so busy; we work all the time. It's a constant battle to put the work down and get away from it . . . and [Ravelry helps make that possible]."

In addition to teaching, writing for publications, blogging, and mentoring other, less experienced designers, Shannon was, until late 2009, the editor of British knitting magazine *YARN Forward*. Since then, she has been working on her own publishing company, Cooperative Press, and running the Knitgrrl Studio. In addition, in 2010 she began teaching a variety of online classes, which she enjoys especially because "I can reach students I may have never gotten the opportunity to teach in person, and it's easier on both teacher and student—they get to follow along at their own pace." With a new book coming out this year (tentatively titled *The Knitgrrl Guide to Professional Knitwear Design: Create, Sell, Communicate, and Keep Your Knits About You*), Shannon continues to promote her belief that knitting is never one-size-fits-all.

SILKE JACKET
by Shannon Okey for knitgrrl.com

When I worked for a German company, my coworker Silke was so very precise in her clothing choices that it was somewhat astonishing to me. A designer piece marked down to $5? She wouldn't buy it if it was half an inch too long in the sleeves. The precision of this jacket's fit— simplicity yet elegance— reminds me of her. The Alchemy yarn is breathtaking and a joy to knit, too! Knitting the mohair-silk blend as a carry-along with the silk/wool adds an interesting texture without being too over the top.

Difficulty: Intermediate
Skills Used: Basic increasing and decreasing, cables

SIZE

S (M, L, 1X)

Finished Measurements
Chest circumference: 32 (34, 36, 38)"
Length: 25 (26, 27, 29)"

MATERIALS

- [MC] Alchemy Yarns of Transformation Sanctuary (30% silk, 70% wool; 125yd per 50g); color: Citrine; 5 (6, 6, 7) skeins

- [CC] Alchemy Yarns of Transformation Haiku (40% silk, 60% mohair; 325yd per 25g); color: Citrine; 1 (1, 1, 1) skein

- 36" US 8 (5mm) circular needle, or size needed to obtain gauge

- 1 cable needle

- Stitch holder or waste yarn

- Stitch markers

- 1 button, 1½" diameter (decorative not functional)

- 8 hook-and-eye closures

- 2 yd ⅝" grosgrain ribbon for front opening

- Coordinating sewing thread

- Tapestry needle

Sample knit by Andi Smith of KnitBrit

GAUGE

20 sts and 24 rows = 4" in St st

PATTERN NOTES

On charts, only the RS rows are shown. On WS rows, work all sts as they appear.

The two fronts are asymmetric; you will have different stitch counts on each side.

SPECIAL STITCHES

L5: Work 5 sts in linen st with MC only.

STITCH PATTERN

LINEN STITCH:

(worked flat over an odd number of sts)

Row 1 (RS): K1, *sl 1 wyif, k1, rep from * to end.

Row 2 (WS): Sl 1 wyib, *p1, sl 1 wyib, rep from * to end.

DIRECTIONS

With MC, cast on 120 (128, 140, 160) sts and work 5 (5, 7, 7) rows of linen st, starting with a WS row.

Next row (RS): BO 10 (10, 12, 12) sts, work to end of row in linen st—110 (118, 128, 148) sts.

Next row (WS): L5 in MC only, join CC and with both yarns held together, p9 (11, 13, 15), pm, p19 (19, 19, 24), pm, p36 (40, 45, 50), pm, p19 (19, 19, 25), pm, p to last 5 sts, drop CC and L5 with MC only.

Row 1 (RS): L5 with MC only, *with both yarns held together, k to 1 st before marker, kfb, sm, kfb, rep from *, cont with both yarns to last 5 sts, L5 with MC only—118 (126, 136, 156) sts.

Row 2 (and all even rows): Work sts as est.

Rep Rows 1 and 2 until you have 270 (302, 312, 332) sts.

Work 4 (4, 6, 6) rows as est *without* increasing, then divide body and sleeves, keeping continuity of linen st and St st, as follows:

Next RS row: Discontinue CC, and, keeping continuity of L5 at beg and end of row, work 42 (47, 50, 53) sts, place next 59 (65, 65, 70) sts onto waste yarn or stitch holder, cast on 10 (10, 12, 12) sts, work 76 (86, 91, 96) sts, place next 59 (65, 65, 70) sts onto waste yarn or stitch holder, cast on 10 (10, 12, 12) sts, work rem 34 (39, 41, 43) sts—172 (192, 206, 221) sts.

Next row (WS): L5 at beg and end of row, work rem sts as they appear.

ESTABLISH CABLE PATTERN:

Row 1 (RS): L5, p0 (1, 1, 0), k2 (2, 2, 0), p1, work Chart 1, *work Chart 2, rep from * to last 14 (15, 15, 11) sts, work Chart 1, k2 (2, 0, 0), p1 (1, 1, 0), k0 (1, 1, 0), L5.

Row 2 (and all WS rows): L5, work sts as they appear to last 5 sts, L5.

Keeping continuity of sts as est, rep 8 rows of Chart 1 and Rows 1 and 2 of Chart 2 until cable section is 2 (3, 4, 6) inches long.

Continuing with Chart 1 as set, work Rows 3–33 of Chart 2 once, then rep Rows 35–41 until desired length. BO in patt with RS facing.

Sleeves

Work each sleeve separately.

Move sts from holder to needle, CO 10 (10, 12, 12) sts and join to work in the rnd in St st using both yarns held together until sleeve measures 10 (10, 11, 11)" from the underarm—69 (75, 77, 82) sts.

Next row: P, decreasing 0 (0, 2, 1) sts evenly across row—69 (75, 75, 81) sts.

Switch to MC only and work k2, p1 rib for 2 (2, 2, 2½, 2½) inches. BO in patt with RS facing.

FINISHING

Wet block sweater, being careful not to "swish" too much and felt the mohair trim. (You can also steam-block gently if you prefer.) When completely dry, sew grosgrain ribbon to either side of cardigan's inner facing and then stitch on hooks and eyes: 7 for the front and 1 at the neckline tab. Sew decorative button on top of the neckline tab.

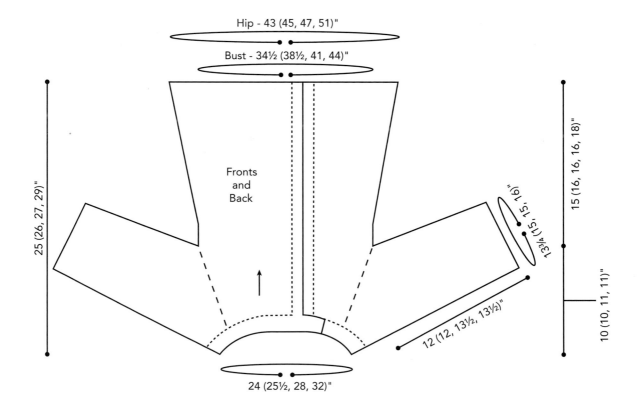

Hip - 43 (45, 47, 51)"

Bust - 34½ (38½, 41, 44)"

Fronts and Back

25 (26, 27, 29)"

15 (16, 16, 16, 18)"

13¾ (15, 15, 16)"

12 (12, 13½, 13½)"

10 (10, 11, 11)"

24 (25½, 28, 32)"

Stitch Key

☐ = K on RS, p on WS

• = P on RS, k on WS

Ⓜ = Make 1

⩔ = (K1, p1, k1) all in same st

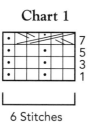 = C5F

= C5B

Chart 1

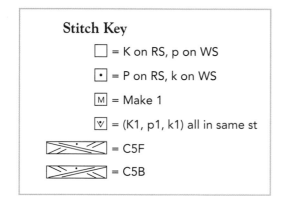

7
5
3
1

6 Stitches

Chart 2

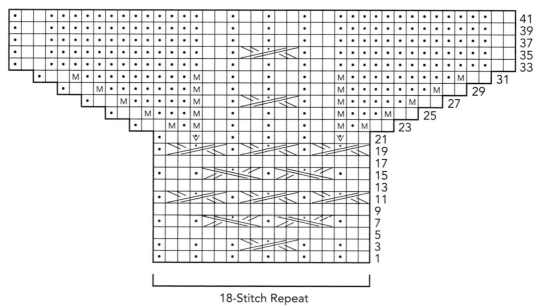

41
39
37
35
33
31
29
27
25
23
21
19
17
15
13
11
9
7
5
3
1

18-Stitch Repeat

Jordana Paige, Jordanapaige.com

The entrepreneurship bug bit knitting bag designer Jordana Paige at the tender age of 18—and it bit hard. An avid knitter since high school, she was frustrated by the impracticality of the average tote bag for carrying her knitting projects. Recognizing an unfulfilled need in the market, she had barely started college when she developed the concept for a fashionable but practical knitting bag with enough pockets and sleeves to hold all of the notions, yarn, and assorted paraphernalia that knitters typically bring along with their projects. In 2003, local press featured the teenaged Jordana and her first "Knitters' Purse," but the tone of the accompanying article was bemused and even a bit patronizing, as if it were impossible to believe in the wisdom of one so young.

Undeterred by her own lack of experience or by the distinct lack of enthusiasm from the manufacturers' representatives she approached, after months of research she finally found a manufacturer willing to make the bags to her exacting specifications. That first year, cold-calling yarn shop owners to market her bags was definitely her greatest challenge in launching a business. Today, however, not only are her bags featured in hundreds of yarn shops around the United States, but they suit the needs of knitters to perfection, and they are made of environmentally friendly pleather in an assortment of fashionable colors and styles.

Although her parents gladly supported her initiative (their garage was her first shipping and receiving warehouse), and even provided the financial backing she needed to start the fledgling company, it wasn't long before the business was entirely self-supporting. Equally impressive is the fact that while Jordana was busy establishing her entrepreneurship bona fides, she simultaneously completed a college degree in marketing.

In a small coastal California town known for its laid-back beach culture, she now works out of a large green warehouse with a bright purple door. Ensconced in her cozy office there, she is, at 26, an experienced, one-woman business phenomenon, controlling every aspect of the company from marketing and invoicing to packaging and shipping.

"I used to think I had to 'grow the business' all the time, that I had to be big. So often, we see huge businesses and think they instantly achieved that scale, but we didn't see the incremental, slow progression of steps they took to get there. It finally dawned on me that I don't have to jump from nothing to being a giant company."

Only 8 years have passed since that first basic "Knitters' Purse" was developed, yet today Jordana Paige knitting bags are sold by more than 300 retailers and yarn shops nationwide, as well as in the U.K., Australia, and Canada. Through her Web site, she also sells her bags directly to consumers. "I love the autonomy. I don't think I could work for somebody else, because I enjoy being my own boss."

In addition to her knitting bag collection, in mid-2008 Jordana launched a self-published pattern line that includes a variety of garments. Although there are only a handful of patterns so far, each is a gem—notable for its expert shaping and stylish details. While the pattern line remains secondary to the bag business, her goal is to add several new patterns each year to the collection. Supplementing her self-published patterns are the designs she has published in online and mainstream knitting magazines such as *Knitty.com* and *Vogue Knitting* (where her very first submission was accepted in 2003, before she actually knew how to write a pattern!).

Her pattern-writing skills are self-taught. "After *Vogue*, I thought, 'This is kind of fun,' so I started submitting more ideas to magazines and books as a way to build my pattern-writing skills. Lots of knitters want to be designers, but it's important to figure out and really understand how to write good patterns." That initial exposure was just the impetus she needed to educate herself. Since the success of that first effort, her work has also appeared in books such as *Big Girl Knits* (Potter Craft, 2006) and online sites such as *Stitch Diva Studios*.

Since first producing a design knit from the top down for *Stitch Diva*, many of her sweater designs feature this technique, and it has become her favorite construction method. "I'd never designed that way before, but I realized, 'This is great! Top-down, no seams; it's so much easier. And it's easier to write the patterns, too.'"

Although she is a regular at Stitches and other knitting conventions, she credits the Internet for much of her company's success. She has had a strong online presence since launching her company Web site in May 2003. Not until 2006, however, did she join the blogosphere, realizing that a blog could support her business and showcase new products, as well as give her a forum in which to discuss design challenges.

Although Jordana's photogenic older sister models each new pattern as it makes its debut, in pre-Ravelry days it wasn't so simple to see how well those patterns would flatter a variety of body types. But her fans began to share photos of themselves wearing completed garments made from her patterns. Recognizing their potential value to other knitters, she asked for more photos, and she posts them on her blog with her own comments. These customer stories have become one of the most charming features of her blog. "My favorite part of designing knitwear is seeing peoples' finished garments, their yarn choices, and the modifications they've made—seeing what they've done with [the pattern]. I always look at a pattern as just an idea, a starting point. Sometimes I think other peoples' choices look better than my original design. I love that they serve as sources of inspiration for people."

She is emphatic that she could not run her business as effectively without such steady feedback from customers. "I often poll customers to ask, 'What do you think of this?' when I'm coming up with new colors or styles for the bags. I introduce new designs and new colors every year, and that feedback is critical."

Once Ravelry appeared, it was only a matter of time until one of Jordana's customers suggested starting a fan group and even offered to moderate it. The site has had a tremendous impact on her business in terms of the frequency and quality of feedback she receives about both her bags and her designs, allowing her to be ever more responsive to her customers' needs. "I love the fact that I can search for any pattern and that people can contact me directly with questions. I can see that people are making my designs; that's actually my favorite part of the site, since I used to have to search the blogs and read comments to get feedback. With Ravelry it's all in one place. It shows me what's popular, making it easier for me to gauge what will sell."

Her thoughts on the impact of knitters on social media and vice-versa are influenced by her experiences as a knit-preneur. "Knitting is one of the trends that first made blogging big. Knit bloggers were there from the beginning; knitting and social media go together. To an extent, we've transitioned from the stitch 'n' bitch knitting circle to the equally social form of putting the craft online." In addition, she cites online craft store Etsy.com as the key to viability for many small business owners, from indie dyers and spinners to designers of novelty buttons and needle cases.

Her bag design process is still informed by her own early frustrations as a knitter who could never find the perfect knitting bag. Layout for the inside pockets is critical because they provide the bags' most important function. "Unless it has those features on the inside, it's not a knitting bag. It's got to have enough pockets to hold a huge assortment of tools." She doesn't use zippers because the yarn can get caught on them, so she regularly experiments with other kinds of clever snaps and fold-overs as snag-free alternatives. She considers fashion trends and styles, but the ultimate test of each new design is its functionality. "I want each bag to be a lasting one; an investment that will stay in style for a long time." She uses durable straps and materials because, "at Stitches, people show me what they can fit into them, and it amazes me how much they can hold. But helping each knitter choose the right bag in the right color is the most fun part of doing the shows."

When she started her business, the knitting trend was at an all-time high, and excitement within the industry was palpable. "It was easier to pick up the phone, make those cold calls, and find yarn shop owners who were willing to try something new because products were flying out of their shops. While that has subsided somewhat, the shops that haven't made it seem to be the ones that were trying to get in on a cyclical trend while it was hot. Those still in business today are really committed to serving knitters who have moved beyond the furry novelty-yarn scarf. And these knitters are the die-hard ones who like interesting garment construction, who are interested in challenging themselves, who will try lace and cables. It's still a booming industry."

Knitters' Guide to Essential Blogging Terminology

Etsy—noun: this online mega-store is the place to find an incredible variety of handcrafted items, including delectable hand-dyed and hand-spun yarns, stitch markers, fabulous buttons, needles and needle cases, and project bags. And that's just for starters!

DELYSIA CAMISOLE
by Jordana Paige

Breezy and light, Jordana contrasts the streamlined silhouette of the 1920s with feminine details of lace and ribbon in a camisole that looks equally stylish on its own or over a T-shirt.

Difficulty: Easy
Skills Used: Basic increasing and decreasing, lace knitting

SIZE

XS (S, M. L, 1X, 2X)

Finished Measurements
Chest: 30 (34, 38, 42, 46, 50)"
Length: 28¾ (28¾, 30¼, 30¼, 31¾, 31¾)"

MATERIALS

- Blue Sky Alpacas Alpaca Silk (50% alpaca, 50% silk; 146yd per 50g); color: Ice #113; 5 (5, 6, 7, 8, 8) skeins
- 24" US 5 (3.75mm) circular needle, or size needed to obtain gauge
- 1 cable needle or double-pointed needle
- Stitch marker
- 3 buttons, ½" diameter
- 4yd ⅜"-wide ribbon
- Tapestry needle
- Sewing needle and thread

GAUGE

20 sts and 32 rows = 4" in St st

PATTERN NOTES

Delysia is worked from the top down. After adding the buttonholes, the piece is joined and worked in the round in stockinette stitch with columns of eyelets. The lace straps are worked separately and attached by weaving ribbon through the eyelets.

DIRECTIONS

Body

Loosely CO 120 (136, 152, 168, 184, 200) sts.

LACE BAND:

Row 1: Sl 1, k3, *k2tog, yo, rep from * to last 4 sts, k4.

Row 2: Purl.

Row 3: Sl 1, k1, yo, k2tog, *k2tog, yo, rep from * to last 4 sts, k4.

Row 4: Purl.

Row 5: Sl 1, k3, *k2tog, yo, rep from * to last 4 sts, k4.

Row 6: Purl.

Rep Rows 1–6 twice more.

Body

You will now join the piece to form a rnd, overlapping the button bands.

With RS facing, sl 4 sts from right needle onto cn or dpn and hold to back, so that the first and last 4 sts are overlapping, *k st on left needle together with the first st on the cn, rep from * once, pm to indicate beg of rnd, **k st on left needle together with first st on cn, rep from ** once, M1, [k4, M1] to end, k2—146 (166, 186, 206, 226, 246) sts.

Next rnd: Knit.

Rnd 1: K14 (16, 18, 19, 20, 21), yo, k2tog, k41 (47, 53, 61, 69, 77), ssk, yo, k28 (32, 36, 38, 40, 42), yo, k2tog, k41 (47, 53, 61, 69, 77), ssk, yo, k14 (16, 18, 19, 20, 21).

Rnds 2–4: Knit.

Rep these 4 rnds until garment measures 16 (16, 17, 17, 18, 18)" from bottom of lace band.

WAIST BAND:

Next rnd: K3 (3, 3, 5, 3, 3) *k2tog, k12 (14, 13, 12, 20, 18), rep from * to last 3 (3, 3, 5, 3, 3) sts, k to end of rnd—132(156, 174, 192, 216, 234) sts.

Next rnd: *K3, p3, rep from * to end.

Rep this last rnd for 4 inches. BO loosely.

Right Strap

Cast on 12 sts.

Row 1 and all WS rows: K2, p to last 3 sts, k3.

Row 2: K8, yo, ssk, yo, k2.

Row 4: K1, k2tog, yo, k4, [yo, ssk] twice, yo, k2.

Row 6: K6, [yo, ssk] 3 times, yo, k2.

Row 8: K1, k2tog, yo, k2, [yo, ssk] 4 times, yo, k2.

Row 10: K4, [yo, ssk] 5 times, yo, k2.

Row 12: K1, k2tog, yo, k2, [yo, ssk] 4 times, yo, [sk2p, k1.

Row 14: K6, [yo, ssk] 3 times, yo, sk2p, k1.

Row 16: K1, k2tog, yo, k4, [yo, ssk] 2 times, yo, sk2p, k1.

Row 18: K8, yo, ssk, yo, sk2p, k1.

Row 20: K1, k2tog, yo, k6, yo, sk2p, k1.

Rep these 20 rows 17 (17, 18, 18, 19, 19) times. BO, leaving about 10" of yarn for seaming.

Left Strap

Cast on 12 sts.

Row 1 and all WS rows: K3, p to last 2 sts, k2.

Row 2: K2, yo, k2tog, yo, k8.

Row 4: K2, [yo, k2tog] twice, yo, k4, yo, ssk, k1.

Row 6: K2, [yo, k2tog] 3 times, yo, k6.

Row 8: K2, [yo, k2tog] 4 times, yo, k2, yo, ssk, k1.

Row 10: K2, [yo, k2tog] 5 times, yo, k4.

Row 12: K1, k3tog, [yo, k2tog] 4 times, yo, k2, yo, ssk, k1.

Row 14: K1, k3tog, [yo, k2tog] 3 times, yo, k6.

Row 16: K1, k3tog, [yo, k2tog] 2 times, yo, k4, yo, ssk, k1.

Row 18: K1, k3tog, yo, k2tog, yo, k8.

Row 20: K1, k3tog, yo, k6, yo, ssk, k1.

Rep these 20 rows 17 (17, 18, 18, 19, 19) times. BO, leaving about 10" of yarn for seaming.

FINISHING

Block to measurements on schematic. Lay straps on top of garment. Weave ribbon through eyelets, being careful not to twist ribbon. Secure ribbon by hand-sewing with thread to wrong side of garment. Sew cast-on and bound-off edges of straps to garment. Sew on buttons.

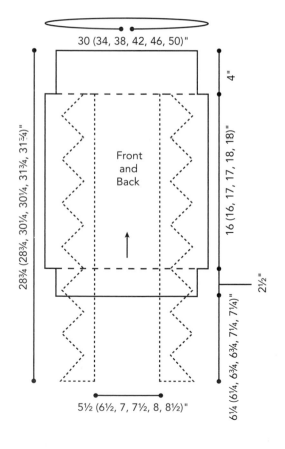

30 (34, 38, 42, 46, 50)"

4"

16 (16, 17, 17, 18, 18)"

28¾ (28¾, 30¼, 30¼, 31¾, 31¾)"

Front and Back

2½"

5½ (6½, 7, 7½, 8, 8½)"

6¼ (6¼, 6¾, 6¾, 7¼, 7¼)"

Knitters' Guide to Essential Blogging Terminology

Meme—noun: a series of questions, thoughts, or ideas that are transmitted across the online knitter's community from blogger to blogger like a virulent, old-fashioned chain letter.

Stitch Key

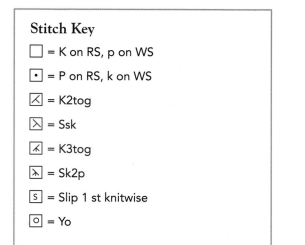

☐ = K on RS, p on WS

• = P on RS, k on WS

⟋ = K2tog

⟍ = Ssk

⟋ = K3tog

⟑ = Sk2p

S = Slip 1 st knitwise

○ = Yo

Lace Band Chart

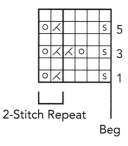

2-Stitch Repeat

Beg

Right Strap Chart

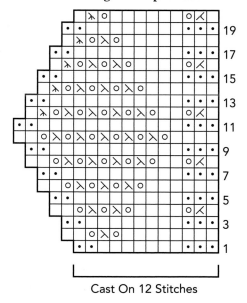

Cast On 12 Stitches

Left Strap Chart

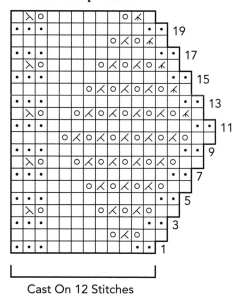

Cast On 12 Stitches

Hilary Smith Callis, The Yarniad

Growing up in a Danish and Swedish farming family in California's Central Valley, Hilary Smith Callis was surrounded from her earliest childhood by generations of skilled knitters. She has vivid memories of sitting with her maternal grandmother, painstakingly working to master the Continental knitting style she uses to this day. It was slow going: "I worked on the same garter stitch scarf for years, and I would pick it up whenever the urge struck to do something crafty."

Although she put aside her knitting in favor of other activities through high school and college, once she began her job as "the token humanities person" at NASA's Ames Research & Visitor Center south of San Francisco, the long commute provided just the motivation she needed to revive the hobby, because it gave her a creative outlet to balance her science-oriented day job. In late 2006, aware of her tendency to make substantial modifications to every pattern she knit, she studied a sweater pattern that was the jumping-off point for designing her own garments—the popular Drops Jacket from Garnstudio (to date she has made two of them).

An intuitive knitter, Hilary rarely draws more than a very quick, rough sketch of her concept, preferring to work from the image she sees in her mind's eye. She seldom writes up a pattern as she creates an original design, choosing instead to swatch, swatch, and swatch some more until the fabric and styling take on the qualities she envisions. Only once the project has been completed does she commit the pattern to paper. A kimono-style wrap cardigan, simple but classic, was her first effort to capture one of the many ideas in her head.

Ravelry opened her eyes to the infinite number of variables that existed for each pattern that tempted her, and reading knitting blogs revealed the kinship that was growing among passionate knitters. In mid-2007 she started writing her own blog simply as a way to document and photograph her projects, "even though it seemed so self-indulgent, and I was positive that no one but my mother would read it." "The Yarniad" name is a direct reference to Hilary's college years as a classics and art history major, and her Latin-titled blog categories ("Res Completa" for finished projects, "Res Originales" for her original designs, etc.) are further riffs on her continuing love for the precision of the dead language. "Classics is one of my great loves . . . but the Greek and Latin word for knitting is 'plecto.' I didn't like the look or the sound of that, so I came up with my own."

Her dormant creativity reawakened with her first successful design efforts. And with an eye for body-conscious, feminine styles that are fashionable but not trendy, she quickly developed an online following. As each new design appeared in her blog, feedback and comments increased, and it was clear that the traffic to her site extended well beyond her mother. When blogger Teresa Gregorio of Canaryknits featured The Yarniad in 2008 as part of its regular spotlight on indie designers, Hilary realized that because of the Internet and online social networking, and despite her lack of an actual plan to make it happen, she had established herself as a bona fide designer.

Like many knit bloggers in their twenties, she has made successful re-interpretations of stylish garments from the nationwide lifestyle and clothing retailer Anthropologie, where the sources of inspiration seem endless. One of her personal projects, the Julia Livilla Cardigan, with its juxtaposition of an elegant, simple stockinette body paired with a crisp pleated ruffle down the front, is just one example of her ability to put her own refined spin on a mainstream design. "In a city like San Francisco, you see people putting together all sorts of clothing combinations, with such a variety of fashion influences—in any neighborhood it's inspiring just to walk down the street."

Although she is more knowledgeable now, having tried different fit and style techniques and mastered an ever-growing assortment of stitches, her original designs still begin with an idea that fixes itself in her imagination and won't let go. "I just let it flow naturally; it doesn't work if I force something. And I usually stick with my first idea—it's a more intuitive process. I have a better idea how to make garments fit. . . . There's less trial and error. Holding onto the image in my head, I try to get it right the first time."

Describing herself as a die-hard "wool girl" who loves the springiness and the memory of that classic fiber, she'd always rather design something simple that doesn't rely on excessive stitch variety or complicated styling to make it interesting. She prefers to let the yarn tell the story in her efforts to design pieces that flatter everybody who wears them. Yet with a preference for streamlined but comfortable garments, her fit and finishing techniques are especially important to ensure that her creations complement a variety of figure types. So perhaps it should come as no surprise that her blog has attracted passionate followers. "I never thought people would be interested in what I was doing with it. Why would anyone care? But I get comments regularly, especially after I post photos of a new completed project. People are always asking me to write up my patterns. That's one of the really wonderful things about blogging and the Internet—the constant feedback and encouragement." In 2009, she received further recognition that her designs are worthy of a wider audience when *Knitty.com* published one of her designs.

Ravelry has become the go-to resource for many knitters with questions or curiosity about what yarns will fit a specific pattern, or to find a project that will work with a yarn already in the stash, and that is true for Hilary as well. She uses it as a tool for learning about techniques, patterns, and yarn the same way she used blogs before there was Ravelry.

With no plans to quit her day job at NASA, she struggles to make more time for knitting and design, and she hopes one day to devote her efforts to designing full-time. As her original creations become more popular and she receives more requests from her blog readers for patterns, she's given more serious thought to the trade-off between doing something she loves versus making a reasonable income in a more mainstream profession—a conundrum that faces many new designers.

The staying power of the knitting trend factors into her considerations. In this new technology-based era, more people are interested in creating something "old technology" with their hands. She follows the huge uptick of interest—also reflected in the blogs—in cooking, sewing, scrapbooking, and other crafts. Many have rediscovered the "domestic arts" as a means to express who they are at a more basic level; some, like Hilary, consider it a reclamation of lifestyle goals that fit in with increased commitment to green technology and protection of the environment. From her perspective, it is a natural progression for the knitting population to embrace both the fragility of our environment and a desire to be more thrifty in our use of materials.

KOUKLA CARDIGAN
by Hilary Smith Callis

Named for the Greek word for "doll," this double-breasted babydoll sweater is flattering and just sweet enough not to give you a toothache. The fitted, empire-waist bodice is knit in pieces and seamed, then stitches are picked up from the cast-on edges and the skirt is worked down in one piece from there. The fronts and back are split to make room for pockets, which are worked as you go and give the sweater some sass. Look out for notes on customization, which have been provided to help you attain the perfect fit. Wear Koukla with your favorite skirt or straight-leg jeans and boots for a modern look.

Difficulty: Intermediate
Skills Used: Basic increasing and decreasing, picking up stitches, short rows, following two sets of instructions at the same time

SIZE

XS (S, M, L, 1X, 2X)

Finished Measurements
Chest: 30 (34, 38, 42, 46, 50)"
Length: 22½ (23½, 24¼, 25, 25, 25¾)"

MATERIALS

- Rowan Yarn Kid Classic (70% lambswool, 26% kid Mohair, 4% nylon; 153yd per 50g); color: Lavender Ice (841); 7 (7, 8, 9, 10, 11) skeins

- US 7 (4.5mm) circular needle, 40" for size XS–M, 60" for size L–2X, or size needed to obtain gauge

- Spare US 7 (4.5mm) circular needle (16" length or longer)

- 4 buttons, 1¼" diameter

- Coordinating thread and needle

- 4 sew-on snaps, size 2 or 4

- Tapestry needle

- Stitch markers

- Scrap yarn

GAUGE

20 sts and 28 rows = 4" in St st

PATTERN NOTES

The jacket is knit in pieces, beginning with the back, fronts, and sleeves above the empire waist and then the full length (the "skirt") is picked up and worked..

Three-needle join: Hold the two pieces on two needles held parallel in the left hand. Insert a third needle into the first stitch on the front needle knitwise, then into the first stitch on the back needle and knit these 2 sts together. Repeat across row until the specified sections are joined.

w&t: Wrap next stitch and turn work. Bring yarn to front and slip next stitch, bring yarn to back and return st to left-hand needle. Turn work, bring yarn to the back, and knit to the end of the row.

DIRECTIONS

Back

CO 67 (77, 87, 97, 107, 117) sts. Work 3 (3, 3, 3, 5, 5) rows in St st, starting with a purl row.

Inc row (RS): K1, M1R, k to last st, M1L, k1—2 sts increased.

Rep last 4 (4, 4, 4, 6, 6) rows 4 times more—77 (87, 97, 107, 117, 127) sts.

Work in St st until piece measures 4 (4½, 4¾, 5, 5¼, 5½)", ending with a WS row.

Note: The placement of the empire waist will vary for different body types. The piece should now reach from the below your bust to your underarm. Adjust the length as needed for a proper fit, ending with a WS row.

SHAPE ARMHOLES:

BO 2 (3, 3, 4, 4, 4) sts at beg of next 2 rows.

Dec row (RS): K1, ssk, k to 3 sts before end of row, k2tog, k1.

Work 1 row even.

Rep the last 2 rows 3 (5, 7, 9, 11, 14) times more—65 (69, 75, 79, 85, 89) sts.

Work even until piece measures 9 (10, 10¾, 11½, 12¼, 13)" from CO edge, ending with a WS row.

SHAPE NECK:

K16 (17, 19, 20, 22, 23), BO center 33 (35, 37, 39, 41, 43) sts, k to end.

Cont with right shoulder only.

Next row (WS): Purl.

Dec row (RS): K1, ssk, k to end.

Rep last 2 rows 3 times more—12 (13, 15, 16, 18, 19) sts rem.

Next row (WS): Purl.

Bind off.

Break yarn and rejoin at left shoulder.

Starting with a WS row, p 1 row.

Dec row (RS): K to last 3 sts, k2tog, k1.

Rep last 2 rows 4 times more—12 (13, 15, 16, 18, 19) sts rem.

Next row (WS): P.

Bind off.

Left Front

CO 49 (56, 64, 71, 76, 84) sts.

Work 3 (3, 3, 3, 5, 5) rows in St st, starting with a p row.

Inc row (RS): K1, M1R, k to end of row.

Rep last 4 (4, 4, 4, 6, 6) rows 4 times more—54 (61, 69, 76, 81, 89) sts.

Work in St st until piece measures same as back from CO edge to beg of armscye, ending with a WS row.

SHAPE ARMHOLES:

Next row (RS): BO 2 (3, 3, 4, 4, 4) sts, k to end of row.

Next row (WS): Purl.

Note: Sizes L, 1X, and 2X will begin neckline shaping before armscye shaping is complete. Please read through the rest of this section before continuing.

Dec row (RS): K1, ssk, k to end.

Next row (WS): Purl.

Rep the last 2 rows 3 (5, 7, 9, 11, 14) times more—48 (52, 58, 62, 65, 70) sts.

Sizes XS, S, and M only: Cont in St st.

When piece measures 6 (7, 7¾, 8, 8¾, 9½)" from CO edge, begin shaping neckline.

Next WS row: BO 21 (24, 28, 29, 30, 34) sts, p to end.

Next row (RS): Work armscye shaping if necessary, k to last 3 sts, k2tog, k1.

Next row (WS): Purl.

Rep the last 2 rows 14 (14, 14, 16, 16, 16) times more.

BO rem 12 (13, 15, 16, 18, 19) sts.

Right Front

CO 55 (62, 70, 77, 82, 90) sts.

Note: *Because the right front will be on the outside when the cardigan is worn, you will be creating a vertical hem to finish the exposed edge. The vertical hem will be worked as follows for the entire length of the right front piece:*

RS rows: K5, sl 1 pwise, work to end as specified in patt.

WS rows: Work as specified in patt to last 6 sts, p6.

Maintaining vertical hem over the 6 sts on the right edge as laid out above, work 3 (3, 3, 3, 5, 5) rows in St st, beginning with a p row.

Inc row (RS): K to end of row, M1L, k1.

Rep last 4 (4, 4, 4, 6, 6) rows 4 times more—60 (67, 75, 82, 87, 95) sts.

Work in St st until piece measures same as left front from CO edge to beg of armscye, ending with a RS row.

SHAPE ARMHOLES:

Next row (WS): BO 2 (3, 3, 4, 4, 4) sts p to end.

Note: *Sizes L, 1X and 2X will begin neckline shaping before armscye shaping is complete. Please read through the rest of this section before continuing.*

Next row (RS): K to last 3 sts, k2tog, k1.

Next row (WS): Purl.

Rep the last 2 rows 3 (5, 7, 9, 11, 14) times more—54 (58, 64, 68, 71, 76) sts.

Sizes XS, S, and M: Cont in St st.

When piece measures 6 (7, 7¾, 8, 8¾, 9½)" from CO edge, begin shaping neckline.

Next RS row: BO 27 (30, 34, 35, 36, 40) sts, *including the 6 vertical hem sts,* k to end, working armscye shaping if necessary. At this point, the vertical hem is complete.

Next row (WS): Purl.

Next row (RS): K1, ssk, k to end, shaping armscye if necessary.

Rep the last 2 rows 14 (14, 14, 16, 16, 16) times more.

Purl 1 row.

BO rem 12 (13, 15, 16, 18, 19) sts.

Sleeves (Make 2)

CO 52 (57, 61, 69, 75, 82) sts.

Work 5 rows in St st, starting with a p row.

Next row (RS): P all sts to form turning ridge.

Next row (WS): Purl.

Work in St st until piece measures 1 (1, 1, 1½, 1½, 2)" from turning ridge, ending with a WS row.

SHAPE SLEEVE CAP:

BO 2 (3, 3, 4, 4, 4) sts at beg of next 2 rows.

Dec row (RS): K1, ssk, k to last 3 sts, k2tog, k1.

Work 3 rows even.

Rep last 4 rows 0 (1, 1, 2, 1, 0) times more.

Rep dec row.

Work 1 row even.

Rep last 2 rows 13 (11, 13, 13, 17, 19) times more—18 (23, 23, 27, 27, 32) sts.

BO 2 (2, 2, 3, 3, 3) sts at beg of next 4 rows.

BO rem 10 (15, 15, 15, 15, 20) sts.

Sleeve cap should measure 5½ (5½, 6, 6½, 7, 7)" from beg of cap shaping.

Assemble the Bodice

Using yarn and tapestry needle, sew left and right fronts to back at shoulders and side seams. Fold sleeve hem to inside and fasten down by sewing CO edge to straight line of purl bumps on inside of fabric. Sew sleeve seams, and sew sleeves into armscyes. Block lightly if desired.

Skirt

With RS facing, starting at left front edge, pick up and k48 (55, 63, 70, 75, 83) from the left front, pm, 65 (75, 85, 95, 105, 115) from the back, pm, and 54 (61, 69, 76, 81, 89) for the right front including the 6 vertical hem sts—167 (191, 217, 241, 261, 287) sts total. If you do not have the exact number of sts specified at this point, simply increase more or fewer sts on the increase row.

Next row (WS): P to last 4 sts, k4.

Note: Over the skirt portion of the sweater, you will continue the vertical hem on the right

front and you will create a garter stitch edging on the left front as follows:

Every RS row: Work patt as est to last 6 sts, sl 1, k5.

Every WS row: Work patt as est to last 4 sts, k4.

Next row (Inc row) (RS): Inc 33 (34, 33, 34, 34, 33) sts evenly across the row using M1L to 200 (225, 250, 275, 295, 320) sts.

Work in St st until skirt measures 5 (5, 5, 5, 4¼, 4¼)", or desired length to pocket, ending with a WS row.

CREATE POCKETS:

Next row (RS): K to 30 sts before the first marker, mark this stitch and this row, k to 3 sts

before first marker, p3, remove this marker, and turn work. You will now work the left front only and place the rest of the skirt sts on a spare needle or scrap yarn.

Work piece in St st for 5 inches (or desired length of pocket), creating ribbing at the pocket edge by repeating the following 6 rows until length is reached (and remembering to maintain 4 garter sts at left front edge):

Row 1 (WS): Purl.

Row 2 (RS): Knit.

Row 3: K3, p to end.

Row 4: Knit.

Row 5: Purl.

Row 6: K to last 3 sts, p3.

Break yarn.

Place left front sts on spare needle or scrap yarn, rejoin yarn to right front at stitch marker, placing right front sts on needle. Remove marker. P3, k27, mark this row and the last st worked, and k to end, remembering to maintain the vertical hem.

Work piece in St st until length of right front matches left front, creating ribbing at the pocket edge by repeating the following 6 rows until length is reached:

Row 1 (WS): Purl.

Row 2 (RS): Knit.

Row 3: P to last 3 sts, k3.

Row 4: Knit.

Row 5: Purl.

Row 6: P3, k to end.

Break yarn.

Place right front sts on spare needle or scrap yarn and back sts on needle.

Place sweater WS up with top of the sweater away from you and unfinished bottom closest to you. On the left front piece (which will be on your right), count 30 sts to the right of the side seam to the marked stitch and row. Pick up and k 30 sts from these purl bumps (folding to the side along the line of purl bumps you counted can help), pm, k across the back sts on the needle, pm. Next, pick up and k 30 sts from the purl bumps of the right front piece in a straight line to the marked stitch. The 30 sts picked up from each front will create the pocket linings.

Work back and forth in St st until length of piece matches that of the left and right fronts. Break yarn and place back sts on spare needle.

Starting at the left front edge, rejoin yarn and k to 30 sts before end of needle. K remaining 30 left front sts together with 30 pocket lining sts using a three-needle join (see pattern notes).

K across the back sts, k the first 30 sts of the right front together with the 30 pocket lining sts using the three-needle join, k to end of row, working vertical hem over last 6 sts.

Work in St st for 2", or until desired total length of sweater, ending with a WS row. Maintain vertical hem throughout, and maintain 4 garter sts on left front edge until ¾" before desired length of sweater. For remaining ¾", work the 4 edge sts in St st

On next WS row, BO 6 sts (this completes the vertical hem) and k to end to form turning ridge.

Work in St st for 4 rows to form hem at the bottom of the sweater.

Break yarn, leaving a tail 3 times longer than the total width of the hem. Do not bind off, but turn hem to inside and sew down the live sts to the purl bumps on the inside of the sweater. Secure last st and break yarn.

Collar

With RS facing and starting at the right front edge (not including the vertical hem sts), pick up and k130 (140, 150, 160, 160, 170) sts all the way around the collar edge (matching this number of sts precisely is not important). Work in reverse St st (p on RS rows and k on WS rows) for 1", ending with a RS row.

SHAPE COLLAR WITH SHORT ROWS:

Next row (WS): K to last 2 sts, w&t.

Next row (RS): P to last 2 sts, w&t.

Next row: K to 2 sts before last wrapped st, w&t.

Next row: P to 2 sts before last wrapped st, w&t.

Rep last 2 rows 7 (8, 10, 11, 11, 14) times more.

After last w&t, k to end of needle, working wraps together with their sts. On next row, p across all sts, working wraps with their sts.

K 1 row.

BO all sts pwise.

FINISHING

With yarn and tapestry needle, fold vertical hem to inside and sew vertical hem in place.

Fold edge of collar to inside and sew in place.

Wash and block sweater. Blocking will smooth out the appearance of the pockets from the outside. Fasten all loose ends and weave in.

The jacket closes with snaps placed beneath the buttons. Sew 2 snap halves ½" in from the edge, one just below the collar and one just above the waist on each side. On the left front, sew the female halves to the RS; on the right front, sew the male halves to the WS. Try on the jacket; and with the fronts overlapped as shown in the photograph, mark the desired positions for the remaining snap parts and then sew them in place. Sew on buttons over the snaps.

Knitters' Guide to Essential Blogging Terminology

WIP—noun "Work in Progress"; the incomplete knitting projects that take up precious space in a knitter's bag, curl up in baskets, mushroom on the kitchen counter, rest beside the bed, and colonize any horizontal surface where a knitter can safely store them until they become "FOs."

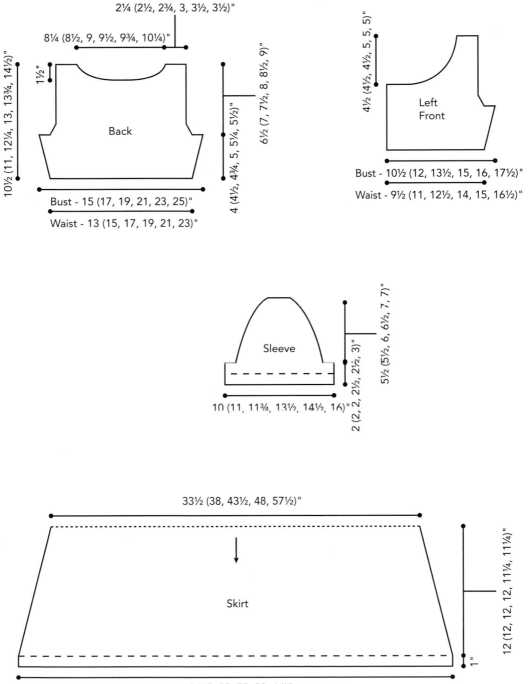

2¼ (2½, 2¾, 3, 3½, 3½)"

8¼ (8½, 9, 9½, 9¾, 10¼)"

1½"

10½ (11, 12¼, 13, 13¾, 14½)"

Back

6½ (7, 7½, 8, 8½, 9)"

4 (4½, 4¾, 5, 5¼, 5½)"

Bust - 15 (17, 19, 21, 23, 25)"

Waist - 13 (15, 17, 19, 21, 23)"

2¼ (4½, 4½, 5, 5, 5)"

4½ (4½, 4½, 5, 5, 5)"

Left Front

Bust - 10½ (12, 13½, 15, 16, 17½)"

Waist - 9½ (11, 12½, 14, 15, 16½)"

Sleeve

5½ (5½, 6, 6½, 7, 7)"

2 (2, 2, 2½, 2½, 3)"

10 (11, 11¾, 13½, 14½, 16)"

33½ (38, 43½, 48, 57½)"

Skirt

12 (12, 12, 12, 11¼, 11¼)"

1"

40 (45, 50, 55, 59, 64)"

Ann Weaver, Weaverknits

When Ann Weaver strides into an Irish pub and simultaneously sheds her jacket, whips out her latest knitting project, and orders up a foamy artisanal beer, she radiates good cheer and a kind of shooting-sparks intelligence. She has worked as an artist's model, a secretary, a baker of organic breads, a sculptor, a Macy's salesperson, a waitress, and—oh, yes—a teaching fellow at Harvard, where she did her PhD coursework in Assyriology. Perhaps more remarkable still is that at various times, she has done two or more of these things concurrently. An impressive collection of chic eyeglasses and a veritable rainbow of hair colors give her a chameleon quality; from one blog post to the next, readers never know which Ann they will see. The word "predictable" is not in her vocabulary, and she lives her life according to her conviction that, "What you do from 9-to-5 is not who you are."

Once her mother taught her the basics of knitting when she was 7, Ann felt compelled to learn as much as possible about it, much as she has with other passions in her life. She has knitted steadily ever since, although her early efforts were limited almost exclusively to "small, rectangular projects." Living in New York City in the mid-1990s, she indulged in an early version of "tagging," the art of guerilla knitting that involves covering utilitarian objects in public spaces (such as parking meters and lamp posts) with knitted cozies. Yet in the decade since she began knitting sweaters, the craft has served more as a means for her to explore the world of fiber and the notion of identity—how we define ourselves at least in part by what we choose to wear.

She particularly enjoys making garments that are "edgy but not too obvious." And indeed, her sweaters have a clean, modern style that is both androgynous and easy to wear, with one or two unusual, stand-out elements that make her fans sit up and take notice. Several of her patterns have been published in online magazine *Knitty.com,* where the editor "really 'gets' my style." Ann readily acknowledges that each knitting publication has its own "look," so she has made an art of gauging the audience for each and tailoring her design submissions accordingly. That analysis paid off when British magazine *YARN Forward* published two of her designs in the Fall 2009 issue and *Interweave Knits* included three of her projects for Holiday 2009. Editors of the new publication *Circular Knitting Redefined* are also among those who understand what drives her; she has three designs in the book.

Seeking inspiration in couture, she looks for pieces that combine elements of high fashion with those of hand-made designs. Taking cues from the construction of high-end designer garments, she looks for those that reveal attention to detail from choice of fabric to finishing techniques. "If I buy $70 worth of materials, I can make a sweater [like the ones I'd see at] Neiman Marcus. It's about getting the details right and about finding something made lovingly, not whipped out by a sweatshop worker." A garment's wearability is her ultimate consideration.

Ann's own knitting is energized by the wider resurgence of interest in hand crafts. With her own not-always-happy experiences working in corporate environments, she appreciates that during any economic downturn, people turn to things they can make and do for themselves, whether it's knitting or planting a vegetable garden, to fulfill a desire for control over at least one part of their lives. Knitting has been part income-generating fall-back and part source of comfort during her own employment challenges. And she shares the knitting community's gratitude and astonishment at the ways in which the Internet has facilitated her desire for control over her work.

The knitting blogosphere has granted her access to a world far bigger than her Weaverknits site and her own designs. It has provided her with an endless variety of creative fiber options, including spinning, that she can use for both profit and barter. In addition, it has proven a versatile corollary to her many other interests, such as the old-school punk rock aesthetic and the do-it-yourself community. Since she learned to spin in 2006 and began selling her homespun yarns via the crafters' online shop Etsy.com, she has become an expert at employing the barter system to acquire knitting paraphernalia and, of course, more yarn.

There are many free pattern PDFs available on the Weaverknits blog because she believes, "It's not all about finances, it's about giving back to the community that supports me. It's being part of something bigger than myself, saying, 'I made this—here, you have it. How many free patterns have I downloaded and made, after all? It's about sharing with those who share with me."

A perfect example of this conviction is her Wheels of Fury hat, designed for and inspired by her indomitable father, Tom Weaver. After a motorcycle accident left him paralyzed from the waist down, he didn't miss a beat in his teaching career and began entering wheelchair races for fun. The hat, with its embroidered flames spurting from the back end of an intarsia wheelchair, is available as a free download on the Missability disability awareness site and on Stitchlinks.

Ann started her blog in 2007 after discovering the seemingly infinite number of knitting blogs she could link to via Ravelry. "With blogging, I'm able to reach a much larger community." And as a forum for her very funny stream-of-consciousness knitting commentary, she ensures that Weaverknits's readers get to know her in all her colorful quirkiness. A fan of colors that she describes as "murky," the site itself is an elegy to all things "grellow," a shade of yellow tinged with gray and green that she finds particularly appealing.

Photos are liberally splashed between her written musings to illustrate the details of her various knitting projects. In addition to this documentation, there are personal stories about her family in Michigan, her in-laws, and her husband, Chris (for whom she has made several pairs of the short hand-knitted socks he likes to wear for cycling), as well as her riffs on a range of subjects from politics and pets to the tribulations of the workplace. What communicates clearly through both the blog and the knitwear designs is that Ann's idiosyncratic creative vision is part of her charm, and that charm is manifest in her designs.

The Johnny Rotten Jacket that follows expresses her aesthetic perfectly; with its in-your-face color combination and mock-tailoring details, it reinvents the very punk rock style it professes to emulate. But that should come as no surprise from an individual who regularly reinvents herself and has mastered the art of finding happiness wherever she finds herself. Her coworkers in the organic bakery, for example, "are more intelligent, thoughtful, and well-informed than any of my administrative coworkers *ever*. All of them read. All of them know about current events, even the obscure BBC-only stuff. It's fantastic."

JOHNNY ROTTEN JACKET
by Ann Weaver

This piece was inspired by a photo of Johnny Rotten, lead singer of the Sex Pistols, in a blue plaid jacket, as well as a conversation I had with one of my friends a few years back:

Me: You know, I'd like to get a suit custom made for myself, a man's skinny suit tailored to my measurements. A real classic punk rock suit, a London Calling suit.

Friend: You need a Johnny Rotten suit.

Me: Oh yes, yes I do. To wear to my state bureaucrat job. I mean, it's a suit, it's appropriate, what could they say? I think it should be pinstriped.

Friend: Blue and orange pinstriped.

Me: Holy cow. Yes.

The bespoke Johnny Rotten Suit never materialized, and I quit my state job soon afterward. When presented with the opportunity to design for this book, however, the idea immediately came to mind, and I began to engineer a pinstriped knit fabric.

   The result is even better than I initially envisioned: Pinstriped, blue and orange, fitted, stunning—and I made it myself. Which is totally punk rock.

Difficulty: Intermediate
Skills Used: Stranded knitting, slip-stitch patterning, turned hem facings, increasing and decreasing in pattern, seaming, following multiple sets of instructions simultaneously, single crochet edging

SIZE

XS (S, M, L, 1X)

Finished Measurements
Chest: 32 (35, 38, 41, 44)"
Length: 20½ (21½, 22, 23½, 25)"

MATERIALS

- [MC] Berroco Peruvia (100% Peruvian Highland wool; 174yd per 100g); color: Aquamarina 7143; 5 (6, 8, 9, 10) skeins

- [CC] Berroco Peruvia (100% Peruvian Highland wool; 174yd per 100g); color: Naranja 7110; 2 (2, 2, 3, 3) skeins

- 24" US 9 (5.5mm) circular needle, or size needed to obtain gauge

- 24" US 8 (5mm) circular needle

- 16" US 9 (5.5mm) circular needle

- Size E/4 (3.5mm) crochet hook

- 3 buttons, 1¼" diameter

- Stitch markers

- 2 stitch holders or waste yarn for holding live stitches

- Tapestry needle

GAUGE

16 sts and 24 rows = 4" in St st using larger needles

21 sts and 28 rows = 4" in patt stitch using larger needles

PATTERN NOTES

Carry the CC yarn very loosely across the WS of the work on Rows 5 and 10 to avoid puckering the fabric, and measure gauge after pattern swatch has been steam blocked. Note, however, that gauge in pattern will differ greatly from gauge in stockinette because the slip-stitch Pinstripe Pattern creates a fabric with significantly less stretch. Make a large gauge swatch in pattern to assure that your finished garment will fit correctly.

With the exception of the hem facings, the entire jacket is worked in the Pinstripe Pattern as in the chart.

Note: *The border sts on either side of the main pattern are only worked at the beginning of body rows for sizes XS, M, and 1X and on the sleeves. For sizes S and L, omit these border sts when working the body, working only the main 8 sts.*

When you are shaping the garment, the CC slip stitch rows (Rows 5 and 10) are always worked as set with no decreases, and the decreases are continued in the next appropriate row.

Slip the first st of each row that is worked in MC and work the 1st st of each row that is worked in CC. Slipping these sts makes working the single crochet trim easier.

BUTTONHOLE:

Row 1: Work 3 sts, BO next 3 sts, work to end of row.

Row 2: Work to gap created by bound-off sts in previous row. CO 3 sts over the 3 bound-off sts.

Note: *The 2nd of the 3 bound-off sts (the 5th st of the row) is a CC st. Since the buttonhole rows are both MC rows, BO the CC st in MC, and CO the st in its place in MC as well.*

The 2 buttonhole rows are always followed by a CC row (either Row 5 or Row 10 of Pinstripe Pattern). On the row following the 2 buttonhole rows, work the 5th st of the row in CC to reestablish the pattern.

DIRECTIONS
Body

Using MC and smaller needle, CO 169 (183, 199, 215, 231) sts. Pm after the 44th (48th, 52nd, 56th, 60th) st and after the 45th (49th, 53rd, 57th, 61st) st to indicate the right side seam and pm after the 80th (88th, 96th, 104th, 112th) st and after the 81st (89th, 97th, 105th, 113th) st to indicate the left side seam.

Work in St st for 1½", ending with a k row.

Change to larger circular needle and p 1 row. This row forms a turning ridge for the hem. Join CC and begin to work in Pinstripe Pattern, following the chart.

Work Rows 1–10 (1 rep) of patt.

Work 0 (1, 1, 0, 1) reps of Rows 6–10 of patt.

Work Rows 1–10 of patt 3 (3, 3, 4, 4) more times.

WAIST SHAPING:

Next row (Row 1 of patt): *Work to 2 sts before marker, ssk, slip marker, work st between markers, slip marker, k2tog, rep from * once, then work to end of row—165 (179, 195, 211, 227) sts rem.

Work Rows 2–10 of patt with no shaping.

Next row (Row 1 of patt): *Work to 9 sts before marker, ssk, work to 2 sts before marker, ssk, slip marker, work st between markers, slip marker, k2tog, work 5 sts, k2tog, rep from * to end of row—157 (171, 187, 203, 219) sts rem.

Work Rows 2–7 of pattern with no shaping.

Next row: Continuing in patt, work Row 1 of buttonhole.

Next row: Work Row 2 of buttonhole.

Work Row 10 of patt.

Next row (Row 1 of patt): Work to 8 sts before 1st marker, ssk, work to 6 sts after 2nd marker, k2tog, work to 8 sts before 3rd marker, ssk, work to 6 sts after 4th marker, k2tog, work to end of row—153 (167, 183, 199, 215) sts.

Work Rows 2–10 of patt with no shaping. Work Rows 1–2 of patt one more time.

Next row: Cont in patt and work Row 1 of buttonhole.

Next row: Work Row 2 of buttonhole.

Work Row 5 of pattern.

Next row (Row 6 of patt): Work to 6 sts before 1st marker, M1R, work to 6 sts after 2nd marker, M1L, work to 6 sts before 3rd marker, M1R, work to 6 sts after 4th marker, M1L—157 (171, 187, 203, 219) sts.

Work Rows 7–10, then Rows 1–5 of patt.

Next row (Row 6 of patt): Work to 7 sts before 1st marker, M1R, work to 1st marker, M1R, slip 1st marker, work st between 1st and 2nd markers, slip 2nd marker, M1L, work to 7 sts after 2nd marker, M1L, work to 7 sts before 3rd marker, M1R, work to 3rd marker, M1R, slip 3rd marker, work st between 3rd and 4th

markers, slip 4th marker, M1L, work to 7 sts after 4th marker, M1L, work to end of row—165 (179, 195, 211, 227) sts.

Work Row 7 of patt.

Next 2 rows: Cont in patt and work Rows 1 and 2 of buttonhole.

Work Row 10 of patt.

BEGIN NECK SHAPING:

Read through the following section before continuing. You will continue shaping the waist and, **at the same time,** decrease at the neck as follows:

Dec 1 st on each end of next on every RS row a total of 10 (10, 10, 10,12) times, then every 6 (6, 6, 6, 6) rows a total of 4 (5, 6, 7, 7) times as follows: K1, ssk, work to last 3 sts in pattern, k2tog, k1.

Next row (Row 1 of patt): *Work to marker, M1R, slip marker, work st between markers, slip marker, M1L, repeat from * once, then work to end of row—169 (183, 199, 215, 231) sts rem.

Work 19 (19, 19, 19, 29) more rows in patt as you continue neck shaping.

DIVIDE FRONTS AND BACK:

Next row (Row 1 of patt): Work to 4 (5, 6, 6, 6) sts before 1st marker, BO next 8 (10, 12, 12, 12) sts, removing 1st and 2nd markers, work to 4 (5, 6, 6, 6) sts before 3rd marker, BO next 8 (10, 12, 12, 12) sts, removing 3rd and 4th markers, work to end.

Left Front

Work the sts for the Left Front only. Place rem sts on holders or lengths of waste yarn. Cont with neckline decreases as est as you shape the armhole as follows:

Next row (WS): Work even, working neckline decrease as est.

Next row (RS): BO 3 (4, 4, 4, 4) sts, work to end of row.

Next row: Work even, working neckline decrease as est.

Dec 1 st at armhole edge on next 3 (3, 5, 5, 6) MC RS rows as follows: K1, ssk, work to end—24 (26, 26, 30, 33) sts rem for Left Front when all shaping is completed. Work even until piece measures 8 (8½, 9, 9½, 10)" from beg of armhole shaping, ending with a WS row.

SHOULDER SHAPING:

As you shape the shoulder, you will BO at the beg of every RS row, **except** the CC row. Work Row 5 normally and cont binding off on the next RS row.

***Row 1 (RS):** BO 4 (4, 4, 4, 4) sts, work to end.

Row 2 and following WS rows: Work even.

Row 3: BO 4 (4, 4, 4, 5) sts, work to end.

Row 5: BO 4 (4, 4, 6, 6) sts, work to end.

Next row (WS): BO rem 12 (14, 14, 16, 18) sts.***

Right Front

Return Right Front sts to needle and join MC with WS facing. Join CC when necessary.

Note: Remember to continue working the neck shaping while shaping the armhole.

Next row (WS): BO 3 (4, 4, 4, 4) sts work to end of row.

Next row (RS): Work even, working neckline decrease as est.

Dec 1 st at armhole edge of next 3 (3, 5, 5, 6) MC WS rows as follows: P1, p2tog, work to end of row—24 (26, 26, 30, 33) sts rem for Right Front when all shaping is completed.

After completing armhole and neck shaping, work even until Right Front measures approximately 8 (8½, 9, 9½, 10)" from beg of armhole shaping. End with a RS row.

SHOULDER SHAPING:

BO at the beg of every WS row, **except** the CC row. Work Row 10 normally and cont binding off on the next RS row.

****Row 1 (WS):** BO 4 (4, 4, 4, 4) sts, work to end.

Row 2 and following RS rows: Work even.

Row 3: BO 4 (4, 4, 4, 5) sts, work to end.

Row 5: BO 4 (4, 4, 6, 6) sts, work to end.

Next row (RS): BO rem 12 (14, 14, 16, 18) sts.**

Back

Return Back sts to needle and rejoin MC with WS facing.

Work 1 row even.

BO 3 (4, 4, 4, 4) sts at beg of the next 2 rows.

Dec 1 st at each edge of next 3 (3, 5, 5, 6) MC RS rows as follows: K1, ssk work to last 3 sts,

k2tog, k1—60 (64, 66, 74, 84) sts rem after armhole shaping is completed.

Work even until Back measures approximately 8 (8½, 9, 9½, 10)" from beg of armhole shaping. End with a WS row.

Next row: Work 24 (26, 26, 30, 33) sts, BO next 12 (12, 14, 14, 18) sts, work last 24 (26, 28, 30, 33) sts.

Working the left shoulder sts only, work shoulder shaping as for Right Front from ** to **.

Rejoin MC yarn to the right shoulder sts at the neck edge with WS facing. Rejoin CC when necessary. Work shoulder shaping as for Left Front from *** to ***.

Sleeves (Make 2)

Using MC and smaller circular needle, CO 57 (57, 57, 65, 65) sts. Work in St st for 1½", ending with a WS row.

Change to larger circular needle and p 1 row. This row forms a turning ridge for the hem. Join CC and begin to work in Pinstripe Pattern from chart including the edge sts at the beg and end of the row.

Work in patt until piece measures approximately 8½ (9½, 10½, 11½, 12½)" from turning edge row, then beg increasing as follows:

Inc 1 st at each end of every Row 1 of patt 5 (8, 5, 5, 6) times **and, for sizes M, L and 1X only at each end of Row 6** as follows: Work 1 st, M1R, work to last st, M1L, k last st. Add a CC stripe after you have worked 4 incs by working 2nd st of next CC row in CC—67 (73, 77, 85, 89) sts.

Cont to work straight, if necessary, until sleeve measures approximately 17½ (17½, 18, 18½, 18½)". End with a WS row.

SHAPE SLEEVE CAP:

When binding off in MC, carry CC along by wrapping MC over it.

BO 4 (5, 5, 5, 5) sts at beg of next 2 rows.

BO 2 (2, 3, 3, 3) sts at beg of next 2 rows.

Dec 1 st at each edge of every 2nd (2nd, 3rd, 3rd, 3rd) MC row 10 (11, 10, 10, 12) times as follows: On RS rows, work 1 st, ssk work to last 3 sts, k2tog, k1. On WS rows, work 1 st, p2tog, work to last 3 sts, p2tog tbl, p1—37 (38, 44, 52, 52) sts.

BO 2 sts at beg of next 4 (4, 6, 6, 6) MC rows—29 (32, 32, 40, 40) sts.

BO 4 sts at beg of next 4 (4, 4, 6, 6) MC rows—13 (16, 16, 16, 16) sts.

BO rem sts in MC.

Lapels

LOWER RIGHT LAPEL:

Using MC and larger 16" circular needle, CO 3 sts.

Row 1 (RS): Kfb, k2.

Row 2 (WS): Purl.

Row 3: Join CC, k 1st st in CC, k 2nd st in CC, wrapping yarn twice, sl next st, k last st in CC.

From this point on, work in Pinstripe Pattern, with 2nd st on RS corresponding to 8th st in the patt rep.

Inc in patt every **RS** MC row by kfb in 1st st. Add CC sts at inc edge as necessary to work in patt. Work a total of 20 (23, 23, 29, 29) inc rows—24 (27, 27, 33, 33) sts.

BO all sts in MC.

LOWER LEFT LAPEL:

Using MC and larger 16" circular needle, CO 3 sts.

Row 1 (RS): K2, kfb.

Row 2 (WS): Purl.

Row 3: Join CC, k 1st st in CC, k 2nd st in CC, wrapping yarn twice, sl next st, k last st in CC.

From this point on, work in patt, with 2nd st on RS corresponding to 8th st in the patt rep.

Inc in patt every **WS** MC row by pfb in 1st st. Add CC sts at inc edge as necessary to work in patt. Work a total of 20 (23, 23, 29, 29) inc rows—24 (27, 27, 33, 33) sts.

BO all sts in MC.

Steam-block lower lapels, weave in ends, and pin to right and left neck edges of body, matching the tapered ends of the lapels with the beg of the body neck shaping and matching the inc edge of each lapel with the jacket edge with WS of lapel facing the RS of the body. Sew to neck edge.

Upper Collar

Using MC and larger 24" circular needle, with WS facing, pick up and k4 (8, 8, 8, 8) sts along left front of neck just above where lower lapels end, 24 (24, 28, 28, 36) sts along back neck, and 3 (7, 7, 7, 7) sts along right front of neck. Join CC and work 10 rows of Pinstripe Pattern, working both beg and end of row border sts in chart.

Beg with Row 1, work 18 rows in patt, and inc 1 st in patt at each end of every MC row as follows: On RS rows, work 1st st, kfb, work to last 2 sts, kfb, k1; on WS rows, work 1st st, pfb, work to last 2 sts, p1.

BO all sts loosely in MC.

FINISHING

Steam-block all pieces. Sew shoulder seams. Ease sleeve caps into armholes and sew, being careful to match stripes as closely as possible. Sew sleeve seams, including hem facings. Turn hem facing and sleeve facings under at turning row and steam flat. Sew facings to WS of work.

Using MC and size E/4 crochet hook and beg at lower right corner of jacket edge, work sc border around front and lapels of jacket. At turned hems, draw crochet hook through both layers of fabric to close hem.

For the sections where the 1st st of each row has been slipped, work 1 sc in each edge loop; for those areas where you have not, or if you have not slipped the 1st st of each row, work 1 sc in every other edge loop. Work up the right edge, around the lapels, working 3 sc in each corner st of the lapel for ease, and down the left edge. Cut yarn and draw through loop. Weave in ends. Sew buttons to jacket.

Steam all seams flat. Tack collar and lapels in place if desired. Tacking these in place keeps the lapels flat when wearing the jacket unbuttoned.

Stitch Key

▨ = With MC, k on RS, p on WS

⊟ = With MC, slip 1 purlwise

▨ = With CC, k on RS, p on WS, wrapping yarn around needle twice

⊟ = With CC, slip 1 purlwise

Pinstripe Pattern

9
7
5
3
1

End   8-Stitch Repeat   Beg

Knitters' Guide to Essential Blogging Terminology

Lemming Effect—noun: when a popular project inspires large groups of knitters to knit it simultaneously.

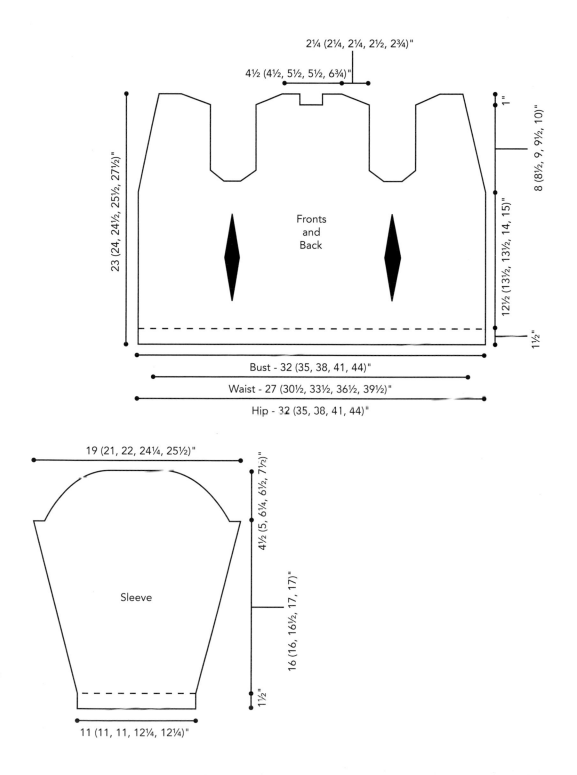

2¼ (2¼, 2¼, 2½, 2¾)"

4½ (4½, 5½, 5½, 6¾)"

23 (24, 24½, 25½, 27½)"

1"

8 (8½, 9, 9½, 10)"

Fronts
and
Back

12½ (13½, 13½, 14, 15)"

1½"

Bust - 32 (35, 38, 41, 44)"

Waist - 27 (30½, 33½, 36½, 39½)"

Hip - 32 (35, 38, 41, 44)"

19 (21, 22, 24¼, 25½)"

4½ (5, 6¼, 6½, 7½)"

16 (16, 16½, 17, 17)"

Sleeve

1½"

11 (11, 11, 12¼, 12¼)"

Melissa Wehrle, Neoknits

From the reception area on into the heart of its labyrinthine offices, the New York City knitwear company for which designer Melissa Wehrle works is an exercise in controlled chaos. Sweaters, jackets, and knit tops spill from racks, hooks, shelves, and every other available horizontal surface. Yarn color cards are tacked willy-nilly to every wall surface, where they resemble a dizzying candy store of color trends and possibilities. It is both inspiring and overwhelming, and it offers a sharp contrast to Melissa's own organized style.

Wearing one of her own lace cardigan designs, she pulled out a notebook bursting with sketches for original sweater designs. From the first glimpse, it was clear that there were more design concepts within those pages than one woman could possibly knit in a lifetime.

Melissa's selection as the featured designer in *KnitScene* magazine's Fall 2009 issue was a recent major coup—and a great surprise. With four of her designs splashed across its pages along with a profile highlighting her accomplishments, it established her as an indie designer to watch. *KnitScene*'s editor, Lisa Shroyer, said of Melissa, "Her projects are fairly simple, on-trend and yet classic; and her blog, design aesthetic, and overall persona are youthful and hip in a very friendly way."

In the magazine issue's exclusive design collection of menswear-inspired garments, Melissa's aesthetic combined what Shroyer called "girly details" such as feminine waist shaping, with classic tweed yarns, leather buttons, and tabbed cuffs in a nod to the boyfriend/grandpa-chic theme. "Melissa really excels at designing classic garments that are timeless in appeal, but that ever so subtly pick up on current trends."

A bachelor's degree from New York's Fashion Institute of Technology prepared her well for the life of a sweater designer. Her ongoing research into fashion trends does double duty as she puts her knowledge to good use in both her professional capacity and in her own independent designs. The difference is that in her blog, Neoknits, she can explore her own creativity without concern for retail fashion trends.

Neoknits is the principal sounding board and showcase for her original designs. She started the blog in 2004 after joining a Stitch 'n Bitch knit-along for one of the projects in Debbie Stoller's first book. Melissa quickly discovered that many of the other participants had their own blogs. At the time, she was working on her Granny Smith sweater pattern, never intending to publish it. "But I posted it on the blog, and the response was very positive—everybody said they loved it and wanted to know how soon the pattern would be available for sale." With its tight focus on knitting, the blog has become an important vehicle to promote her designs and sell her patterns, despite the fact that many of her favorites are "secret" projects in the works for mainstream magazines, about which she cannot post pre-publication.

Challenging herself to "push the boundaries of what I know about pattern-making" is a perpetual goal. "It's easy to write a pattern for a stockinette stitch pullover, but when you get into lace stitches there's more math—making it fit with the repeats and the sizing, making sure multiple lace stitches work together in the pattern-writing process. Some people design for the challenge of mastering a particular technique. My designs are inspired by the silhouette, the stitch. For me it's all about the fit, the timelessness, the fashion of it."

She is especially conscious of sizing issues. "Working in the industry, I have experience fitting garments on plus-size models, so I have a grasp of what looks good on larger figures. Grading up a pattern accurately is the challenge. My experience in the industry has really helped me understand fit issues. Proper fit is absolutely sacred."

Gaps in her own wardrobe are often where she finds inspiration. "My strongest designs come from things that I want and need myself. When I perceive a hole out there that can't be filled [by walking into a clothing store], I have to create it myself."

Her career in the knitwear fashion industry, with access to all that delicious fiber, is, ironically, the source of one of her greatest frustrations. "When you're working on a Fair Isle pattern or even a stripe, sometimes the color you need is not available in the right yarn, or you find the perfect yarn but you can't find two colors that work together. Color is *the* big frustration for me because I'm so spoiled."

Like many of today's new generation of serious knitters, Melissa learned the basics of the craft as a child, from her grandmother. But the hobby didn't stick. She didn't pick up her knitting needles again until 2000 while at FIT, where she studied knitwear design. At that point, her enthusiasm grew to the point that she decided to make a career of it. But work-related knitting commitments kept her from completing more than one or two sweaters for herself in an entire year, an unhappy result of transforming her hobby into a job. So she joined some of the local Stitch 'n Bitch groups and is currently a member of three groups that meet regularly around New York City.

"Being with a group motivates me to finish things, to share them, to have the [group members] badger me to keep going." In addition, she gets sizing and design input as well as votes from the group on which designs to submit to magazines. "All the members have different body types, and all have different opinions. They're such a good sounding board for me, such good PR people."

Melissa's online life spills over into her day-to-day activities. She has met up in person at coffee shops and on yarn quests with other knitters she has "met" online, and she sells her original patterns on Ravelry, where she checks in for messages a couple of times a day. "I get a lot of questions about my patterns—sizing issues and ease—and want to be responsive to those. I want to help the [knitters making my designs] as best I can, balancing that with my other commitments and deadlines."

Neoknits is clearly the blog of a knitter's knitter. Offering tutorials for her favorite techniques such as buttonholes, shaping, and fit, the site is full of useful information, relayed in clear language with helpful photos. With her independent design career really taking off since 2007, Melissa serves up frequent posts about her latest publication successes.

Melissa acknowledges that her design aesthetic is fairly consistent across the continuum of her work. She has a real talent for flattering shaping techniques, and delicate lace details abound in her designs. A review of her project photo gallery reveals a definite bias toward working with finer yarns and smaller-size needles. Over the decade of her design career, the evolution of her style has been gradual and subtle. Ravelry fans note that Melissa's designs occasionally share details in common, yet each has its own individual appeal. She serves up garments that acknowledge current fashion trends while simultaneously featuring enough classic elements that they never go out of style. That makes her patterns good investments and her projects wardrobe staples that reside permanently at the front of the closet.

ORIGAMI SHRUG
by Melissa Wehrle

Origami is the Japanese art of taking a flat piece of paper and turning it into something that has dimension. The unique construction of this shrug follows this same principle. The body of the garment is knit in the round, and when it is flat, it does not look like anything special. But when worn, it transforms into a drapey shrug, showcasing your handiwork and most precious silky yarn beautifully.

Difficulty: Intermediate
Skills Used: Basic increasing and decreasing, lace knitting, knitting in the round

SIZE

XS (S, M, L, 1X, 2X, 3X)

Finished Measurements
Width: 36½ (39, 40¼, 41½, 43, 44, 46½)"
Length (when worn): 22 (24½, 25½, 26½, 28, 29, 30)"

MATERIALS

- Handmaiden Fine Yarns Double Sea (70% silk, 30% seacell; 273yd per 100g); color: Topaz; 4 (4, 5, 5, 5, 6, 6) skeins

- 32" US 6 (4mm) circular needle, or size needed to obtain gauge

- 24" US 4 (3.5mm) circular needle

- Tapestry needle

- Stitch marker

- Clear beading elastic (optional)

GAUGE

19 sts and 29 rows = 4 in patt st

PATTERN NOTES

The body is knit in the round with one seam along the center of the bound-off edge. Two openings are left at either side of the seam to act as armholes.

The lace stitch is reversible, so when worn the folded back collar will match the body.

To choose the correct size, take a measuring tape and make a circle with the measurement at the smallest rib point—this corresponds with the outside circumference of the shrug. Slip the circle behind your neck and stick both arms through. Remember that the actual shrug will give more than the measuring tape, but if it's too big, go down a size, or if too small, go up.

To add or take away volume and length, shorten or lengthen the jersey section right above the rib.

STITCH PATTERN

Reversible Lace Pattern: (multiple of 12 sts)

Note: Pattern is also charted on page 120.

Rnd 1: *K2tog, yo, rep from * to end.

Rnds 2–4: Knit.

Rnd 5: *K3tog, k4, yo, k1, yo, k4, rep from * to end.

Rnd 6: *K4, yo, k1, yo, k4, sl 1–ssk–psso, rep from * to end.

Rnd 7: *P3tog, p4, yo, p1, yo, p4, rep from * to end.

Rnd 8: *P4, yo, p1, yo, p4, p3tog tbl, rep from * to end.

Rnd 9: *P3tog, p4, yo, p1, yo, p4, rep from * to end.

Rnd 10: *Yo, k2tog, rep from * to end.

Rnds 11–13: Purl.

Rnd 14: *P4, yo, p1, yo, p4, p3tog tbl, rep from * to end.

Rnd 15: *P3tog, p4, yo, p1, yo, p4, rep from * to end.

Rnd 16: *K4, yo, k4, k1, yo, sl 1–ssk–psso, rep from * end.

Rnd 17: *K3tog, k4, yo, k1, yo, k4, rep from * to end.

Rnd 18: *K4, yo, k4, k1, yo, sl 1–ssk–psso, rep from * to end.

Rep Rnds 1–18 for patt.

DIRECTIONS
Body

With larger circular needle, CO 348 (372, 384, 396, 408, 420, 444) sts. Place marker and join in the round, being careful not to twist. K 1 round. Change to lace patt and work until piece measures 7 (8½, 9½, 9½, 11, 11, 11)".

Change to smaller circular needle.

Dec Rnd: K2tog [k2tog, k2] 86 (92, 95, 98, 101, 104, 110) times, k2tog—260 (278, 287, 296, 305, 314, 332) sts.

Work even in k1, p1 rib until body measures 9 (10½, 11½, 11½, 13, 13, 13)".

Inc Rnd: [M1, k3] 86 (92, 95, 98, 101, 104, 110) times, M1, k2—347 (371, 383, 395, 407, 419, 443) sts.

Change to larger circular needle. K all rnds. Work until body measures 14½ (16½, 17½, 18, 19½, 20, 20½)". BO all sts loosely.

FINISHING

Block body to measurements. With piece laid flat, on the BO edge, pin sides together 6 (6, 6½, 6½, 7, 7½, 8)" in from each end for armholes. Sew BO edge together between the two pins, leaving the armhole open at each side. Weave in all ends. If needed, 2 rows of clear beading elastic can be woven in at top and bottom of rib on the inside to help hold the rib shape.

Stitch Key

☐ = K on RS, p on WS

• = P on RS, k on WS

☒ = K2tog

☒ = K3tog

☒ = Sl 1-ssk-psso

☒ = P3tog

☒ = P3tog tbl

☐ = Yo

Lace Pattern

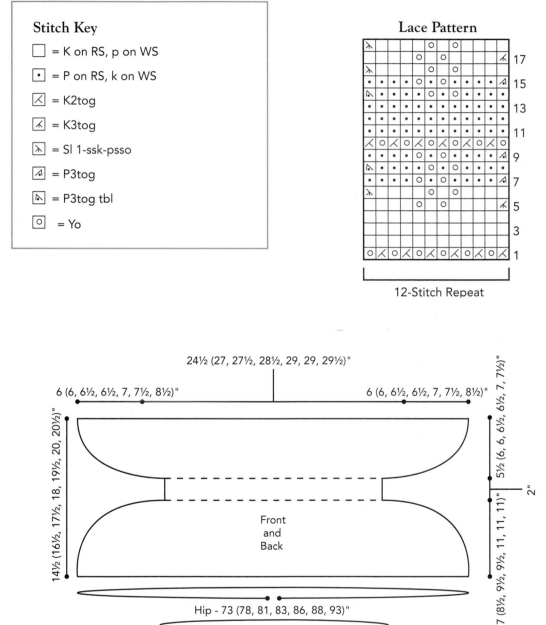

12-Stitch Repeat

24½ (27, 27½, 28½, 29, 29, 29½)"

6 (6, 6½, 6½, 7, 7½, 8½)"   6 (6, 6½, 6½, 7, 7½, 8½)"

5½ (6, 6, 6½, 6½, 7, 7½)"

14½ (16½, 17½, 18, 19½, 20, 20½)"

2"

Front
and
Back

7 (8½, 9½, 9½, 11, 11, 11)"

Hip - 73 (78, 81, 83, 86, 88, 93)"

Waist - 43 (46, 48, 49, 50, 52, 55)"

Hip - 73 (78, 81, 83, 86, 88, 93)"

Julie Weisenberger, Cocoknits

Apassionate knitter and designer since she first learned the craft in Austria during a college study abroad program, by the age of 24 Julie knew that knitting was key to the career she wanted. It never occurred to her, however, to start at the bottom of the design ladder and work her way up. Instead, she started her own knitwear company, Julie Hoff Designs, personally assembling a knitting cooperative of women in a small Irish village who hand-knit her designs for sale in the United States. The demands of running a successful company—not to mention marriage and mothering daughter Hanna—eventually took precedence over the hobby knitting that had brought her so much pleasure. By the early 1990s, when shoulder pads and big hair were still de rigueur, her colorful intarsia sweater designs were carried by high-end boutiques and department stores such as Henri Bendel, Mark Shale, and Nordstrom. She also designed patterns for Kristen Nicholas, who was then the creative director at Classic Elite Yarns and was profiled in Melanie Falick's original version of *Knitting in America* (Artisan/Workman Publishing Company, 1996).

Then Julie's second daughter, Emma, was born with severe disabilities. Dealing with a never-ending consortium of doctors, hospitals, and therapists made it impossible to focus on running her business. Her energy exhausted, she closed it down in 1997, and put away her knitting entirely for several years.

A confluence of events reignited her passion for knitting several years later, when Oakland, California, yarn shop Article Pract opened its doors and Julie wandered in on a whim to have a look around. She soon picked up her needles again, charmed and inspired by the abundance of new yarns on the market. "The yarn selection for knitwear designers was extremely limited even a decade ago, and now it's amazing! I felt like Rip Van Winkle, being completely out of it for years and then waking back up to realize, 'This is *so* much better, and *so* much more fun.'" It wasn't long before the owner of Article Pract persuaded her to teach classes at the shop. She had improvised the sweater samples she used in those classes to demonstrate finishing techniques and was surprised when students clamored for her to create patterns for them. As a designer for whom math calculations come easily, her response at first was, "Just knit it." The designs seemed self-evident to her, but she was persuaded to write them up, recognizing that for most knitters the process is not intuitive.

Once she had created the first set of patterns, her dormant entrepreneurial spirit was reawakened as well. She began to envision a concept for a new business. Her plan revolved around the Internet and developed around the same time that Ravelry was unveiled in 2006. First, she created Cocoknits, the Web site featuring her original designs, even as she wondered how to market herself on the Internet, and how she would identify an audience for her patterns. Miraculously, she found that Ravelry could do all of that for her. Her site is "absolutely reader-driven," in that readers vote for their favorite designs every month. Although she has never done any advertising, her Ravelry fan group ("Cuckoo for Cocoknits") has definitely helped to spread the word about her wearable, deceptively simple designs.

Cocoknits is an extremely interactive site in that every month Julie posts three new pattern prototypes, and the one receiving the most votes gets written up into a pattern first, translating into higher sales figures by satisfying consumer demand. The others usually follow within a few weeks, bringing the total number of original designs available for sale on her site to well over 50 in just 4 years.

Julie believes that the Internet is directly responsible for the success of her business model. "I could *never* do this without the Internet; I put the designs up on the site, but I only write up the ones my readers really like." Taking that thought a step further, she acknowledges the Internet's importance in making it possible for her to run a business at all—because her daughter's special needs make it impractical to work at a standard 9-to-5 career. "The Internet allows me to work from home, and to work when I can. It allows me to set goals that I do my best to reach, but the world won't end if I can't meet them as planned." She remains pleasantly astonished by her successful reincarnation as a hand-knits designer, Version 2.0. "I'm absolutely making it up as I go along, but it's working for me. It seems like I've come out of nowhere because I wasn't knitting for so long, but I'm not a beginner by any means."

The unique features in Julie's knitted designs often result from the marriage of techniques she first learned in Europe and then adapted for American knitters. Her reputation for ingenious garment construction began with this collection of interesting and unusual details. Many of her garments are nearly seamless, yet have set-in sleeves. Yokes are knit seamlessly, using an original technique she calls "English-tailored shoulders" that allows the knitter to make set-in sleeves without having to seam them. Knitters from all over the world email to thank her for the simplicity, beautiful shaping details, and wearability of her designs. It is her conviction that often, "the simplest solution is the most elegant."

Her garments are "modeled" by a dressmaker mannequin rather than by a "skinny model in a lifestyle shot," a deliberate effort to make it easier for knitters to visualize themselves wearing her designs. Further, Ravelry's links to finished-project photo galleries make it possible for knitters to see each of Julie's designs modeled by real people of all shapes and sizes.

In addition to her independent design work, Julie continues to teach several classes at Article Pract. Her 12-week sweater design class always sells out, and satisfied students have helped to spread the word about her patterns. "My niche is impeccable shaping and interesting yarn texture. Great yarn and accents like beautiful buttons speak for themselves; you don't need a complex garment design on top of that. Well-fitting, simple design is what I always return to." The distinction between "homemade" and "handmade" is a flashpoint for her, and her goal is to ensure that her patterns fall clearly into the second category.

Direct contact with the people who knit her designs is equally essential to Julie's success; she hears from customers regularly via all the online channels, and their input influences her work. Much as she loves cables and complex colorwork, she does not wear that type of garment herself; like many designers who are sensitive both to the currents of fashion and to the best characteristics of knitwear, she always returns to what she herself wants to wear. Although at first she questioned whether there would be sufficient demand for the simple styles that dominate her site, she quickly realized that this is just what her customers want. "I feel so lucky that people have responded [positively] to my designs, and that I don't have to apologize for all the stockinette that makes them so quick to knit!" Constantly seeking ways to improve the drape and fit of her garments, Julie regularly develops new construction techniques that fit her mantra of simple elegance.

In addition, she has a streak of the inventor in her. Her patent-pending Knitters' Blocks are available for purchase on her site and are also distributed to yarn shops nationwide by Bryson. In a true "necessity is the mother of invention" moment, Julie was rushed for time to pin and block a new sweater, and she seized upon several extra carpet squares left over from a home improvement project. Impressed by how well the dense backing held her pins in place, and how effectively the carpet surface wicked moisture away from the knitted pieces, she realized that she was onto something. She approached the carpet tile manufacturer to work with her on the development of interlocking blocking squares that would be portable yet sturdy, would absorb water but not mildew, could be safely ironed, and could be flexibly sized to accommodate a wide range of projects. Today, her Knitters' Blocks are sold in sets of 9 or 18, and the smaller set can be carried in a knitting project bag.

While the challenges of meeting her daughter's needs continue, this time around Julie's business is "pleasantly constant" rather than frenetic. She still has "tons of ideas" for new sweaters; and thanks to the Internet, there is room in her life for the knitting career she always knew she could have.

BUTTON TUNIC
by Julie Weisenberger

From the time Julie's daughter could toddle she was a collector. Her pockets were constantly full of pebbles, flowers, and little sticks . . . anything that caught her eye. So when she found these fabulous buttons it seemed natural to design a functional garment that would both show off the buttons and please little collectors. It will please the knitter, too, because it is knit top-down in the round with no seaming.

Difficulty: Beginner
Skills Used: Basic increasing and decreasing

SIZE

1 (2, 4, 6) year(s) old

Finished Measurements
Chest: 18 (21, 23, 25)"
Length: 12 (14, 16, 18)"

MATERIALS

- Sublime Yarns Organic Cotton DK (100% cotton; 120 yds per 50g); [MC]: 96 Bone, 2 (3, 4, 5) skeins; [CC]: 97 nutmeg, 1 (1, 2, 2) skeins

- 16"–24" US 6 (4mm) circular needle, or size needed to obtain gauge

- 1 set US 6 (4mm) double-pointed needles or a second US 6 (4mm) circular needle of any length

- 8 buttons, 1" diameter
- Needle and thread to sew on buttons

GAUGE

22 sts and 28 rows = 4" in St st

PATTERN NOTES

Tunic is knit in the round from the top down.

Use either double-pointed needles or two circular needles to begin in the round. Switch to one circular needle when the work is big enough.

Front and back are identical, so you can decide which side will be the front.

SPECIAL STITCHES

LLI (left lifted increase): Insert left needle into left leg of stitch two rows below last completed stitch. Knit this stitch through the back loop.

RLI (right lifted increase): Insert right needle into right leg of stitch just below next stitch, place it onto left needle and knit it, then knit the stitch on the needle.

DIRECTIONS

Yoke

CO 60 (64, 72, 76) sts. Join, being careful not to twist.

Set-up rnd: *K10 (12, 14, 14), pm, k20 (20, 22, 24), pm, rep from * once. Use a distinct or different color marker in the final position to indicate beg of rnd.

INCREASE FOR YOKE:

Rnd 1: *Kfb, k to 1 st before m, kfb, sm, rep from * around—68 (72, 80, 82) sts.

Rnd 2: Knit.

Rep these two rnds 10 (14, 15, 16) more times—32 (42, 46, 48) sts for each sleeve and 42 (50, 54, 58) sts each for front and back. Yoke incs are complete.

Body

DIVIDE SLEEVES FROM BODY:

Next rnd: Remove all markers as you encounter them in this rnd. Place first 32 (42, 46, 48) sts on holder or scrap yarn for first sleeve, using knitted or backward loop cast-on, CO 4 (4, 5, 5) sts, pm, CO 4 (4, 5, 5) sts for underarm, k42 (50, 54, 58) sts of back, place next 32 (42, 46, 48) sts on holder for second sleeve, CO 4 (4, 5, 5) sts, pm, CO 4 (4, 5, 5) sts for underarm, k42 (50, 54, 58) sts of front—100 (116, 128, 136) sts on needle. First underarm marker indicates the new beg of rnd.

Work 2 rnds in St st.

Next rnd (Inc rnd): *K2, LLI, k to 2 sts before next marker, RLI, k1, sm, rep from *.

Rep the Inc rnd every 4th (5th, 6th, 7th) rnd 9 more times—140 (156, 168, 176) sts. Cont in St st until tunic measures 11 (13, 15, 17)" from top of shoulder.

Pocket

Switch to contrasting color and k 1 rnd, then cont in Rev St st.

Tip: *If you would rather not purl, turn tunic inside out, and, with WS facing, yo, and k to the last st of the rnd, ssk the last st and the yo. You can now continue knitting with the WS facing until the tunic is complete.*

Work 4 (4½, 5, 5½)" with CC in Rev St st.

Work 8 buttonholes as follows:

Next rnd: *Work 7 (8, 8, 10) sts, [BO next 2 sts, work 16 (18, 20, 20) sts] 3 times, BO 2, work 7 (8, 8, 10) sts, rep from * once more.

BO and complete the buttonholes as follows:

BO normally to buttonhole, [yo onto right-hand needle, then pull 1st st over yo] twice, rep from * through last buttonhole, BO the end of the rnd. Cut yarn and secure.

Sleeves (Make 2)

Place 32 (42, 46, 48) sts held for sleeve onto dpns or two circular needles. Beginning at center of underarm, pick up and k4 (4, 5, 5) sts, k sleeve sts, pick up and k4 (4, 5, 5) sts—40 (50, 56, 58) sleeve sts. Work 3 more rnds of St st (or to desired length) and BO.

FINISHING

Weave in loose ends and block tunic.

Turn pocket up 3 (3½, 4, 4½)". Mark for buttons. Sew buttons in place with thread. Button pockets in place.

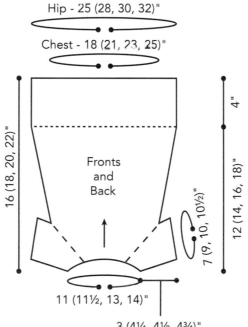

Hip - 25 (28, 30, 32)"

Chest - 18 (21, 23, 25)"

16 (18, 20, 22)"

Fronts and Back

4"

12 (14, 16, 18)"

7 (9, 10, 10½)"

11 (11½, 13, 14)"

3 (4¼, 4½, 4¾)"

PART 2

Accessories
(*or* A Little Luxury Goes a Long Way)

Knitwear designers often self-select into one of two camps; those who knit garments, and those who prefer the near-instant gratification of accessories. Even within this second group, some design only socks while others focus their creative energies on hats, shawls, or baby blankets. These designers understand both the unique challenges and the great rewards of creating beautiful projects from small quantities of yarn.

Lace lovers (so often the guilty parties in the misappropriation of luxurious sock yarn) will find special projects of charming delicacy from designers who are passionate about lace knitting. For those who prefer a cozy hat or pair of mitts for colder climates, well, your interests are represented here, too. As diverse a group as these designers are, they share a common goal for tough economic times: to stretch our budgets—as well as each skein of irresistibly beautiful yarn—and to accommodate every knitterly indulgence without breaking the bank.

Wendy Bernard, Knit and Tonic

Read a few entries in Wendy Bernard's popular Knit and Tonic blog, and you realize that her entire life is fodder for the stories she shares. From the strange and often hilarious characters she encounters at the gym or yoga class to the antics of her 7-year-old daughter (known to readers as "Girlfriend"), from her obsessions with knitting and temari balls to the neuroses of her terrier mix Rocko, nothing is sacred. Since she started writing the blog in 2005, everything in her life has been scrutinized through the lens of her wry and sometimes poignant perspective, and somehow it always comes back to knitting.

"I relate everything back to knitting, but I couldn't just write about the knitting all the time. The 'Tonic' is just my take on my life." Most readers agree that Wendy's life sounds pretty fabulous, but she disputes that impression. "My life may sound fabulous, but it's actually pretty boring. It's just that I have a huge imagination. Everything I write about is true, and I use my take on it to make it interesting. I really write only a little bit about knitting, but I always make a point about knitting that relates to whatever else I was writing about."

So it's not surprising to learn that Wendy is one of those apocryphal bloggers we've all heard about; a knitter whose amusing and compulsively readable posts attracted the notice of a literary agent. Her first book, *Custom Knits* (STC Craft, 2008), evolved from her blog and is now in its fourth printing. A follow-up is due out in 2011. That second book will pick up where *Custom Knits* left off, with techniques to customize patterns to fit individual needs. Nearly 1,700 Ravelry members post photos of their versions of Wendy's designs on her Knit and Tonic fan group, where it is clear that readers have embraced her encouragement to customize their projects.

As someone who has worked alternatively as a hairdresser, a pharmacy technician, and a corporate marketing executive, Wendy really hit her stride as a knitwear designer. The funny thing is, she doesn't subscribe to the "designer" label. "My readers taught me a lot about designing. I'm a process person, so I figure it out as I go. I try something new and then show it off on the blog. I developed a lot of confidence in my ability to make up a sweater pattern and not feel like I had to use a written pattern."

When she first succumbed to the knitting obsession, she "was knitting just to knit, to the point that one day I had my family over and pulled out a big box of scarves, hats, and mittens, and said, 'Hey, anybody want any of these?'"

Now, she makes it a point to be responsive to the knitters who make her patterns. "I have a very personal relationship with readers. Even though I can't respond to every comment, I reply to questions every day." Although she spends just a few minutes a day on Ravelry, she writes blog posts at least three times each week.

Having knit seriously for only the last 6 years, Wendy belongs to the generation of knitters who have always had the resources of the Internet at their fingertips. Contrary to fears expressed within the online knitting world that Ravelry would be the downfall of the independent blog—because members simply wouldn't have time both to document their projects on Ravelry and to write frequent blog posts about them—she believes that Ravelry is a wonderful add-on to the online community, another way for knitters to connect and communicate. "Serious bloggers continue to post on their own sites, and only the casual ones have gone by the wayside. There aren't a million bloggers out there anymore because they're the ones sharing their projects on Ravelry instead."

Since she began designing, Wendy has published patterns on *Knitty.com*, in *Interweave Knits* and *KnitScene*, and has designed others for Blue Sky Alpacas and Stitch Diva Studio. When she designs for magazines, she works more within the framework of traditional knitwear design. "My aesthetic is more fashion than function in that way."

As an intuitive process knitter with a passion for top-down knitting, Wendy has found that legions of like-minded knitters are supportive of her methods. It perplexes her to learn that some knitters "are afraid to try certain fibers, or afraid of learning a new technique. My feeling is, it's . . . all just knits and purls. I have no fear. I may not be good at something, but I'm not afraid to try it."

For every project in her first book, she figured out on her own how to achieve the results she wanted, and she cites both Elizabeth Zimmermann and Barbara G. Walker as liter-ary knitting mentors. Determined to assuage any fears her readers might have about working in such a free-form way, she was careful to strike a friendly and encouraging tone in *Custom Knits*. And with her reputation for stylish designs accompanied by easy-to-follow directions, for the most part readers have been willing to trust her instincts and come along for the ride.

"I have a curious nature when I knit and design, so that's why I like unique construction [techniques]. It's also fun to blog about how I'm doing things. I'd rather do a more interesting construction because it's more interesting to blog about. And once you start putting your own imprint on things you can never leave well enough alone."

The southern California climate is a big influence on her design process, although she relates it more to a general warm-weather design aesthetic than to specific fashion influences. "When most people think about a sweater, they think about its warmth. Because we don't really need that [in southern California], I try to design things that are functional in my own climate and for my own lifestyle. Everything I knit is something I would personally wear. I don't design for anybody but me and my friends; we have an active lifestyle and don't require a lot of warmth." For example, one of *Custom Knits*'s designs features optional short rows at the back of the neck to create a closer fit for greater warmth, an element she wouldn't ordinarily consider. "The last thing I think about is a warm neck. So my design influences are very much those of the California lifestyle and what we would or would not wear here."

For someone living in a sunny climate, Wendy has a substantial yarn stash that lives in Rubbermaid containers, in old luggage, in quilt storage bags, and under the bed. "You basi-cally open up a drawer and yarn will fly out at you." To keep her stash from descending into total chaos, she hosts periodic destashes on her blog and donates yarn that she has received free to churches, to senior centers, and to local schools where knitting is taught to the children.

"My main goal as a designer is to empower other people to get out of that 'I can't do it', or 'I'm afraid, or this won't look good on me' mindset. Almost every day, I get a letter from someone who tells me, 'I was so afraid to try this, but I did it and it turned out so fabulous. I'm so excited, and I'm no longer afraid.' I love hearing that." And unlike some designers, Wendy is thrilled when a knitter changes one of her designs to suit her own taste. "When I create a new design, I try to think ahead: 'OK, if someone wanted to do *this* to it, would it still work?' That's the whole idea of knitting, isn't it? It's not to knit patterns, it's to knit for yourself or for your family, to make things that the people you love will love to use."

TEXTURED TAM AND MITTS

By Wendy Bernard

There's nothing more satisfying than casting on for a tam and matching mitts and being able to wear them or give them away the following weekend. This slouchy tam and matching fingerless mitts feature a simple slip-stitch texture. Overlapping tabs are the perfect accents for the contrasting buttons that give this project its stylish flair.

Difficulty: Intermediate
Skills Used: Knitting flat and in the round in the same piece, increases and decreases, maintaining stitch pattern, slipping stitches

SIZE

Youth L/Women's XS (Women's S/M)

Finished Measurements
Tam: 17¼ (20)" circumference at brim, unstretched
Mitts: 6½ (8)" circumference at wrist, unstretched; 6 (7½)" long

MATERIALS

- Lorna's Laces Swirl Chunky (83% Merino, 17% silk; 120yd per 113g); color: Pond Blue #5ns; 1 skein for Tam and 1 skein for Mitts

- 16" US 10.5 (6.5mm) circular needle, or size needed to obtain gauge

- 1 set US 10.5 (6.5mm) double-pointed needles

- Stitch markers

- Tapestry needle

- One 1" button for Tam

- Two 1" buttons for Mitts

GAUGE

14 sts and 18 rows = 4" in St st

12 sts and 18 rows = 4" in patt stitch

PATTERN NOTES

Both the Tam and Mitts begin with a strip of ribbing of which a number of sts are bound off to form a tab. Next, the piece is joined in the round. The mitts feature a thumbhole that is formed by working in the round to the thumb, then worked flat, and then joined in the round to the top. For a slouchier Tam, work an extra inch before beginning crown decreases.

STITCH PATTERN

Slip-Stitch Weave (even number of sts)

Rnds 1 and 3: Knit.

Rnd 2: *Sl 1 wyib, p1, rep from * to end.

Rnd 4: *P1, sl 1 wyib, rep from * to end.

DIRECTIONS

Tam

BRIM:

With circular needle, CO 57 (65) sts. Work 1x1 rib for 6 rows.

BODY:

Next row (Inc row) (RS): BO 5 sts and shape Body as follows: *k2, M1, rep from * to 2 sts before end, k1, kfb—78 (90) sts. Pm for beg of rnd and join, leaving BO sts free.

Work Slip-Stitch Weave until piece measures 3 (4)" from Inc row to needles, ending on a Rnd 2 or 4 of Stitch Pattern. Using beg rnd marker as first marker, place 5 additional markers so that there are 13 (15) sts between each of the 6 markers.

Shape Crown: On the next k rnd, *k2tog, work to 2 sts before marker, ssk, sm, rep from * to end. Repeat this round, maintaining stitch pattern on Rnds 2 and 4 and change to dpns when necessary, until 6 sts rem. Cut off yarn, leaving an 8" tail. Thread it through rem sts and fasten to inside of crown.

FINISHING

Weave in loose ends. Block flat or over plate with same circumference as tam at its widest circumference. When dry, tack brim tab to opposing side. Sew button onto tab and brim as shown.

Left-Hand Mitt

CUFF:

CO 25 (29) sts. Beg with RS row, work 1x1 rib (beg with k st) for 8 rows.

BASE OF HAND:

Next rnd (RS): BO 6 sts in patt, then inc (kfb) 3 sts evenly to end—22 (26) sts. Place 26 live sts on 3 dpns, leaving tab free. Pm and join.

Beg with Rnd 2 of Stitch Pattern and work until piece measures approx 1½ (2)" from end of ribbing to needles, ending on second or fourth rnd of Stitch Pattern.

THUMBHOLE:

Begin working back and forth in rows.

Next Row (WS): Sl 1, p to end of row.

Next Row (RS): Sl 1 wyib, patt as est to end.

Cont, in rows, slipping the first st of each row and purling WS rows for 5 (7) rows.

HAND:

Begin working in rounds again.

Next row (RS): Work in patt to end, pm, join in rnd.

Cont in rnds for 1 (1½)", ending with a k rnd. Change to 1x1 rib for 5 rnds, BO in patt.

Right-Hand Mitt

CUFF:

CO 25 (29) sts. Beg with a WS row, work 1x1 rib (beg with a p st) for 8 rows.

BASE OF HAND:

Next row (WS): BO 6 sts in patt, cont with a p row, and inc (pfb) 3 sts evenly to end—22 (26) sts. Turn, do not join, work Row 1 of Stitch Pattern to end. Place live sts onto 3 dpns, pm, and join in rnd.

Begin working in rounds. Beg with rnd 2 of Stitch Pattern, work until piece measures approx 1½ (2)" from ribbing to needles, ending on a second or fourth rnd of Stitch Pattern.

THUMBHOLE:

Work as for Shape Thumbhole on Left-Hand Mitt.

HAND:

Work as for Hand of Left-Hand Mitt.

FINISHING

Weave in all ends. When dry, tack cuff tab to opposing side. Sew button onto tab and cuff as shown.

Knitters' Guide to Essential Blogging Terminology

Squee!—exclamation: expression of delight or satisfaction, such as when a Raveler scores a skein of yarn she'd been coveting.

Woot!—exclamation: see "squee!"

Kat Coyle, katcoyle.com

A self-described daydreamer, artist, and designer, Kat lets creative inspiration lead her where it will. She doesn't try to second-guess the process that works so well for her, preferring to follow her muse wherever it takes her. Her blog portrays a color-saturated world that is richly detailed and imaginative, where collage photos and gouache paintings of fantastical flora and fauna share space with her knitting projects. A finely honed color sensibility is at the heart of her creativity and, in fact, her main interest in art *is* color—its endless combinations, its emotional resonance, its visual pleasures. Color is the impetus that drives her intuition about what "works" in design. When it comes to knitting, she applies the same experimental focus that yields such brilliant results in her painting and photography, although the traditional garments that result from these efforts are not necessarily what she considers "art."

For years after her mother taught her the basics, she knit only simple projects. "I was never that committed to it until about 12 years ago, when I became completely obsessed, even though this was before the trend really took off. It had been a passing fancy for so many years, and then I just got really, really into it. I was living alone, and it was a great way to pass the time. Coming from an art background and being a painter, I was always trained to think about 'meaning' and 'intention.' Compared to that, knitting was such a relief—something I could do just for fun, to relax."

An intuitive knitter, she often works fluidly without writing up patterns. This is only a problem when other knitters ask for her patterns. "I have a really hard time going all the way to the end with a pattern unless I have a deadline and someone is waiting for it." Fortunately, she keeps a lot of notebooks, does a lot of doodling and drawing, and writes up detailed notes for each new design.

Her knitted projects are charmingly idiosyncratic, revealing those fine-art roots. The designs manage to be both whimsical and accessible and are always identifiably, definitively her own. For example, not many knitwear designers regularly make skirts, but Kat has made enough of them to consider them something of a specialty. She has an even dozen to her credit, the latest of which—called Petal for the round silk chiffon flowers that decorate its hem—made its debut in *Twist Collective* (Summer 2009). Yet her reason for developing this specialty is utterly pragmatic: "I got into making skirts because I like to wear them." A review of her site's skirt gallery shows that they include a range of clever, flattering details such as lace panels and hems, unique construction techniques, and ribbon embellishments, all of which result in garments that manage to be both timeless and of-the-moment wearable.

Her adventures in blogging started in 2005. "I never had a plan. I just decided one day that I would join the blogging bandwagon. At first I didn't know where I was going to go with it or what kind of persona I wanted to present to the world. I thought I'd just talk about whatever, and that's exactly what I do." The site features her latest paintings and crafts projects as well as knitting experiments and news about her adored son, Felix, who at 6 is a huge fan of her knitted toys and dolls.

In addition to managing her site, she checks in frequently on Ravelry to answer questions that crop up about her patterns. "They [Jess and Casey, the founders of Ravelry] really figured it out—they knew what was missing on the Internet for knitters. It's so user-friendly ... and it's obvious they created it out of love." But her impression of the role of the Internet in supporting traditional handcrafts goes beyond Ravelry and into Big Tent theory. "The Internet brings everybody together. Being an artist can be lonely because you're busy making stuff by yourself. But now you can take a photo of what you've done and put it up there. A big part of making art is showing it. There's a lot of fulfillment in sharing what you've created; it's part of the process. I see the Internet as one giant place to show off what you are creating."

Besides her book, *Boho Baby Knits* (Potter Craft 2007), Kat's designs appear frequently in *Interweave Knits*, *KnitScene*, and *Knitty.com*. She also channels some of her creative energy into the Los Angeles Wisdom Arts Understanding Lab, a nonprofit arts center where she teaches children's knitting classes. "The thing about art classes in elementary schools is that they're very structured. . . . They don't encourage real creativity. I take a lot of my glitzy novelty yarns to my classes so the kids can use them. They *love* the sparkly stuff." Photos of completed knitting projects by Wisdom Arts students often show up on her site, and their exuberance makes it clear that she never tells them to color "inside the lines."

When developing a new design, she knits for a "fantasy of a person," sketching and doodling a series of scenarios in which her fantasy person wears the knitted creation that dominates her imagination at the time. "I'll imagine somebody romantic, or somebody headstrong; I come up with a whole idea of who wants to wear a given outfit." In addition, she is captivated by extreme fashion. "I love to see how extravagant designers can get. I like fashion that's sculptural, but not really that wearable—that's what inspires me." But because so much of the fine artist and so much of her experimental nature comes out in her knitting, she doesn't really think of herself as a fashion-driven knitter—even though most of what she makes is garments. "I don't come at it from that point of view. I want to make something new; I focus on what I'm making and try to solve the problems inherent in that project. I don't think of myself primarily as a garment maker." According to her dreamy vision, a scarf thus finds itself repurposed as a table drape, and a circular shawl becomes an ethereal and graceful skirt.

Like many artists, Kat returns periodically to certain themes until she is satisfied that she has exhausted their creative possibilities. Her newest challenge is to explore further options in shawls and lace stitches. "The thing about shawls is that they're more painterly, like a canvas. Sweater construction is sculptural, but working on a rectangle or a circle and not worrying about how it's going to fit the body is very freeing. The first skirts I made were like sarongs, just wrapping about the body similarly to a shawl." Acknowledging her preference for working with fine-gauge natural fibers, she has begun a deeper exploration of lace stitches, thinking about the various shapes that are formed with "holes and string."

Although Kat has become known as a knitwear designer first and foremost, her fine arts background is never far from her thoughts. Her quirky aesthetic is assimilated into every element of her knitting, and she approaches each new project as a means to make an artistic statement, using fiber as her paint and knitted fabric as her canvas.

Knitters' Guide to Essential Blogging Terminology

Muggle—noun: a non-knitter, someone who "just doesn't understand" the obsession.

LACE FLOWER PIN
by Kat Coyle

Knitting small accessories can be creatively satisfying and a good canvas to express your adventurous spirit; knit with colors you might not wear in a garment but look great as an accent. If you search flea markets for little treasures, this is the perfect project for using one-of-a-kind buttons. The button chosen to adorn the center determines a great deal of the personality of the pin; use wood, shell, rhinestone, or vintage plastic—it's up to you.

It's also a great project for using leftover yarns. Look into your stash for inspiration. The base of the pin is made with worsted-weight wool and worked flat in garter stitch with short-row shaping, then sewn together to form a circle. The flower part of the pin is a simple lace-edging pattern, ruffled along the long flat edge and sewn together to form a circle. It is sewn to the base with a button in the center. A pin back is then added to the wrong side.

Difficulty: Intermediate
Skills Used: Garter stitch short rows, lace knitting, buttonhole stitch (sewing), short-row shaping

SIZE

One size

Finished Measurements
4½" diameter (from petal to petal)
3¼" diameter (circle base)

MATERIALS

- You will need approximately 20 yards of MC and 13 yards of CC for each flower. The pin is shown with two color combinations.

- [MC 1] Rowan Yarn Kidsilk Haze (70% Super Kid Mohair, 30% silk; 229yd per 25g); color: Blushes 583

- [CC 1] Patons Classic Wool Merino (100% pure new wool; 223yd per 100g); color: Natural Mix 00229

- [MC 2] Rowan Yarn Kidsilk Haze (70% Super Kid Mohair, 30% Silk; 229yd per 25g); color: Pearl 590
- [CC 2] Cascade Yarns The Heathers 220 (100% Merino; 220yd per 100g); color: Walnut Heather 8013
- US 6 (4mm) needles, or size needed to obtain gauge
- 1 button, 1"–1¼" diameter for each pin
- Pin back, 1¼" long for each pin
- Wool felt, 2¾"-diameter circle for each pin
- Sewing thread to match felt
- Sharp sewing needle
- Tapestry needle

GAUGE

18 sts and 30 rows = 4" in St st with MC, unblocked

20 sts and 28 rows = 4" in St st with CC, unblocked

Note: *Gauge is not important for this project.*

PATTERN NOTES

The Circle Base is worked in garter stitch with short-row shaping.

w&t: Wrap next stitch and turn work. Bring yarn to front and slip next stitch, bring yarn to back and return st to left-hand needle. Turn work, bring yarn to the back, and knit to the end of the row.

DIRECTIONS
Circle Base

With CC, CO 8 sts.

Row 1: K8.

Row 2: K6, w&t, k to end of row.

Row 3: K5, w&t, k to end of row.

Row 4: K4, w&t, k to end of row.

Row 5: K3, w&t, k to end of row.

Row 6: K2, w&t, k to end of row.

Row 7: K1, w&t, k to end of row.

Row 8: K8, picking up wraps as you encounter them and knitting them together with the stitch they wrap.

Rep these 8 rows 7 more times. BO all sts and cut yarn, leaving a long tail for seaming.

Lace Flower

With MC, loosely CO 5 sts. Rows 2, 4, and 6 contain double yarnovers. In the following rows, treat the yo2 as two stitches; you will always work (k1, p1) in the double yarnover.

Row 1: Knit.

Row 2: K2, yo2, k2tog, k1—6 sts.

Row 3: K2, (k1, p1) in yo2, k2—6 sts.

Row 4: K4, yo2, k2—8 sts.

Row 5: K2, (k1, p1) in yo2, k4—8 sts.

Row 6: K2, yo2, k2tog, k4—9 sts.

Row 7: K5, (k1, p1) in yo2, k2—9 sts.

Row 8: K9—9 sts.

Row 9: BO 4 sts, k to end—5 sts.

Rep the last 8 rows 7 more times.

BO all sts and cut yarn, and leave a long tail for seaming.

FINISHING

Wet-block Lace Flower, placing pins at each point tip to open up lace, and pin flat edge to about 12" in length.

With tapestry needle and tail end, sew together the cast-on and bound-off edges of the Circle Base and neatly weave in tail ends. Slightly full the Circle Base by soaking and agitating (by hand) in hot soapy water. Rinse in cold water, then hot water, and then cold water. Lay flat to dry, shaping into a neat circle.

With tapestry needle and tail end, sew together the cast-on and bound-off edges of the Lace Flower, basting the long tail through flat edge, and pull gently closed to make a flower shape.

Place the Lace Flower on top of the Circle Base, and sew securely together at center. Neatly tack down the Lace Flower petals to the Circle Base by making one small stitch at the bottom of each "V" shape between petals. With sewing thread and sharp needle, sew button to center of the Lace Flower. With sewing needle and thread using the buttonhole stitch, sew the felt circle to the back of Circle Base. Sew pin back to the mid-upper section of felt.

Jared Flood, Brooklyn Tweed

Brooklyn Tweed holds pride of place on the blogroll for many knitters, and for Jared Flood that ride to the top has been a source of wonderment and gratitude. Now a poster child for the ascendency of knitting blogs in the cultural zeitgeist, his roots as a knitwear designer and photographer of stylish knitting began while watching a college friend knit her way through classes several years ago. Enchanted, he decided on the spot to resurrect the childhood hobby he'd learned from his craft-obsessed mother. But he quickly exhausted the skill set of the friend who agreed to teach him because, not content with garter-stitch scarves, he was determined from the outset to make sweaters and other garments.

Right out of college, he headed to New York City with few personal contacts and no job prospects. He started knitting sweaters soon after his arrival in the city, and he launched Brooklyn Tweed later in 2005 while working as a college admissions counselor. Having a full-time 9-to-5 job was challenging for the self-professed "night person," who shifts into his most creative mode around midnight. The blog began as a way of maximizing his lengthy periods of downtime at work and as a means of combining his two great creative loves, photography and knitting.

Brooklyn Tweed's format and style immediately differentiated it from other knitting blogs. Jared's blog readership grew quickly as readers were drawn into the dreamy urban streetscapes and inviting domestic still lifes he created as backdrops for the knitting project photos. Insightful, process-oriented knitting commentary and those artfully photographed projects combined to give the blog its captivating aura. Clearly, Jared the photographer understood the photogenic qualities of knitted fabric just as Jared the knitter understood how to style his FOs into fiberlicious subjects.

At that time, Pam Allen was the editor of Interweave Knits. She had first learned about Jared through her colleagues' blog gossip and was curious enough to take a look for herself. "I was completely impressed with his workmanship. I'd been seeing lots of extraordinarily imaginative designs with clever engineering expertise, but they weren't beautifully made. When I first saw Jared's work, it was like somebody had opened a window and let in the fresh air. It was beautifully crafted and had clearly been knit with care and attention. His pieces were traditional but not stodgy. He made wonderful modern use of traditional techniques and design elements. It was gratifying to see a young knitter put that kind of attention into doing beautiful knitting." Having struggled to find attractive and wearable men's projects for *IK*, Allen invited Jared to design one for the magazine.

He rose to the challenge in part because he believes that "men are at a bit of a disadvantage in knitting. There are not as many fashionable, technique-friendly garments available for us as there are for women." Although he began by adapting women's patterns to fit male bodies, he knew he needed to learn more. Reading widely, from Elizabeth Zimmermann's writings about knitting as well as Internet tutorials, taught him to think differently about technique and construction. He felt encouraged to embrace his natural bias toward traditional techniques and seamless design, which he considers unique to knitting. "What I enjoy most about knitting is the process. I really think about ways of making that enjoyable—of making something that is both a joy to make and a joy to wear."

The Cobblestone pullover (*Interweave Knits*, Fall 2007) was a smashing success and brought a surge in traffic to his blog as well as attention to Jared as a designer. The Koolhaas hat (*IK,* Holiday 2007) was his next major hit; at any given time on Ravelry, there are hundreds of knitters making it. The publication of these two patterns created a perfect storm of talent, timing, and opportunity, and it led to the appearance of his cabled Green Autumn mittens on the cover of *Vogue Knitting*'s Fall 2008 issue. If Jared was unprepared for the resulting attention and by the discovery that people had begun referring to him as a "designer," he nonetheless embraced the title. Even now he sounds both perplexed and immensely flattered by his rapid rise.

"I'm a really private person, so the blog is focused on knitting, not my personal life. But it has brought me dream opportunities. From the very beginning I wanted it to be a beautiful place for people who really love knitting, [and] for it to be about techniques, fiber, materials—all the things we explore on our own but don't necessarily share with other people. I care about real knitting in the old style. That's what keeps me coming back—the endless variety of things to learn about the craft."

Jared draws a lot of inspiration from Ravelry's visual feast. Thinking mostly about what he himself wants to wear, he is less fashion-driven than process-oriented. He evaluates designs according to those features that allow for the most wearable but interesting techniques and construction. Sometimes he approaches a design by considering whether he'd enjoy photographing it. Any project that he can visualize as an indispensible element in an entire ensemble is one he'll want to make. "The fashion aspect is subconscious. Living in New York City, I see inspiring street fashion [all around me], every day."

A second opportunity to collaborate with Pam Allen came in 2009. Allen, who was then the Creative Director at Classic Elite Yarns (although she has since left that position), invited Jared to design a signature collection of patterns for the yarn company. In addition to selecting the project yarns, he was given an unprecedented level of creative control to photograph, style, and participate in the design and layout of the booklet. This collaboration between designer and yarn company ventured into uncharted territory when Allen and CEY agreed to have Jared promote the projects and link to the booklet on both his blog and Ravelry.

Moving a traditional yarn company known for classic fibers into the twenty-first century was a challenge for Allen. But, "It helps us to support someone like Jared. I loved the idea that he could take his wonderful aesthetic and harness that to promote our yarns." According to their arrangement, some of the booklet's patterns were made available for sale on his own site from the first day of release, and the rest were available exclusively in the booklet. Nine months after its publication, all of the booklet's patterns became available on Jared's site, where it was announced that they are part of a larger collection available through CEY. In turn, CEY has provided a unique calling card for him to introduce his designs into yarn shops all over the country without having to sacrifice the market he had already established online.

That online connection has been a huge benefit from the start. Jared offers all of his designs for sale on Ravelry, and he marvels at the ways in which the site supports independent knitwear designers. His fan group alone has nearly 4,000 members, and all are making one or more of his projects. He may also be unique in having a separate group on Ravelry, more than 400 strong, dedicated to KALs (knit-alongs) of his designs, where groups of knitters convene to work on the same project at the same time. "It's been so affirming . . . to be compensated for my work this way. Because of Ravelry, I have the online presence I need to be able to do this as a career. It's exciting to be a designer in this environment because so much is changing. Those of us who started with no intention of doing this full-time are now in a position [because of the Internet] to be able to negotiate with the big yarn companies [and publications] in a way that was not possible before." In addition, his online presence creates an active global fan-base for his work and led to international travel and teaching opportunities in 2009 and 2010.

Now 27 and still a serious knitter for only 6 years, Jared is also impassioned about the future of knitting in relation to the seismic changes wrought by blogging and social networking. A return to "real knitting" among practitioners of his generation is the most heartening sign of knitting's renaissance, by which he means a deep understanding of traditional knitting techniques. Those techniques have been successfully translated into what people today want to wear. Twenty- and thirty-something knitters are undergoing a transformation from "knitting hobbyists who've jumped on the latest craft trend" to "serious knitters who've chosen to make the craft a meaningful part of their daily lives."

Further, he detects in this movement an interest in going deeper, in understanding stitch architecture, design principles, and fiber properties in ways that could not have happened without the Internet. With the Internet acting as community clearinghouse, social lubricant, and instructional engine, Jared sees knitters embracing the craft while learning from each other in ways their ancestors could not have dreamed of. "In the knitting community, we're here because we want to be here."

With his penchant for rustic, tweedy yarns and traditional-with-a-twist designs, his goal has always been to create classic garments that are not part of one specific trend. Everything he makes could have been knit "50 years ago or 50 years from now. I think about that a lot; the timeless aspect of knitting, the tradition we're connected to, and how if you tap into that you're set. Knitting is part of our cultural fabric."

WOODSMOKE SCARF
by Jared Flood

A light, airy, and warm scarf—knit long for many drapey wraps and trimmed with a dainty lace edging in a contrasting color for a sophisticated, elegant look under jackets, or thrown on with a T-shirt.

Difficulty: Easy

Skills Used: Basic lace techniques including yarn overs and decreasing. The pattern uses a knitted-on lace edging technique and garter stitch grafting.

SIZE

One Size

Finished Measurements
Length: 81"
Width: 9"

MATERIALS

- [MC] Beaverslide Dry Goods Fingering Weight (100% wool; 440yd per 100g); color: Woodsmoke Heather; 1 skein*

- [CC] Beaverslide Dry Goods Fingering Weight (100% wool; 440yd per 100g); color: Lichen Frost; 1 skein*

- 36" US 6 (4mm) circular needle, or size needed to obtain gauge

- 1 set US 6 (4mm) double-pointed needles

- Size H/8 (5mm) crochet hook

- Waste yarn for provisional cast-on

- Tapestry needle

- Rustproof blocking wires or blocking pins

    *__Note:__ You will need approximately 150yd of MC and 115yd of CC.

GAUGE

14 sts and 32 rows = 4" in garter st, blocked

PATTERN NOTES

This scarf is a simple rectangle of garter stitch trimmed with a lace border in a contrasting color. You will start the scarf with a provisional cast-on, and after the rectangle is knit, you will remove the provisional cast-on and pick up stitches all the way around, allowing you to work the knitted-on lace border around the perimeter of the scarf.

DIRECTIONS
Body

With circular needle and scrap yarn, chain 302 sts. With circular needle and MC, k 300 sts into bumps of crochet chain, leaving one at either end. Cont. with MC, work garter st (k all rows) until you have worked 16 garter st ridges (32 rows) with MC.

Place a marker on needle, and beg at the corner, use the working needle to pick up 1 st from each ridge along the short side of rectangle (16 sts); place a marker at the corner, unravel provisional cast-on, and slip 300 live sts from the cast-on edge onto needle; at the next corner, place marker, then pick up 16 sts from rem side, as before, picking up 1 st per ridge. When you reach last corner, place a marker.

149

You have now picked up sts around the entire perimeter of garter stitch rectangle—632 sts.

Border

You will now work the border, knitting the lace perpendicular to the body of the scarf and joining it to the scarf at the end of every even row by knitting together 1 stitch from the border with 1 stitch from the body. Rows 1, 3, and 5 contain double yarnovers. In the following rows, treat the yo2 as two stitches; you will always work (k1, p1) in the double yarnover.

Provisionally CO 5 sts with scrap yarn.

Switch to CC and work Border Edging as follows: Work Row 1, turn. Work Row 2, and at the end of the row, join edging to scarf by knitting together 1 st from each.

BORDER EDGING:

Row 1: Sl 1 wyif, yo, k1, yo2, k2tog, k1.

Row 2: K2, (k1, p1) in yo2, k2tog, k tog 1 st from border and 1 st from body, beginning at one corner.

Row 3: Sl 1 wyif, yo, k2, yo2, k2tog, k1.

Row 4: K2, (k1, p1) in yo2, k1, k2tog, k tog 1 st from border and 1 st from body.

Row 5: Sl 1 wyif, yo, k3, yo2, k2tog, k1.

Row 6: K2, (k1, p1) in yo2, k2, k2tog, k tog 1 st from border and 1 st from body.

Row 7: Sl 1 wyif, yo, k7.

Row 8: BO3, k2, k2tog, k tog 1 st from border and 1 st from body.

Cont working the 8 rows of Lace Edging Chart, consuming live sts from center rectangle until you reach corner marker.

Next even row: Work to end of row, but work k1 instead of joining to the body. This row does not join the body and edging.

Work 3 rows normally, joining the edging and body on next even row.

Next even row: Work to end of row, but work k1 instead of joining to the body. This row does not join the body and edging.

Cont in this manner, trimming center rectangle with lace edging, and working a pair of chart rows omitting join stitch at each corner marker.

When you have worked your way all the way around the perimeter of therectangle you will have returned to the cast-on edge of Lace Edging. Unpick provisional CO and graft them to live edging sts on your needle.

Weave in ends.

Block severely, as for lace, using blocking wires or pins. Air dry.

Stitch Key

☐ = K on RS, p on WS

▪ = P on RS, k on WS

☒ = K2tog

◼ = K2tog 1 st from Body with 1 st from Edging

⬛ = No Stitch

⊟ = Slip 1 purlwise wyif

⊙ = Yo

⌒ = BO

Lace Edging Chart

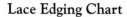
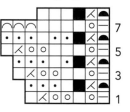

Chrissy Gardiner, Knittin' Mom

Chrissy Gardiner traces the beginning of her knitting career to the birth of her son, Owen, now 5. After bouncing around the country in a series of software design and programming jobs, she and her husband had finally settled in Portland, Oregon, at the end of 2004. At home with toddler daughter Sydney, and the newborn Owen, she rediscovered her craft-loving roots while trying to figure out her next career move. Although she had been knitting since high school, an entrepreneurial knitwear design business was not something she'd ever considered. "Even 5 years ago, I never would have imagined that this is what I'd be doing now."

Her son's playgroup met in a friendly coffee shop/yarn shop. There, she bought the yarn to make an entrelac baby blanket, and found herself "totally in love with it. I was so happy to be knitting again that I couldn't stand it." Through other group members she discovered *Knitty.com* and the "whole universe of knit bloggers." She also met other Portland knitters and quickly grew serious about her own knitting.

By 2005, she had decided that having a blog of her own would be fun, and she called it Knittinmom in a nod to her two children. "But I never expected anybody to read it besides maybe my family." With that limited audience in mind, it made sense to include lots of photos of Sydney and Owen, and to document the family's efforts to live a more "green" existence. "When I started it, I never intended for it to be only about knitting. It's . . . my diary that I let other people read." Over time, the blog has evolved in an organic way. "People like hearing about what I'm designing and how my design business is going. Long-time readers feel like they've been on that journey with me."

Knowing that she didn't want to go back into the corporate world, but uncertain as to what her next career incarnation would be, Chrissy turned her mind to puzzling out how she could convert her knitting passion into a viable business. "I don't necessarily think of myself as a very creative person, and it took me a long time to get over that—to think that I might have something that other knitters would want." But she had become so obsessed with knitting that her husband teased her about how much time she devoted to it. The lightbulb finally went on when she realized that knit designing was something she could do when "the rest of the world was sleeping."

Although she has built a solid reputation as a sock designer, and her company Gardiner Yarnworks features more sock designs than anything else, that was in no way her goal out of the starting gate. "I didn't even know how to knit socks. The very first design I ever did was the Ziggy Scarf. I had originally submitted it to *Knitty.com* and got rejected. That was an ongoing joke—*everything* I sent to *Knitty* got rejected for the longest time, until finally Amy Singer accepted one of my designs."

Once she had mastered sock knitting, she was hooked, and began submitting ideas for them as well as for a range of other projects to the mainstream knitting magazines. *Cast On* accepted a pattern, and as a bonus asked her to write an accompanying article on how to knit socks on two circular needles. She also submitted a range of ideas to *Interweave Knits*, where they accepted her sock patterns but nothing else. "So that's how I became known as a sock designer."

Once several of her designs were accepted into magazines, Gardiner Yarnworks took off. "I finally felt like I was ready to strike out on my own; I felt like I had had enough practice, and I knew what I needed to do to get the patterns out there, test-knitted, tech-edited, and formatted."

Now, she is so busy adding to her own pattern line, teaching sold-out sock workshops at Portland yarn shops, serving on the board of the Association of Knitwear Designers (AKD), writing her blog, and running Sydwillow Press (a new independent publishing venture) that she seldom has time to submit to magazines anymore. "I feel like I've struck the perfect balance, even though every 6 months or so I have a meltdown and decide I can't do this anymore. It's a cycle, and once I have my 6-month freak-out, I'm fine."

Her idea for Sydwillow Press (a division of Gardiner Yarnworks) percolated at the back of her mind for nearly 3 years before she was ready to take action. She'd played with the idea of writing a book based on her blog, but after attending Cat Bordhi's "Visionary" self-publishing retreat, decided instead to capitalize on her strengths by writing a sock book. While the sock knitting bookshelf is somewhat crowded at the moment, very few of those volumes are dedicated to knitting socks from the toe up. Chrissy was convinced there was room for one more. "It took me a *long* time to get to the point where I felt qualified to publish my own book." *Toe-Up! Patterns and Worksheets to Whip Your Sock Knitting into Shape* came out in 2009 with enthusiastic endorsements from the knitwear design community.

Sharing her home with a couple of small, inquisitive children can provide inspiration at the most unlikely times. A new sweater design "was inspired by somebody I saw walking down the street as I was driving my kids to school. If I see something that strikes me, I file it away in the back of my head. But when I find time to do a new design, a lot of my patterns are commissioned so there's already a market [for them]. Sometimes I dig through my yarn and ask myself what I feel like doing."

Often, it's her favorite stitch dictionaries that provide the spark. "Sometimes I'll just sit down with a big stack of those and look through them. Then I'll open up Knit Visualizer [a charting software] and play with different stitch combinations."

An unintended consequence of Ravelry's robust design community is that now, "everybody has their own stitch dictionaries and publishes the ideas they come up with. It stretches me and challenges me to be original. One of the things I've been having fun with lately is combining the stitch patterns in different ways, like my Path of Flowers stole; I play around until something clicks."

Chrissy has made it her business to master a wide variety of knitting challenges. "I am definitely a very good generalist; there isn't much that I have not at least touched on or tried at some point." Her successful experiments have wound up in publications such as *More Big Girl Knits* (Potter Craft, 2008); the Bountiful Bohus Sweater was the result of her first steeking experience. Other books in which her patterns have appeared include: *Color Style* (Interweave Press, 2008), *Knitting Socks with Hand-Painted Yarns* (Interweave Press, 2009), *Designer One-Skein Wonders* (Storey Publishing, 2007), and *Fiber Gathering* (Wiley, 2009).

The availability of her patterns in so many publications has helped draw attention and traffic to her blog. "This is such a personality-driven industry. People really like to read designer blogs; they like feeling that they know you personally in some way." And when a blog is well-written, effectively communicating the blogger's individual personality and style, readers get a real sense of the person behind it. "This is a fascinating byproduct of living in the

Internet age. Sometimes I wonder if I'm too candid on my blog. My kids are on there, and there are people who think I'm crazy for doing that. But I'm generally an open person, and it's fun to have people feel like they can just come up to me at Sock Summit or TNNA and start talking about my kids."

As someone who spends a lot of time online, Chrissy has personal experience with the impact of social media on knitting and the ways online contacts can trigger personal connections. Citing Sock Summit (an annual event) as an example, she routinely sees people organize meet-ups with like-minded knitters they've previously only met online, but who they feel are their friends.

"It's like the old-fashioned quilting bee where you get together to practice a craft. It's all about socializing and building community." Such meet-ups, where individuals bond over their favorite indie dyer or designer, are common occurrences at knitting conventions. Although they start out with that one shared interest, more common ground is often discovered once they meet face to face. "I first met my business partner, Donna, at our local knitting guild, which is something I learned about online. One of my sample knitters is also someone I met online, but I probably never would have met either of these people if not for knitting and the online knitting world. It brings you together with people who could end up being your best friend, and you never would have met them otherwise."

Knitters' Guide to Essential Blogging Terminology

Convo—noun or verb: an abbreviation for "conversation." To exchange personal information with another person, specifically about yarn (as in swaps, trades, or destashing) or other knitting accoutrements. As in: "Convo me to discuss a swap." Close cousin of "PM."

PM—verb: to send a personal message between two bloggers or Ravelers through private messages rather than through public comments or online forums.

CHUTES AND LADDERS SOCKS
by Chrissy Gardiner

This sock combines three of my great loves in life—cables, lace, and socks! The pattern is a relatively simple combination of cable crossing and faggoting that knits up with stunning results. I tried to keep the pattern as a single-skein project, so the cuff length gets shorter as the foot size goes up. If you'd like a longer sock, pick up a second skein, just in case. One advantage of knitting from the toe up is that you can knit to your very last inch of yarn!

Difficulty: Intermediate
Skills Used: Backward loop cast-on, picking up stitches, short-row shaping, basic lace, basic cabling

SIZE

Women's S (M, L)

To fit foot circumference: 6–7 (7–8, 8–9½)"

Finished Measurements
Circumference: 6¼ (7½, 8½)"
Cuff Length: 6 (5, 4)"

MATERIALS

- Sundara Yarn Sock Yarn (100% superwash Merino; 350yd per 100g); color: Winter Pine (Limited Edition Color). Indie dyer Sundara always has similar colors, but often does not repeat specific colors by name; 1 skein (for a longer cuff or very long foot, buy 2 skeins)

- Two US 1 (2.25mm) circular needles, any length, or size needed to obtain gauge

- Stitch marker

- Cable needle

- Tapestry needle

GAUGE

32 sts and 36 rows = 4" in St st

35 sts and 37 rows = 4" in patt st

PATTERN NOTES

w&t: Wrap next stitch and turn work. Bring yarn to front and slip next stitch, bring yarn to back and return st to left-hand needle. Turn work, bring yarn to the back, and knit to the end of the row.

T2F: Place 1 st on CN and hold in front, p1, k1 from CN

T2B: Place 1 st on CN and hold in back, k1, p1 from CN

T3B: Place 2 sts on CN and hold in back, k1, [p1, k1] from CN

DIRECTIONS
Toe

Using the backward loop cast-on, CO 7 (9, 11) sts on the first needle. Turn and k across these sts. Using the second needle, pick up and k8 (8, 12) sts along the CO edge. There are now 15 (17, 23) sts total across both needles. Place a marker to indicate the beg of the rnd. Needle 1 will hold the 7 (9, 11) heel/back of leg sts. Needle 2 will hold the 8 (8, 12) instep/front

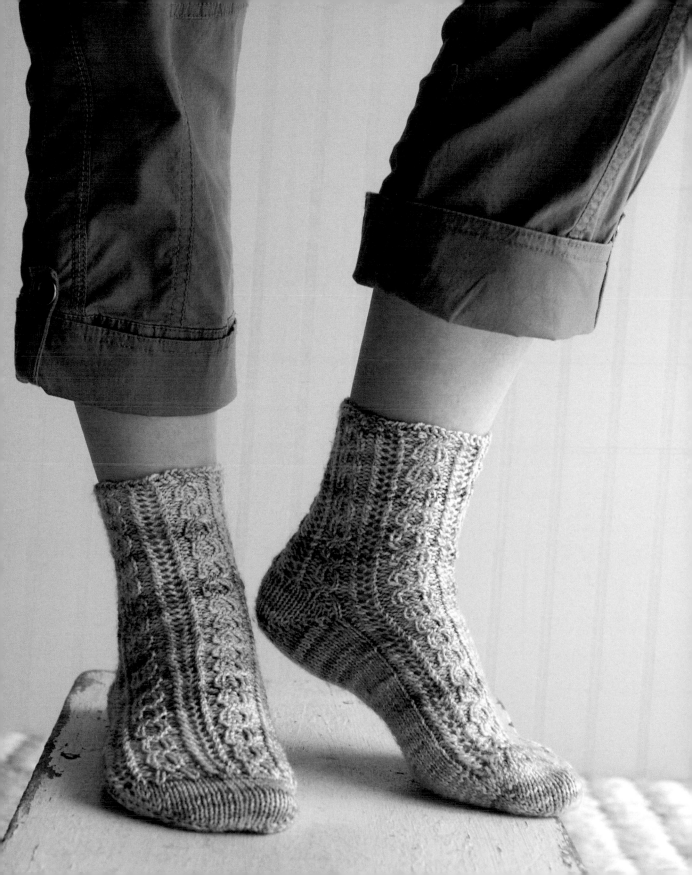

of leg sts. In the st instructions, heel and instep sts are divided using a "ll."

Rnd 1: Kfb, k to last 2 heel sts, kfb, k1 ll kfb, k to last 2 instep sts, kfb, k1—19 (21, 27) sts; 9 (11, 13) heel and 10 (10, 14) instep.

Rep Rnd 1 an additional 3 times—31 (33, 39) sts; 15 (17, 19) heel and 16 (16, 20) instep.

Next Rnd: Knit.

Next Rnd: Kfb, k to last 2 heel sts, kfb, k1 ll kfb, k to last 2 instep sts, kfb, k1—35 (37, 43) sts, 17 (19, 21) heel and 18 (18, 22) instep.

Rep last two rnds an additional 5 (7, 8) times—55 (65, 75) sts; 27 (33, 37) heel and 28 (32, 38) instep.

K 1 rnd even.

Foot

Rnd 1: K across heel sts ll p1 (1, 2), *k2, yo, ssk, p1 (2, 3), k1, p3, k1, p1 (2, 3); rep from *, k2, yo, ssk, p1 (1, 2).

Rnd 2: K across heel sts ll p1 (1, 2), *k2tog, yo, k2, p1 (2, 3), k1, p3, k1, p1 (2, 3); rep from *, k2tog, yo, k2, p1 (1, 2).

Rnd 3: Rep Rnd 1.

Rnd 4: K across heel sts ll p1 (1, 2), *k2tog, yo, k2, p1 (2, 3), T2F, p1, T2B, p1 (2, 3); rep from *, k2tog, yo, k2, p1 (1, 2).

Rnd 5: K across heel sts ll p1 (1, 2), *k2, yo, ssk, p2 (3, 4), T3B, p2 (3, 4); rep from *, k2, yo, ssk, p1 (1, 2).

Rnd 6: K across heel sts ll p1 (1, 2), *k2tog, yo, k2, p1 (2, 3), T2B, p1, T2F, p1 (2, 3); rep from *, k2tog, yo, k2, p1 (1, 2).

Rep Rnds 1–6 until foot measures approximately 2" less than desired finished length from tip of toe.

Heel

The heel will be worked back and forth on the 27 (33, 37) heel sts.

SHAPE BOTTOM OF HEEL:

Row 1 (RS): K to last heel st, w&t.

Row 2 (WS): P to last heel st, w&t.

Row 3: K to the last unwrapped st, wrap it and turn.

Row 4: P to the last unwrapped st, wrap it and turn.

Rep Rows 3–4 an additional 7 (9, 10) times until there are 9 (11, 12) wrapped sts on either side of 9 (11, 13) unwrapped center sts.

SHAPE TOP OF HEEL:

Row 1 (RS): K to first wrapped st (do not k across any wrapped sts), lift wrap and k it tog with the corresponding st, turn.

Row 2 (WS): Sl 1, p to first wrapped st (do not p across any wrapped sts), lift wrap and p it tog with the corresponding st, turn.

Row 3: Sl 1, k to first wrapped st (just past turn from the previous RS row), lift wrap and k it tog with the corresponding st, turn.

Row 4: Sl 1, p to first wrapped st (just past turn from previous WS row), lift wrap and p it tog with the corresponding st, turn.

Rep Rows 3–4 an additional 6 (8, 9) times until a single wrapped st remains on either side.

Next Row: Sl 1, k to last wrapped st, lift wrap and k it tog with the corresponding st but do not turn ‖ work instep sts in next rnd of patt as est.

Next Rnd: Lift the final wrap (at beg of heel sts) and k it tog with the corresponding st, then k to end of heel sts ‖ work instep sts in next rnd of patt as est.

Leg

Begin working the patt around the entire leg as follows, starting with the rnd following the patt rnd just worked across the instep to keep the design going up the leg of the sock. If the next rnd to be worked is 4, 5, or 6, k across the heel sts **for these rounds only** instead of working them in patt to avoid having a partial cable at the top of the heel.

Rnd 1: P0 (1, 1), *k1, p3, k1, p1 (2, 3), k2, yo, ssk, p1 (2, 3), rep from *, k1, p3, k1, p0 (1, 1) ‖ p1 (1, 2), *k2, yo, ssk, p1 (2, 3), k1, p3, k1, p1 (2, 3), rep from *, k2, yo, ssk, p1 (1, 2).

Rnd 2: P0 (1, 1), *k1, p3, k1, p1 (2, 3), k2tog, yo, k2, p1 (2, 3), rep from *, k1, p3, k1, p0 (1, 1) ‖ p1 (1, 2), *k2tog, yo, k2, p1 (2, 3), k1, p3, k1, p1 (2, 3), rep from *, k2tog, yo, k2, p1 (1, 2).

Rnd 3: Rep Rnd 1.

Rnd 4: P0(1, 1), *T2F, p1, T2B, p1 (2, 3), k2tog, yo, k2, p1 (2, 3), rep from *, T2F, p1, T2B, p0 (1, 1) ‖ p1 (1, 2), *k2tog, yo, k2, p1 (2, 3), T2F, p1, T2B, p1 (2, 3), rep from *, k2tog, yo, k2, p1 (1, 2).

Rnd 5: P1 (2, 2), *T3B, p2 (3, 4), k2, yo, ssk, p2 (3, 4), rep from *, T3B, p1 (2, 2) ‖ p1 (1, 2), *k2, yo, ssk, p2 (3, 4), T3B, p2 (3, 4), rep from *, k2, yo, ssk, p1 (1, 2).

Rnd 6: P0 (1, 1), *T2B, p1, T2F, p1 (2, 3), k2tog, yo, k2, p1 (2, 3), rep from *, T2B, p1, T2F, p0 (1, 1) ‖ p1(1, 2), *k2tog, yo, k2, p1 (2, 3), T2B, p1, T2F, p1 (2, 3), rep from *, k2tog, yo, k2, p1 (1, 2).

Rep Rounds 1–6 until leg measures approximately 6 (5, 4)" from top of heel or desired finished length. BO all sts as follows: K1, *yo, k1; pass the rightmost st and the yo over the leftmost st on right-hand needle. Rep from * until all st are bound off.

FINISHING

Weave in ends and block socks lightly.

Norah Gaughan, Berroco Yarn Blog

Norah Gaughan (pronounced *Gawn*), design director at Berroco Yarns, is by any account a rock star in the knitting subculture. Her Ravelry fan group alone has more than 4,500 members, and thousands more subscribe to the Berroco yarn company blog she writes with a colleague. Among her most popular patterns are the Tilted Duster jacket from *Interweave Knits* (Fall 2007) and the cable-intensive Brea Bag from Berroco.com. But these two projects represent the merest speck of her productivity; her Ravelry designer page lists a staggering 427 individual projects and shows cover photographs of 81 books and pattern pamphlets that she has either designed herself or to which she has contributed designs. Yet it is with self-deprecating modesty that she conveys her love of the craft, as if even after 20-plus years in the industry her celebrity is still a somewhat puzzling byproduct of "just doing my job."

While her fans are dazzled as much by the sheer volume of her output as by her command of unique stitch and shaping techniques, at the Berroco office she focuses on creating pattern support for the company's range of fibers. Yet her long and fruitful association with Berroco also allows her to wear many hats. Part of her job is to source yarns from countries as different as Peru and Italy; in this way Berroco achieves the mix of user-friendly fibers and price points that sustains their strong presence in the industry.

Providing pattern support for all those luscious fibers would challenge even the most inspired knitters, but Norah's reputation as a prolific designer is well-deserved. All combined, there are more than 70 new designs in just two of her more recent signature collections for Berroco. One of these is a long-awaited pattern book for men, dominated by textured and cabled traditional sweaters and accessories.

Since her college days, Norah has consistently drawn inspiration both from forms that appear in nature and from mathematical shapes. (For this reason, when membership in her

Ravelry fan group topped 3,000, members made her a "hexagaughan" blanket. Knitters from 11 different countries contributed blocks.) In addition, her designs are known for clever—and often unusual—shaping techniques that flatter a variety of figures.

She credits the Internet for her ability to respond so well to knitters' desires. With her colleague Cirilia Rose, she spends at least 20 hours a week surfing Ravelry and dozens of knitting blogs. "It's fun not to be working in a vacuum, basing [yarn buying and pattern design] decisions solely on the filter of what sales reps and yarn shop owners tell us regarding trends. The end consumer—the person who's really working with the yarn—used to be really hard to get to." Now, with Ravelry and the blogs providing valuable, if informal, market research with the click of a mouse, she has a better sense of which designs will appeal to Berroco customers. When she really loves a new pattern, she is able to see quickly that there are others who like it, too. This access to the online knitting community also makes it easier to sell her more novel garment concepts to Berroco's management because "It's not just me saying it's [a good design]."

As an example, Norah cites her penchant for "designs that are high-waisted; baby-doll style." Although she is occasionally questioned about why she doesn't do more classic waist shaping, because of Ravelry forums and positive online comments she can respond with confidence that "baby-doll shaping is very popular; it's flattering, and it's not just for 16-year-olds."

She is the first to admit that, despite her years of experience, the design process is as much about trial and error for her as it is for a novice designer. Aware that from the perspective of the average knitter she commands one of the highest pedestals in the knitting pantheon, she takes pains to share with knitters the amount of sheer effort that goes into creating each new design. And the Internet is an important vehicle for that effort. In fact, one of the Berroco blog's many charms is that it gives readers a peek into the development stage of new patterns. Her entries regularly explore her thought process and describe the mistakes that eventually yield the desired result.

"I tell stories on myself. I'll explain that I was trying to do one thing: here is what I was thinking—it definitely did not work. So, I had to start over. Things go wrong at every phase of a new design. It's important for readers to understand that even though . . . the first attempt didn't work, eventually we sorted out the problems."

Sketches, yarn swatches, and even photos of inspiring mainstream fashions find their way onto the blog, where they become carefully scattered seeds along the path that leads readers from initial concept to completed design. Following this trail, the reader is treated to a fascinating glimpse into Norah's thought process. This can lead to surprising revelations: "Somebody once asked me a philosophical question about why, as a rule, I don't do top-down designs. I think that decreasing is more effective than increasing, and that you have better control over the shape when things are in pieces, so top-down is just not my thing."

Both the Berroco site and the Ravelry fan group influence her designs indirectly. "I think about it when someone comments, mostly about the design part because that's more personal to me than yarn choices." Those decisions are made by Berroco's owner, with input from yarn shops and sales representatives. "But sitting down and designing a sweater, that's more my decision—that's where I'm directly involved."

The company Web site allows Norah and her team to extrapolate a certain amount of information about the popularity of specific patterns and yarns. Ravelry allows her to track how many projects are in progress using Berroco yarns and pattern books. Pattern information from each new booklet launched by the company is immediately downloaded onto Ravelry; it's been extremely useful market research for the company to see how many of those patterns are "favorited" and how many of the patterns are actually being knit up with Berroco yarns. In this way, the site offers information that is immediately useful, supplementing the anecdotal material that appears in individual user profiles.

"Not only is it fun to see what people are making, but it also gives me some leverage; I see the gallery pictures, so I know they're being made by people of all ages, with all different figure types. [That visual information] frees people to make pattern modifications, to see that the designs will look good on average knitters, not just on the models in the books."

Current fashion trends are a peripheral influence when designing her signature collections with the company's new yarns. "We look at [fashion] magazines, at shapes and at silhouettes, and narrow down our concepts to the ones we want to work with. Once we have settled on a group of sweaters, the fun part is solving the problems [such as], OK, how do I use my own thought process to make that [garment] completely different?"

As a designer who has been knitting for more than half her life, structuring a new collection to include a variety of difficulty levels can be a challenge. She believes that many knitters underestimate their skill level, to the point that they are intimidated at the thought of working their way through some of her patterns. "It seems like I call everything 'Intermediate.' It's gotten to be kind of a joke that I'm always telling knitters, 'It's not as hard as it looks.'"

Yet she always tries to pare down things to make her patterns easier to follow and easier to knit. "I actively look for clever tricks to find the easiest way to do something. So even [with] a fairly hard pattern, if the pattern repeats all end at the same time, that makes it simpler for the knitter. If we have a choice of two things, and one of them makes it easier both for me as the designer and for the knitter, I go for it."

What lies ahead for this designer at the pinnacle of her career?

"As long as I feel like there's something that I haven't done before, something new, something kind of scary because I'm not sure if it's going to work out . . . then it's fresh and new. There are always stitch variations, and variations on those variations. As long as there's still something to learn, I could be discovering new things until I'm 85!"

SPROUTING CLOCHE
by Norah Gaughan

Either a cold winter day or a bad-hair day will benefit from a soft cloche that covers the ears, and if it happens to include both an unusual rib stitch band and graceful stems of leaves all round, so much the better! Lustra's sheen results from a blend of Peruvian wool and Tencel, creating a lovely hand that is delicious next to the skin.

Difficulty: Intermediate
Skills Used: Unusual increasing and decreasing, following charts

SIZE

Fits most women

Finished Measurements
Circumference: 21"

MATERIALS

- Berroco Lustra (50% Peruvian wool, 50% Tencel; 197yd per 100g); color: 3141 Capucine; 1 skein

- US 7 (4.5mm) needles, or size needed to obtain gauge

- US 5 (3.75mm) needles

- Tapestry needle

GAUGE

18 sts and 24 rows = 4" in St st on larger needles

PATTERN NOTES

Ribbed cast-on: Just like a knitted cast-on, but using both knits and purls for a tidy edge. Make a slip knot and put it on the left-hand needle—this counts as the first st. *Insert the right-hand needle into the st purlwise and purl it, transfer the newly made st to the left-hand needle, insert the right-hand needle into the last st on the left-hand needle knitwise and knit it, transfer the newly made st to the left-hand needle, rep from * until you have cast on all your sts.

STITCH PATTERN

K1b, P1 Rib (worked flat on a mult of 2 sts):

Row 1 (RS): *K1 tbl, p1, rep from * to end of row.

Row 2 (WS): * P1, p1 tbl, rep from * to end of row.

Cloche

With smaller needles, CO 98 sts, using the ribbed cast-on.

Work in k1b, p1 rib for 1½", ending with a WS row.

Change to larger needles and k 1 row.

Begin following Leaf Motif Chart as follows:

RS rows: P1, work chart 3 times, p1.

WS rows: K1, work chart 3 times, k1.

When chart is completed, there are 32 sts.

Next row (RS): K1, (k2tog) 15 times, k1—17sts.

Next row (WS): Purl.

Next row: K1, (k2tog) 8 times—9 sts.

Break yarn. With tapestry needle, thread end through remaining loops, tighten, and secure. With the same yarn, sew seam from ribbed CO edge to top of crown. Weave in end.

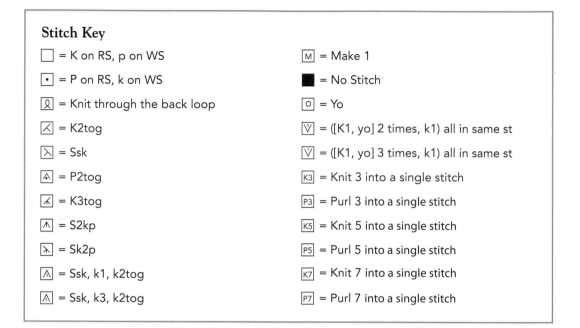

Stitch Key

☐ = K on RS, p on WS

• = P on RS, k on WS

ℚ = Knit through the back loop

⊼ = K2tog

⊼ = Ssk

⊼ = P2tog

⊼ = K3tog

⋀ = S2kp

⋋ = Sk2p

⋀ = Ssk, k1, k2tog

⋀ = Ssk, k3, k2tog

M = Make 1

■ = No Stitch

O = Yo

V = ([K1, yo] 2 times, k1) all in same st

V = ([K1, yo] 3 times, k1) all in same st

K3 = Knit 3 into a single stitch

P3 = Purl 3 into a single stitch

K5 = Knit 5 into a single stitch

P5 = Purl 5 into a single stitch

K7 = Knit 7 into a single stitch

P7 = Purl 7 into a single stitch

Knitters' Guide to Essential Blogging Terminology

Button—noun: the blog, Web site, and vendor logos that appear in bloggers' sidebars telling other bloggers with a single set of tiny images what else the blogger reads and where they shop for knitting supplies.

Leaf Motif Chart

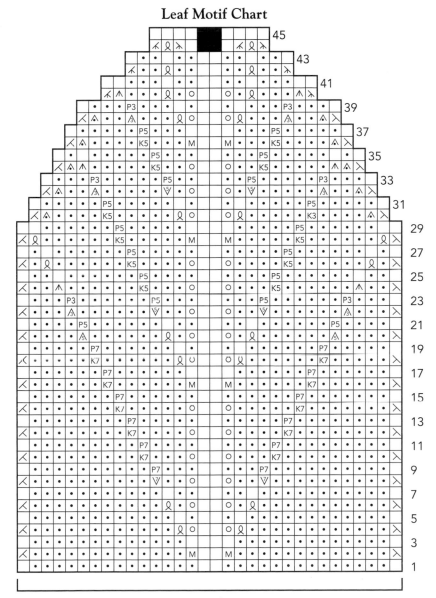

32-Stitch Repeat

Anne Hanson, Knitspot

This master tailor and former costumer of Broadway productions still remembers pestering her grandmother to teach her to knit—when she was all of four years old. Anne knit all through high school and college, designing garments and accessories for family and friends alike. Even then, others encouraged her to start her own knitting business, and she dreamed that someday she'd be able to make a career from her passion. But after twenty years in the fashion industry in New York City, where she did pattern-making and draping for big-name designers, Anne and her husband, David, had had enough of big-city life. While on a visit to friends in small-town Ohio, on a whim they went house-hunting.

Fast forward seven years. Anne and David have made a new life in that same small Ohio town, where they live in a large, gracious historic brick home that they bought despite Anne's reservations. "When we looked at this house, I just cringed. I knew [the renovations] would take years; this *is* Mr. Blanding's Dream House."

In David's hands the house is, indeed, a grand dame undergoing one facelift after another, a state of continual refurbishment that takes much of his time and energy. Anne refers to her husband fondly as the "house artist." He applies his engineering background to each project, and just one example of his expertise is the studio/office where Anne does her design work; it is a masterpiece of efficiency and calm. They have also cultivated a large and bountiful garden from which she draws steady inspiration. For example, her neck-warmer project for this book evolved from her impressions of the climbing hydrangea that grows at the back of the house.

Although she insists she's never had a business plan, when they moved to Ohio Anne was unemployed and actively looking for work. She started her blog both as a way to keep busy and, at the back of her mind, as a means to launch a business. "Of course, when you first start a blog, you have two readers: your mother and your best friend. Slowly, I put myself out there and began to develop a following."

In addition, she began teaching classes at her new local yarn shop. She created patterns for her classes because she couldn't find "the perfect mitt, the perfect hat" to use as teaching tools for her students. Her original patterns were instantly, wildly popular, and her students were eager to buy them. "Then it seemed like every personal project I was working on, they wanted to buy. They'd ask, 'Are you making a pattern for that?' So I wrote them up." From the start, her classic, flattering designs sold briskly in yarn shops (and are carried by more than 75 yarn shops nationwide), and Anne had an epiphany. "I knew if I could get them on the Internet, they'd do very well."

Given her extensive repertoire of stunning lace designs, it is no surprise that her Wing O' the Moth stole, made for a friend's wedding, was the first pattern she put up on her blog, specifically because of blog comments she received while it was in progress. "I fell into a niche; that first shawl attracted all these lace knitters. It's a huge interest area that isn't being fulfilled. I love to design lace; it's a more compositional, painterly kind of project to design. I can go really far out on a tangent with my imagination."

Once her online store opened, her pattern sales quadrupled. A neckwarmer pattern published in *Knitty.com* was followed by two lovely shawl patterns that appeared in *Twist Collective*.

With her husband acting as photographer and Anne modeling her own samples, the Knitspot blog has become synonymous with her extensive, whimsically named collection of ethereal lace shawls. These are whipped up in a variety of gorgeous yarns provided by indie dyers and spinners, all of whom compete to have Anne test-drive their fibers. In addition to contests, charitable knitting, and giveaways, one of the many delightfully interactive elements of Knitspot is Anne's request for help from readers in naming new projects. The resulting names often reflect motifs from nature that appear in the lace; others are borrowed from literary or cultural references. And she still knits almost every sample herself in order to ". . . write the pattern well and to see where the potential pitfalls lie." This care results in a body of work that contains very few errata.

Although her prolific output and the Knitspot site's attractive, professionally designed online store might suggest otherwise, Anne insists she still has no formal business plan. She does, however, have terrific instinct for what works. "I'm a very organized person, but I have no desire to have a plan that's so rigid I miss other opportunities while I'm following it. I'm always open, but you can't light every fire at once. For instance, the sweater patterns: I've been wanting to do a collection of them since I was a teenager. But even after I started my pattern business, it had to get to a point that I could hire [test knitters] to help with that kind of project at the pace my readers have come to expect." With several sweater patterns added to her collection within the last year and more on the way, she has begun to satisfy that ambition.

Her Little Nothing scarf collection was born of her desire to experiment with different lace patterns, and of asking herself, "What's the perfect color and texture to make that stitch pattern pop? What yarn makes it really come to life? It was supposed to be a simple creative exploration, making experimental swatches for myself." She posted about her efforts, and soon readers asked, "What about the pattern? When are we going to get that?" Although the Little Nothing patterns are based on widely published stitch dictionary options such as those in the Barbara G. Walker *Treasuries*, the artistry and deliberate accessibility that goes into Anne's "gateway" versions are readily apparent. "I can't tell you how many people write to me saying they never would have attempted lace knitting if they didn't have my patterns to get them started [thinking about borders, edging, motif repeats, and blocking]. Nothing about a simple project is really that simple if you've never done it before. Little Nothings encourages people to try knitting lace—to take that first step."

As a lifelong knitter, Anne has a long perspective on the cyclical nature of the craft. "I'm always surprised when I hear it's dying down again, because I don't get a sense of that at all. There's a whole group of people that don't *make* anything with their hands all day—they don't get to produce anything quantifiable. But knitting is rewarding and works with that lifestyle; where else in life do they feel that kind of satisfaction? It's thrilling . . . when someone writes to let me know that they have the desire to [challenge themselves], to apply their minds, to try harder and more complex projects. This opposes our larger societal trend to have everything be easier, softer, more disposable, faster."

To that end, she believes that Ravelry supports the knitting community in a vital way; members support each other in their efforts and encourage serious study of the craft, instead of acting as superficial cheerleaders of a fleeting trend. "Knitting is a discipline, and I see more and more people embracing that discipline, making peace with the fact that it can be difficult and slow. I'm grateful for its popularity, and happy that other people find it as fascinating as I do."

HYDRANGEA NECKWARMER

by Anne Hanson

Description: A pretty neck warmer in two sizes that adds a circle of warmth at the neck without bulk. Knit in a climbing vine motif and finished with a knit-on border of leaf lace, this piece works up quickly on circular needles, travels well, and makes a beautiful gift.

Difficulty: Intermediate
Skills Used: Basic increasing and decreasing, lace knitting

SIZE

S (L)

Finished Measurements
Circumference: 16 (18)"
Length: 7 (9)"

MATERIALS

- Woolen Rabbit Opulence (50% silk, 50% Merino; 375 yd per 113g); color: Pussywillow; 1 skein (Approximately 120 (150) yd will be needed)

- 16" US 3 (3.25mm) circular needle, or size needed to obtain gauge

- 1 set US 3 (3.25mm) double-pointed needles

- Tapestry needle

GAUGE

24 sts and 36 rows = 4" in St st, unblocked

22 sts and 30 rows = 4" in Climbing Vine Pattern, blocked

NECKWARMER

Top Edge

With circular needle, CO 84 (96) sts. Place marker and join to beg working in the rnd, taking care not to twist sts.

Rnds 1 and 3: Purl.

Rnd 2: Knit.

Body

Follow the Climbing Vine chart 3 (4) times (or to desired length), or follow the written directions below.

CLIMBING VINE PATTERN:

Rnd 1: *Yo, k2, ssk, k3, k2tog, k2, yo, k1, rep from * to end of rnd.

Rnd 2 and all even-numbered rnds: Knit.

Rnd 3: *K1, yo, k2, ssk, k1, k2tog, k2, yo, k2, rep from * to end of rnd.

Rnd 5: *K2, yo, k2, sk2p, k2, yo, k3, rep from * to end of rnd.

Rnd 7: Sl 1, *(k1, yo) twice, k2, ssk, k3, k2tog, k1, rep from * to end of rnd.

Rnd 9: Sl 1, *yo, k3, yo, k2, ssk, k1, k2tog, k2, rep from * to end of rnd.

Rnd 11: *K5, yo, k2, k3tog, k2, yo, rep from * to end of rnd.

Rnd 12: Knit.

Rep these 12 rnds 2 (3) more times (or to desired length). This completes the body section.

Hem Edging

Follow the Leaf Lace Edging chart 21 (24 times), ending last repeat after Row 7, or follow the written directions below. The edging is worked perpendicular to the body of the neck warmer. You will join the edging to the body by working one st from the edging together with one st from the body at the end of each RS row by purling these two sts together.

Set-up: Using a provisional cast-on, CO 12 sts with waste yarn onto a double-pointed needle.

P 12 sts from provisional cast on with working yarn and circular needle. Continue knitting the edging using one end of the circular needle and one dpn.

With RS facing, beg edging on Row 1.

Row 1 (RS): Yo, k1, yo, k2, (k2tog) twice, k2, yo, k2tog, ptog 1 st from edging and 1 st from body.

Row 2 and all WS rows: Sl 1, p11.

Row 3: Yo, k3, yo, k1, (k2tog) twice, k1, yo, k2tog, p2tog.

Row 5: Yo, k5, yo, (k2tog) twice, yo, k2 tog, p2tog.

Row 7: Yo, k3, k2tog, k2, (yo, k2tog) twice, p2tog.

Row 8: Sl 1, p 11.

Rep these 8 rows 20 (23) more times, ending last rep on Row 7. Remove provisional cast-on and place the resulting 12 sts onto a spare needle. Cut working yarn to a length of 10" and thread onto a tapestry needle. Hold the ends of the edging with WS together and graft the live sts using kitchener stitch.

FINISHING

Weave in all loose ends. Block to finished measurements, reshaping as needed to prevent creasing.

Note: *Stitch key and charts on page 174.*

Stitch Key

☐ = K on RS, p on WS

◩ = K2tog

◪ = Ssk

◩ = Ptog 1 st from edging
and 1 st from body

◩ = K3tog

◪ = Sk2p

☐ = Slip 1 purlwise wyif

⊙ = Yo

Climbing Vine Chart

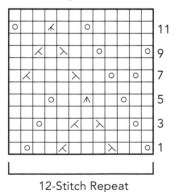

12-Stitch Repeat

Lace Leaf Edging Chart

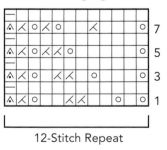

12-Stitch Repeat

Kirsten Kapur, Through the Loops

As an art student at college in upstate New York, Kirsten had every intention of using her creative skills professionally upon graduation. But once she landed in New York City for her first "real" job as an assistant designer in the garment industry, she decided that fashion was not for her. Textile design proved more to her liking, and she worked happily in that end of the industry for the next 10 years, applying her art background to pattern, color, and texture within the fiber universe. Only when her three children were born did she put aside the career to focus on parenting.

The kids inherited Kirsten's wide creative streak; all teenagers now, they are musicians and artists in their own right. Once she learned to knit, they provided her with a constant source of inspiration. Knitting for them has always been a pleasure. "A lot of people complain because their kids don't like to wear handknits, but mine are into it."

Their willingness to wear handknit garments is in brilliant evidence on Kirsten's blog, throughtheloops, where all three regularly model her creations. In fact, she feels very lucky that they like her designs and enjoy wearing them. With their own distinct styles in evidence, her kids use quirky accessories to put their personal stamp on her designs and are never shy about suggesting settings and themes for photo shoots. Their participation has turned the blog into a family project.

When Kirsten started her blog in 2006, her main goal was to connect with other knitters and contribute to blog-supported yarn and dye swaps. Inspired by the first knitting blogs she read, she realized that some of those bloggers were also knitwear designers—and as someone for whom knitting techniques are almost intuitively simple to master, she decided that she could do that, too. "All creative acts, for me, are just things I do. I've never found obstacles to my knitting designs. I'm fearless about crafts, and I feel strongly that we learn from our mistakes. Don't be afraid of ripping out your errors—it's only knitting, and you can do it again."

The intuitive framework of her knitting extends to the yarn choices she makes. She appreciates that indie yarn dyers and spinners often send her new yarns to sample because rather than impose the structure of a new project concept onto the yarn, she channels her "yarn whisperer" tendencies; "sometimes a new design is dictated by the yarn telling me what it wants to be."

Soon after starting her blog, Kirsten was approached by Amy Singer, editor of *Knitty.com*, about contributing a pattern to the online magazine. "That's the wonderful thing about the whole explosion of the online knitting world: We get to find out about the new, up-and-coming designers, and they get a venue to work in." The publicity from her appearance in *Knitty* gave a huge boost to her profile and her blog traffic.

Describing herself as a "very mediocre golfer" in her limited free time, these days she spends what sometimes feels like every waking moment with her knitting in hand. Although her busy schedule doesn't allow for teaching classes or workshops, she has remained very responsive to questions from the knitters who are making her projects. And with nearly 2,400 members in her Ravelry fan group alone, there are lots of questions. "Ravelry has given indie designers like me much more exposure; the site does a lot of things for me that a blog by itself can't do." Where she used to mail out paper copies of all her patterns to purchasers, now Ravelry hosts her files and handles her sales.

Her Ravelry store includes both a generous selection of free patterns and more than two dozen patterns for sale. "Being a knitting designer online, I can design something new one month, and have it up on the site the next month." Most of her favorite patterns are for accessories, particularly hats, shawls, and socks. The most popular of these have inspired knit-alongs. There are close to 3,000 Ravelers making her Thorpe hat and hundreds more working on the One-Day Beret and the Ulmus Shawl.

Although she is best known for her cleverly designed, colorful accessories, her plans include the creation of more garments. The few available on her site have always been popular, and her fearless, intuitive approach to design makes it easy for her to imagine more. Despite her career change many years ago, her inspiration is clearly grounded in her extensive background in fashion and textile design. She absorbs the "idiosyncratic genius" of New York City street fashion and filters her ideas through what her own children find stylish and wearable. Although she wishes she were a member of the design community that finds its inspiration in nature, "I'm not one of those mind-blowing designers who goes to the park, looks at tree bark, and finds a sweater design there."

Part of the charm of the online knitters' community for Kirsten is that designers interact directly with the people making their patterns. It's a bonus to have the ability to answer the end user's questions in person. "I'm so appreciative that people support my work by buying my patterns, and I try to anticipate what kinds of questions will come up. I spend a lot of time helping knitters work out the pattern details, which is great because people point out things to me about my patterns that I might not have seen. Even if it's not an error, sometimes it's how to make the instructions clearer."

Since the inception of throughtheloops, its emphasis has shifted almost entirely away from personal revelations and family anecdotes and onto the knitting. "I keep in mind that this is my business. There are many bloggers out there who speak their minds on issues like politics and [social] controversy. There are times I'd like to do that, but I don't because I want my blog to be about the things that bring us together instead of things that divide us." Reflecting on the blogs she most enjoys reading, she realized that for her their appeal lay mainly in their in-depth knitting commentary, and that helps keep her focused on the content of her own. At first, however, it was a struggle to balance the personal with the professional. When her kids' band began performing in public in 2008, she wanted to promote their efforts. But even those mentions are few and far between. "When people come to read my blog, they come for the knitting, so I don't give them too much of the other stuff."

One notable exception to her blog's knitting and design orientation is the sidebar dedicated to the memory of her late father, a respected microbiologist who struggled with Alzheimer's disease. Like other bloggers who harness the popularity of their blogs to support charitable organizations, Kirsten has her favorite cause: the Fisher Center for Alzheimer's Research Foundation. In her father's memory, she designed Dr. G's Memory Vest, a stylish, cabled V-neck vest. For each donation made to support the foundation's research and awareness outreach, she sends a free copy of the vest pattern to the donor. She's very proud of having raised thousands of dollars to date for the Fisher Center. "I'll never take that link down, and I will continue to encourage people to make donations."

SOCKSTRAVAGANZA

by Kirsten Kapur

Test your knitting skills with these whimsical socks. Cable and Fair Isle techniques keep the knitting interesting, and the Fair Isle cuff and striped toe give you a chance to play with color combinations.

Difficulty: Advanced
Skills Used: Fair Isle, cables

SIZE

One size, adaptable to any foot length

Finished Measurements
8" circumference at Fair Isle cuff, relaxed
5½" circumference at leg, relaxed
The socks will stretch to fit up to 10" circumference leg and foot

MATERIALS

- [MC] Fearless Fibers Tight Twist Superwash Merino Wool Sock Yarn (100% superwash Merino; 480yd per 113g); color: Sloth; 1 skein

- [CC] Fearless Fibers Tight Twist Superwash Merino Wool Sock Yarn (100% superwash Merino; 480yd per 113g); color: Spellbound; 1 skein

- 1 set US 1 (2.25mm) double-pointed needles, or size needed to obtain gauge

- Cable needle

- Tapestry needle

GAUGE

34 sts and 46 rows = 4" in St s

36 sts and 41 rows = 4" in Fair Isle patt st

36 sts and 46 rows = 3" in cable patt

PATTERN NOTES

When working in Fair Isle patt, keep the floats in the back of the work loose to allow the cuff to stretch.

The cable patt is worked across the front of the sock and down the foot. The Rib Pattern is worked across the back of the sock and down the heel flap.

The Fair Isle Chart will rep twice around the sock.

For cable and Fair Isle patts, see charts.

STITCH PATTERN

Rib Pattern (Worked across 36 sts): P1, k2, p2, (k1, p2) 3 times, (k2, p1) 2 times, k2, (p2, k1) 3 times, p2, k2, p1.

DIRECTIONS
Cuff

With CC, CO 72 stitches. Place 18 sts on each of 4 needles and join to work in the rnd.

Work 10 rnds in k1, p1 rib.

Fair Isle Panel

Work Rnds 1–26 of Fair Isle Chart using both MC and CC. The 36-st chart will rep twice around the sock.

Leg

Next rnd (Rnd 37): Using MC, k 1 rnd.

Begin to work from Cable Chart across needles 1 & 2 and in rib patt (see notes) across needles 3 & 4.

On needles 1 & 2, work Rnds 1–24, then Rnds 1–23. Cont in rib on needles 3 & 4.

Work Rnd 24 across needles 1 & 2, then start heel flap on needles 3 & 4 as follows.

Heel Flap

The heel flap will be worked **back and forth** on needles 3 & 4 only. Place all 36 of these sts on needle 4 to make it easier to work the heel flap. Cont to work the rib patt down the heel flap, **except** sl the first st of each row:

Row 1 (RS): Sl 1, k2, p2, (k1, p2) 3 times, (k2, p1) 2 times, k2, (p2, k1) 3 times, p2, k2, p1.

Row 2 (WS): Sl 1, p2, k2, (p1, k2) 3 times, (p2, k1) 2 times, p2, (k2, p1) 3 times, k2, p2, k1.

Rep Rows 1 and 2 until the heel flap measures 2¼". You may adjust the length of your heel flap, making it longer to accommodate a higher arch or shorter to accommodate a flatter arch. End with a WS row.

Heel Turn

Row 1 (RS): Sl 1, k20, ssk, k1. Turn.

Row 2 (WS): Sl 1, p7, p2tog, p1. Turn.

Row 3: Sl 1, k8, ssk, k1. Turn.

Row 4: Sl 1, p9, p2tog, p1. Turn.

Cont in this way, increasing the number of sts that are knit or purled after the slipped st by 1 st on each row, until all of the sts have been used. End with a WS row.

Next row (RS): Sl 1, k to end of heel.

Gusset and Foot

Begin to work in the rnd again. Pick up 1 st in each slipped st at the left edge of the heel flap.

Work across needles 1 & 2 (the top of the foot), cont in cable patt. Using the spare needle (needle 3), pick up 1 st in each slipped st along the second side of the heel flap.

Divide the sts evenly on needles 3 & 4. Work in St st across needles 3 & 4.

Gusset dec rnd 1: Needles 1 & 2: work in cable patt. Needles 3 & 4: k1, ssk, k to last 3 sts, k2tog, k1.

Gusset dec rnd 2: Needles 1 & 2: work in cable patt. Needles 3 & 4: knit.

Rep these 2 Gusset Dec rnds until 36 sts rem on needles 3 & 4.

Once the gusset decs are completed, continue to work foot in cable patt across needles 1 & 2 and in St st across needles 3 & 4.

When the foot is 2" less than the desired foot length, begin toe. **Do not** end cable chart on row 4, 8, 12, 16, 20, or 24.

Toe

In CC, k 1 rnd.

Toe dec rnd 1: With MC, on needles 1 & 2: k1, ssk, work to last 3 sts on needle 2, k2tog, k1; on needles 3 & 4: k1, ssk, work to last 3 sts on needle 4, k2tog, k1.

Toe dec rnd 2: In CC, knit.

Rep these 2 Dec Rnds until 24 sts rem, then work Toe Dec Rnd 1 only, cont to alternate colors on each rnd until 16 sts rem.

FINISHING

Graft toe using the kitchener stitch. Weave in all ends. Block.

Make the second sock in the same way as the first.

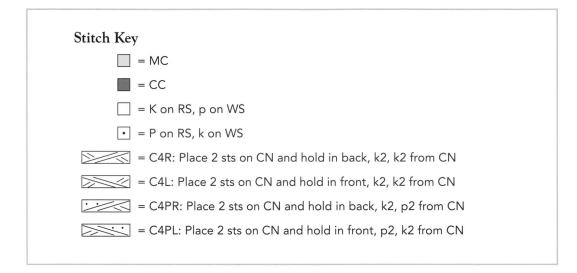

Stitch Key

☐ = MC

■ = CC

☐ = K on RS, p on WS

☐ = P on RS, k on WS

▱ = C4R: Place 2 sts on CN and hold in back, k2, k2 from CN

▱ = C4L: Place 2 sts on CN and hold in front, k2, k2 from CN

▱ = C4PR: Place 2 sts on CN and hold in back, k2, p2 from CN

▱ = C4PL: Place 2 sts on CN and hold in front, p2, k2 from CN

Cable Chart

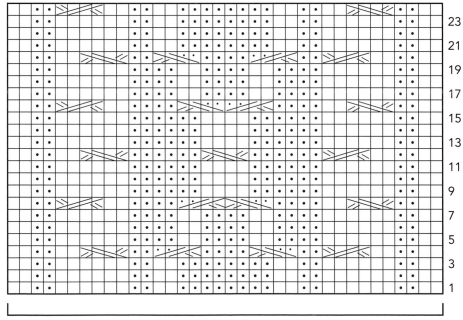

36 Stitches

Fair Isle Chart

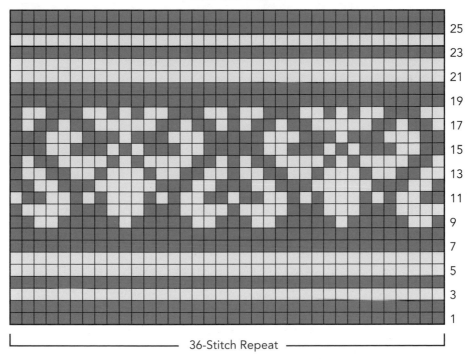

25
23
21
19
17
15
13
11
9
7
5
3
1

36-Stitch Repeat

Knitters' Guide to Essential Blogging Terminology

ISO and Destash—verbs: Ravelry hosts "In Search Of" and Destash forums for knitters in search of specific yarns or wishing to sell off or trade unloved and unwanted yarns from their stash. Bloggers periodically host individual destashing on their own sites for the same purging or income-generating purpose, usually so they can buy more yarn.

Ruth P., Woolly Wormhead

If "Hat Architect" seems a strange title for English designer-blogger Woolly Wormhead, consider this: the converted double-decker bus in which Ruth lives has been fitted out resourcefully with dedicated stash storage that holds enough yarn to make at least 200 hats. She describes herself as an "amiable eccentric and partial recluse, curious traveler, dreadlocked bus-dwelling sort." But that barely scratches the surface. With more than 90 original designs to her credit, Ruth sells her quirky yet wearable hats both online and in the books she self-publishes. Although there are definite themes in her body of work, no two of her hats are alike. "I have a personal pet peeve with this idea that a hat is simply a half-dome blini shape that just sits on heads."

Her approach has always been three-dimensional. "The thing that interests me most is the form, the 3-D shape." Her university textile degree dealt with the creation of three-dimensional fabrics rather than surface design, and the organic shapes of her hats are a testament to that enduring passion. She explores every possibility of a certain design, working in rapid succession as the ideas occur to her and trying to knit a mock-up of each new concept before the inspiration can slip away. "I go through journeys on a particular way of working and then go off on another tangent, working in groups or series."

"Everything I've ever made has been sculptural. That's my big driver; when I start making a hat, the first thing I think of is its direction—will it be a pixie hat, a slouchy beret, or something that hangs forward? I quite like the idea that a hat takes on a dimension of its own." Her versatility is reflected in the fact that she draws on resources ranging from art history and fashion history to favorite characters in literature and how she imagines the hats they might wear.

The minimal materials required for hat-making suit both her space constraints and the lifestyle she describes as "alternative": She and her partner, Tom, share their snug home with adorable toddler son Aran as well as all that yarn. When they are not encamped in Italy, they are living the carefree life of perpetual tourists, traveling throughout Europe in the bus to experience as many other cultures as possible.

A former art teacher in London secondary schools, she especially enjoys the math elements of hat design. They allow her to incorporate unusual techniques that depend on mathematical structure for their construction. "In my head I've waged a little war against plain, boring hats. From a design perspective, a hat has to have only a circumference that fits on the head, but from there you can go in any direction. You've got much more potential to get creative."

The sideways construction of her Lenina hat is just one example of her organic designs. Cabled vertical sections are joined by three-needle bind-off seams, creating the raised pattern that appears to sit on top of the cables. Since cabled hats are typically worked sideways (and she has published more than 30 sideways hat designs), this method results in an unusual structure that is uniquely attractive and highly wearable, yet only moderately challenging. "When you're turning a standard hat on its side, you've got to think about it in a completely different way."

In addition to her self-published books, *Going Straight: A New Generation of Knitted Hats* and *Wee Woolly Toppers*, a collection of 10 hats for babies, Ruth has authored *Kitchener Unravelled: The Complete Guide to Grafting*, which she believes to be the definitive volume on the possibilities of Kitchener stitch. Convinced that only knitters who make lots of socks have steady experience working with Kitchener stitch, she decided to explore its uses in combination with other stitches. Observing that many knitters need to review a Kitchener tutorial each time they want to use the stitch, she developed several inventive ways to incorporate it into a wider range of knitting projects. While there are also several Kitchener stitch tutorials in *Going Straight*, the new book emphasizes its usefulness in more unexpected applications.

Blogging has helped her answer many reader questions and address the details they find difficult. As a member of the Yahoo group UK Handknitters, she first became aware of knitting blogs in 2005 and soon decided to create her own. "The idea that you can have a look at somebody else's life just grabbed me." Other parts of her life crept into her engaging posts right from the beginning, and between her non-traditional lifestyle and her unusual hats, she soon had a large and loyal following.

Returning to the UK several times each year, Ruth teaches sell-out knitting classes and workshops, including the annual I-Knit London and 2009's UK Ravelry Day. Considering herself as much an artist as a designer, she describes her hats as "wearable art." As such, she takes bending the rules in stride, if that's what it takes to create her own vision of what something as simple as a hat can be.

She is perplexed by critics who find her hats too unusual. "Many of my designs are what I consider really safe. If I wanted to make really wacky, weird designs, I'd have no trouble coming up with those ideas." She encourages knitters to "make something that won't be seen on the head of every third person walking down the street." It is her mission to help other knitters get comfortable enough to take creative chances, to experiment with shapes, construction techniques, and forms that may seem strange at first, and to view their knitting as full of unexpected possibilities.

The Internet has impacted Ruth's life in many ways, not least of which is that she first met Tom online. In addition, it makes her business possible on a far larger scale than she could otherwise envision. "I make most of my sales online, which confirms its benefits [for me]—that's where my market is . . . and Ravelry has made it so much easier. People now have options they might otherwise never learn about." Her Ravelry fan group, Wormhead's Hats, has nearly 2,200 international members knitting up hundreds of versions of her projects.

As a former teacher, she is a stickler for high standards in pattern presentation, and she appreciates Ravelry's design forums and the volunteer editors who make a commitment to ensuring those criteria are observed on the site. With her meticulous pattern-writing skills and enormous body of published work, it is not surprising that she was one of the first European members accepted at the professional level into the Association of Knitwear Designers (AKD).

Thanks to the Internet, she has also formed online relationships with other avid knitters and designers. Although she has been knitting steadily since her mother taught her at the age of 3, "I was always a closet knitter—I never had any other friends who knit. It wasn't until I went online that I started to find others, and now I have friends all over the UK [and internationally] who knit."

LENINA CAP
by Woolly Wormhead

Gentle and structured, feminine and quirky, Lenina is full of subtle detail and charm. Inspired by the character of the same name from Aldous Huxley's *Brave New World*, this pattern uses simple cables for detail and is constructed from a series of panels knit sideways. For its technical creativity as well as its wearability, Lenina will no doubt pique the curiosity of everyone who sees it.

Difficulty: Intermediate
Skills Used: Provisional cast-on, three-needle bind-off, basic cables.

SIZE

S (M, L)

Fits head circumference of: 17–18 (20–21, 22–23)"

Finished Measurements
Circumference: 15¼ (18, 20¾)"
Height: 7¾ (8½, 9¼)"

MATERIALS

- Malabrigo Yarn Merino Worsted (100% Merino; 216yd per 100g); color: 97 Cuarzo; 1 skein

- US 7 (4.5mm) straight needles, or size needed to obtain gauge

- 1 spare US 7 (4.5mm) needle for three-needle bind-off

- US H/8 (5mm) crochet hook

- Waste yarn for provisional cast-on

- Tapestry needle

- 6 (7, 8) stitch holders, or spare needles

GAUGE

17 sts and 26 rows = 4" in St st

22 sts and 29 rows = 4" in patt st

PATTERN NOTES

Each panel is knit separately then joined with the three-needle bind-off.

SPECIAL STITCHES

C2F: Place 1 st on CN, k1, k1 from CN

Knitters' Guide to Essential Blogging Terminology

Fiberlicious—adjective: a quality ascribed to yarns that contain luxurious fiber blends and are exquisitely soft, cuddly, and/or beautifully dyed. Close cousin of "fiberluscious."

DIRECTIONS
Panel

Using waste yarn and provisional cast-on, CO 41 (45, 49) sts. Change to main yarn and continue as follows:

Row 1 (WS): K4, [k2, p2] 9 (10, 11) times, k1.

Row 2 (RS): Sl 1, [C2F, p2] 9 (10, 11) times, p2, w&t.

Row 3: K2, [k2, p2] 9 (10, 11) times, k1.

Row 4: Sl 1, [C2F, p2] 9 (10, 11) times, w&t.

Row 5: [K2, p2] 9 (10, 11) times, k1.

Row 6: Sl 1, [C2F, p2] 8 (9, 10) times, C2F, w&t.

Row 7: P2, [k2, p2] 8 (9, 10) times, k1.

Row 8: Sl 1, [C2F, p2] 8 (9, 10) times, k1, w&t.

Row 9: P1, [k2, p2] 8 (9, 10) times, k1.

Row 10: Sl 1, [C2F, P2] 8 (9, 10) times, w&t.

Row 11: [K2, p2] 8 (9, 10) times, k1.

Row 12: Sl 1, [C2F, p2] 7 (8, 9) times, C2F, p1, w&t.

Row 13: K1, p2, [k2, p2] 7 (8, 9) times, k1.

Row 14: Sl 1, [C2F, p2] 7 (8, 9) times, C2F, w&t.

Row 15: P2, [k2, p2] 7 (8, 9) times, k1.

Row 16: Sl 1, [C2F, p2] 7 (8, 9) times, k1, w&t.

Row 17: P1, [k2, p2] 7 (8, 9) times, k1.

Row 18: Sl 1, [C2F, p2] 7 (8, 9) times, w&t.

Row 19: [K2, p2] 7 (8, 9) times, k1.

Break yarn, leaving a 2yd-long tail.

Transfer sts to st holder, to be joined later.

Work a total of 6 (7, 8) panels.

FINISHING

Transfer the held sts for the first panel to the working needle. Carefully remove the provisional cast-on from the 2nd panel and transfer live stitches to spare working needle. Hold the two needles parallel in the left hand, with **wrong** sides of the two panels together. Use the three-needle bind-off to join the first row of the 2nd panel to the last row of the 1st panel, **and, at the same time,** when you encounter a wrapped stitch, pick up the wrap and place it onto the needle, then lift both the wrap and stitch off and twist toward you, and then place back on the needle and then perform the bind-off.

Continue joining all the panels this way, finishing by joining the held sts for the last panel to the CO sts of the first panel.

Thread one of the tails at the crown through the sts at the crown and pull to tighten. Weave in all ends.

For a neat finish at the brim, work a rnd of sc around the lower edge. Take care not to make the crochet too tight.

Lightly block hat.

Note: *Stitch key and chart on page 190.*

Stitch Key

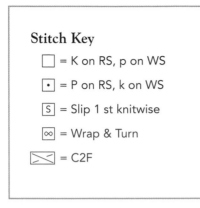

☐ = K on RS, p on WS

• = P on RS, k on WS

S = Slip 1 st knitwise

∞ = Wrap & Turn

⧓ = C2F

Cable Panel Chart

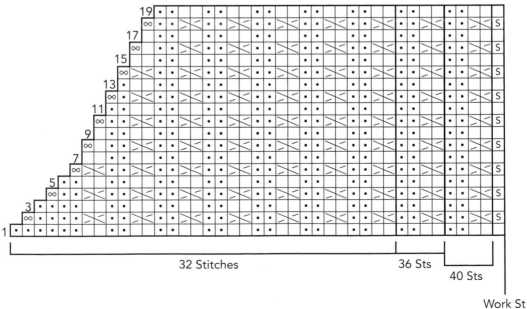

32 Stitches   36 Sts   40 Sts

Work St
On All
Sizes

Clara Parkes, Knitter's Review

At the dawn of the twenty-first century, with her high-tech industry firm in a spasm of consolidation and her colleagues being recast as casualties of the burst high-tech bubble, Clara Parkes read the writing on the wall. It said: "Knit." So after a decade on the west coast, she packed up her belongings and traveled 3,000 miles to re-evaluate her life in the tiny coastal Maine town where her family had spent all the summers of her childhood. And in 2000, in the midst of this period of reflection and "deep creative frustration," the seeds of what would become *Knitter's Review* were sown.

Although she'd been knitting for most of her life and wanted to give the craft a more central role, she quickly realized that only the superstars of the mainstream publishing world made a decent living from knitwear design and writing. But what about an independent newsletter that focused on inspiring people who were doing unusual, knitting-related things with their lives? No one had done that. Even more daringly, no one had created such a newsletter with an exclusively online presence. The light clicked on.

"It's so exciting to write about something that I'm really passionate about. It all made sense to me." This passion carried her forward even when her own mother wondered aloud how Clara could possibly have so much to say about yarn. Even her first readers' reaction was, "Sheep? You've got to be kidding." Nonetheless, in May 2000, she registered the *Knitter's Review* domain name, and by that September she had launched the site. Making it a weekly newsletter was a stretch at the beginning, but, "There's a great story to be told in every single skein." Her first profile covered the award-winning Morehouse Merino sheep farm in New York's Hudson River Valley, where purebred Merino sheep are raised for their ultrafine, deliciously warm wool. From there, the newsletter's readership grew quickly and steadily.

By 2004, when she first became aware of knitting blogs, the mainstream knitting industry was suffering the first of its own "welcome to the twenty-first century" growing pains. "The industry was trying to figure out how to adapt to [the Internet's growing role]—you had all these [indie designers, one-person dye houses, and yarn spinners] with brilliant ideas that they wanted to bring directly to knitters." And "the Internet facilitates the knitting community's desire for instant gratification in a way that mainstream publishers and local yarn shops have struggled to harness to their own advantage."

Yet in a perfect example of the growing synergy between publishing and the Internet, it was because of her online presence with *Knitter's Review* that Clara was approached to write *The Knitter's Book of Yarn* (Potter Craft, 2007). "I wrote it in part to help those brick-and-mortar yarn store owners. Yarn stores have people coming in all the time who are just terrified of making yarn substitutions—who are afraid to try knitting a pattern in any yarn other than the one that was used for the sample." As she developed her concept for the book, she knew it would have to be "a really engaging, fun read, [especially because] some people just laughed when I told them I was writing a whole book about yarn." Now in its third printing, *The Knitter's Book of Yarn* has exceeded even its author's expectations. Her second volume, *The Knitter's Book of Wool*, was published in October 2009 and is also selling well.

Her second book builds on everything she learned while writing the first one and brings it to the next level. "I focused on what kind of wool characteristics work best for different projects." Soft wool, crunchy wool, wool blends—*The Knitter's Book of Wool* encourages knitters to expand their horizons. "Animal fibers are extraordinary. They're not an extruded product, or synthetic. You don't need a centrifuge or sulfuric acid [to treat them]. First, they kept an animal warm, and now they're going to keep a person warm." Picking up where *The Knitter's Book of Yarn* left off, Clara intended *The Knitter's Book of Wool* "to grow with the knitter" as his or her level of expertise increases.

She has always gotten referrals, reviews, and feedback from knitting bloggers. "The growth of *Knitter's Review* was very organic. I had no real marketing budget, so right from the beginning it was just word of mouth. That works best for *Knitter's Review* because it's kind of an esoteric topic. It takes a certain kind of knitter to want to read about yarn; obviously, the site is not about free patterns and other give-aways." Nonetheless, she has attracted more than 34,000 loyal subscribers about whom she says, "I'm more interested in how avid the readers are about the topic, how long they stay. I'm not just about building big numbers, but about having a very stable and passionate reader base that loves yarn and wants to go on the journey with me." Her regular column about everything yarn-related in the online magazine *Twist Collective* has increased the readership of *Knitter's Review* still further.

With the introduction of Ravelry in May 2007, a new means of disseminating her material became available. Her two fan groups (one for *Knitter's Review* and a separate one for *The Knitter's Book of Yarn*) have nearly 1,200 members between them, and she goes back and forth daily between her own site and Ravelry to respond to reader questions and comments. "Ravelry's been great—I get a lot of emails from members. It's total cross-pollination, with yarn information, tutorials—all of that. I emailed (Ravelry co-founder) Jess way, way back in the beginning and said, 'What you're doing is so extraordinary. How can I help you with this?' It's such a wonderful resource that came about at a time when everybody needed it." She is particularly grateful to Ravelry's founders because they have created the kind of broad database she felt pressure to do with *Knitter's Review* but that she freely admits is not her core competency.

Never knowing what will be reviewed next helps keep *Knitter's Review* content fresh. Strict independence from formal associations with individual yarn companies or product manufacturers is her mandate in order to maintain credibility and integrity with her readership. Advertisers, assuming she would work in the traditional publishing model by reviewing every new product they introduced to the market, wanted an editorial calendar to structure their ads. But *Knitter's Review* doesn't work that way, and she has resisted any perception of "being in the pocket of the yarn companies." She remains selective about the yarns and other knitting-related goods she'll review. As a guide, "I pay attention to what people are writing about on blogs, in Ravelry, and in my forums, and that informs my decisions on what to review in each issue."

In addition to knitting, she regularly spins and dyes her own yarns. "I do both to stay personally connected to the process." In fact, her connection to yarn has expanded to include greater awareness of and admiration for the sheep farmers in New England. Her latest challenge is to assist in reviving yarn production in the United States. "It's not simply an issue of aesthetics—it would have a huge impact economically; the farmers are really struggling. They're converting their flocks to meat breeds because they can't afford to raise the other breeds if there's no market for the wool."

She is identifying farmers throughout the United States who are raising the yarn breeds, then bringing more attention to them through the development of effective marketing plans that cater to knitters' needs. Her goal is to raise knitters' awareness of these home-grown materials. "That's a real challenge right now—everything needs to be 'soft.' So therefore [knitters think] the only wool worth buying is Merino, 98 percent of which comes from Australia or New Zealand. But there are hundreds of really incredible breeds—Blue-Faced Leicester, Cormo, Shetland, Corriedale—that produce yarn with incredible character. It's robust with wonderful twist. It's three-dimensional, really lively, and springy." While these yarns have a different feel than Merino, once washed, their softness is comparable.

"Considering all the breeds of sheep that exist [compared with] what's available in yarn stores today, we're seeing just the tip of the iceberg. All we get is strawberry, because we don't know about raspberry and black currant and all the other wonderful flavors out there." Her point is a perfect example of circular logic: the only wool we know to ask for by name is Merino because that's what we see in yarn shops and online vendor sites; yet these vendors stock mostly Merino wool because that's all knitters know to ask for.

Clara is determined both to make other kinds of wool more easily available to knitters and simultaneously to support the sheep farmers who raise these breeds. Considering this streak of altruism that runs so deep through her life and work, it is obvious why *Knitter's Review* and her books earn such intense loyalty from readers: Her passions inform her mission, and her generosity of spirit informs her knitting choices, making her writing compelling, endlessly informative, and richly entertaining.

Knitters' Guide to Essential Blogging Terminology

Frankenstein—verb: to knit a project from an assortment of orphan skeins or remnants of yarn, rather than from yarn purchased specifically for that design.

FOXGLOVES
By Clara Parkes

A simple lace panel down the back of the hand lifts these fingerless mitts from purely practical to charmingly decorative. Worked in a tightly knit plush Merino, they are both warm and versatile.

Difficulty: Intermediate
Skills used: Basic increasing and decreasing, following multiple sets of instructions at the same time

SIZE

Women's M

Finished Measurements
Hand circumference (relaxed): 6½"
Length (cuff to fingertip): 6"
The ribbing makes for a flexible fit. These mitts will comfortably accommodate an 8" hand.

MATERIALS

- Alchemy Yarns of Transformation Temple (100% superfine Merino wool; 128yd per 50g); color Foxglove, 1 skein
- 1 set US 3 (3.25mm) double-pointed needles, or size needed to obtain gauge
- Stitch markers
- Stitch holder
- Tapestry needle

GAUGE

28 sts and 32 rows = 4" in St st

36 sts and 32 rows = 4" in k2, p2 rib patt, unstretched

PATTERN NOTES

To create a tighter, warmer fabric for these mitts, they are knit on needles several sizes smaller than the yarn label specifies. When substituting, seek a yarn that normally would knit up at 6 stitches per inch on US 5 (3.75mm) needles.

STITCH PATTERN

Foxglove Stitch (Worked Over 9 Sts)

Rnd 1: K2, k2tog, yo, k1, yo, ssk, k2.

Rnd 2: Knit.

Rnd 3: K1, k2tog, yo, k3, yo, ssk, k1

Rnd 4: Knit.

DIRECTIONS

Right Mitt

CUFF:

CO 46 sts. Arrange the sts on 3 needles as follows: 19 sts on the first needle, 15 sts on the second needle, and 12 sts on the third needle. Join to work in the rnd.

Set-up round: (K2, p2) twice, (k1, p1) 4 times, k1, (p2, k2) twice, p1, (k2, p2) to end.

Rep this rnd 5 times more.

HAND:

Begin Foxglove Pattern as follows:

Rnd 1: (K2, p2) twice, pm, begin working

Foxglove Stitch over next 9 sts, pm, (p2, k2) twice, p1, (k2, p2) to end.

Rnds 2–8: Work Foxglove Pattern between markers as est and work all other sts in ribbing as set.

THUMB GUSSET:

Rnd 9: Work 25 sts in patts as est, ending just before the single p rib st. Place gusset marker, M1R, p1, M1L, place second gusset marker, work in ribbing to the end of the rnd—48 sts.

Rnds 10–12: Work 25 sts in patt as est, sl the first gusset marker, k1, p1, k1, sl the second gusset marker, work in patt to end of rnd.

Rnd 13 (Increase rnd): Work in patt to first gusset marker, sl marker, M1R, k to center st, p1, k to second gusset marker, M1L, sl marker, work in patt to end of rnd—50 sts.

Rnd 14: Work in patt to first gusset marker, sl marker, k to center st, p1, k to second gusset marker, sl marker, work in patt to end of rnd.

Rep Rnds 13–14 until you have 13 sts between the gusset markers, ending with Rnd 13—58 sts.

Next rnd: Work in patt to first gusset marker, remove it and place next 13 sts on a holder, remove second gusset marker, CO 1 st to bridge the gap, and work in patt to the end of the round—46 sts.

Next 14 rnds: Work in ribbing and Foxglove Stitch patts as est. To re-establish the rib patt in first rnd, p the new st that you CO over the thumb gap.

RIBBED CUFF:

Next rnd: (K2, p2) twice, (k1, p1) 4 times, k1, (p2, k2) twice, p1, (k2, p2) to end. Rep this rnd 5 more times. BO loosely.

Work thumb as instructed below.

Left Mitt

CUFF:

CO 46 sts. Arrange the sts on 3 needles as follows: 19 sts on the first needle, 12 sts on the second needle, and 15 sts on the third needle.

Set-up rnd: (K2, p2) twice, (k1, p1) 4 times, k1, p2, (k2, p2) to last 3 sts, k2, p1.

Rep this rnd 5 times more.

HAND (BEGIN FOXGLOVE STITCH PATTERN):

Rnd 1: (K2, p2) twice, pm, begin working Foxglove Stitch over next 9 sts, pm, (p2, k2) to last st, p1.

Rnds 2–8: Work all ribbing and Foxglove sts in patt as est, slipping markers as you go.

THUMB GUSSET:

Rnd 9: Work in ribbing and Foxglove Stitch patts as est to last st, place gusset marker, M1R, p1, M1L—48 sts. (The end of the rnd will serve as your second "invisible" gusset marker.)

Rnds 10–12: Work in patts as est to gusset marker, sl marker, k1, p1, k1.

Rnd 13 (Increase rnd): Work in patt to gusset marker, sl marker, M1R, k to center st, p1, k to second gusset marker, M1L—50 sts.

Rnd 14: Work in patt to first gusset marker, sl marker, k to center st, p1, k to end.

Rep Rnds 13–14 until you have 13 sts between the first gusset marker and end of rnd, ending with Rnd 13—58 sts.

Next rnd: Work in patt to first gusset marker, remove marker and place next 13 sts on a holder, CO 1 st to bridge the gap—46 sts.

Next 14 rnds: Work in ribbing and Foxglove Stitch patts as est. To reestablish the rib patt in first rnd, p the new st that you CO over the thumb gap.

RIBBED CUFF:

Next rnd: (K2, p2) twice, (k1, p1) 4 times, k1, (p2, k2) to last st, p1.

Rep this rnd 5 more times.

BO loosely.

Thumb

Place the first 7 sts from the holder on a needle. Place the rem 6 sts on another needle.

Join yarn, leaving a generous tail, and use a 3rd needle to pick up and k 3 sts across the top of the thumb opening—16 sts. Join to work in the rnd.

Next rnd: K6, p1, k9.

Rep this rnd 5 times more. BO.

Rep for 2nd mitt.

FINISHING

Weave in ends with a tapestry needle, using the tail from the thumb to close up any gaps at the base of the thumb.

Kristi Porter, The Domestic Sphere

Back in the Blogging Dark Ages of 2002, Kristi started a knit blog. She was a new mother at the time, knitting for fun because she needed something she could "pick up and put down" while tending to her two young daughters. With a college degree in anthropology and graduate studies in social communities, she had always been interested in the online community phenomenon of social networking, although it wasn't called that in those days. "When you're isolated at home with your kids, you need some connection to the outside world. Blogging was a satisfying and easy way to do it. You could do it at 3 o'clock in the morning when you were feeding a baby."

Although she often mentions her family in blog posts, she never strays too far into personal territory. "In the olden days, you could imagine [the blogosphere] as sort of an alternate universe, where your mother was not going to read it and the people you worked with were not going to read it. But now people realize that if you put it out there, it's out there for *everyone*."

There were very few knit blogs in those days—so it was actually possible to read through all of them every day and to stay connected with that entire small community. The commitment and pioneer spirit of these early practitioners (including Amy Singer in her pre-*Knitty.com* days, Bonne Marie Burns of Chic Knits, and Stephanie Pearl-McPhee of Yarn Harlot) was contagious. "They were really thinking about their knitting and talking about it. That made me want to write about what I was doing. There was lots of inspiration and problem-solving resources within that group. And there was a strong sense of community that gave you a real feeling of connection."

Several members of Kristi's family were knitters and crocheters, and she can't remember exactly when she learned the craft herself. One of her strongest memories is of her grandmother crocheting a tablecloth out of super-fine crochet thread. "She worked on it throughout my youth—my entire childhood!" Once completed, it measured 5 feet wide by 10 feet long, and it was given to an aunt who brought it out for special occasions. It was eventually given to Kristi as a wedding gift and is now a treasured family heirloom.

She cut her design teeth early and was knitting her own sweaters by the time she was in high school. "Thank God the eighties were all about big and boxy. I didn't really understand that people knit from written patterns, and it was much more natural to me to make the pieces to fit my own ideas." Once theDomesticSphere blog was underway, she self-published the first of her designs. Then, when Amy Singer started *Knitty,* Kristi had a design in the first issue. She also became *Knitty*'s first technical editor while helping to put that first issue together.

Her publication credentials grew in direct proportion to her reputation for reliable, accurate technical editing skills. To date, her original designs have been included in Amy Singer's *Big Girl Knits* books (Potter Craft), as well as in Shannon Okey's *Knitgrrl* books (Watson-Guptill). She also provides tech editing services to various craft book publishers, and much of the work she does now is a result of the relationships she has built with those publishers. She is the author of three of her own knitting books: including *Knitting Patterns for Dummies* (Wiley, 2007), and *Knitting in the Sun* (Wiley, 2009); and, follow up volume, *Knitting in the Sun for Kids* is due out in Spring 2011. Those book projects also developed organically from her publishing connections. "More often than not, someone says 'Hey, can you do this?' and I just can't say no."

Her pattern-writing skills evolved from her desire to communicate her ideas to others. "It's like music. It's one thing to play it, but if you don't write it down, no one else can play it." Reading other peoples' patterns inspired her to write up more of her own designs; "The more patterns you read, the more you learn in terms of design, technique, and process."

As one of the early knit bloggers, she drew a following right away and quickly discovered the thrill of getting comments from readers who were excited about her designs. "We all like to get that positive feedback. But if you're going to blog over the long haul, you have to do it for yourself. It's a way of recording daily life, and your thoughts, and the details of what you're making—just as some people would keep a journal. That has its own satisfactions regardless of whether you get any feedback. It's good to share, but blogging also provides a valuable personal record—and that's what keeps you going."

Ravelry provides her with a critical lasting record in its own right, in terms of connecting and keeping up with other designers and bloggers. And "if you're thinking about a specific yarn, or making a particular project, it's great to see what people are doing with it, what [a certain] yarn looks like knit up, what modifications knitters are making. That can be enormously useful."

With every original pattern, Kristi is conscious of sending something of herself out into the world. In the past, that was it; it was simply "out there." But chances are she wouldn't just run into somebody wearing a sweater she had designed. Now Ravelry has changed all that. "You can see who has made it, who made comments, or gave feedback—that's really satisfying. You couldn't get that kind of feedback any other way."

She has consistently drawn inspiration from the architectural and structural elements of knitwear design. "Some designers are not numbers people; they just want to create their visions and leave the pattern-writing to somebody else. But I do like the numbers and thinking about the geometry of how the pieces go together. If I can whip out the Pythagorean Theorem to figure out how to do armhole shaping, I'm happy."

From her perspective, the ultimate test of a design's success is its wearability. "Some designs are exquisite, fun to knit and beautiful to look at, but ultimately not practical. Not something you can really wear. I try to design things that are very 'everyday' and that are going to fit real people." Although not a big follower of fashion, she keeps an eye out for unusual designs. "If I notice somebody wearing something interesting, I'll definitely sidle up to them [to see] how the collar is attached, how all the pieces fit together—especially if there's some unconventional construction."

As a lifelong knitter, she believes that part of what's wonderful about the craft is that there are always new layers of complexity to explore and new challenges that will feel "just right" to knitters at every level of expertise. To make her point, she references the book *Flow: The Psychology of Optimal Experience* by philosopher-psychologist Mihaly Csikszentmihalyi. "There are those times when you're doing something [you love], and the rest of the world drops away—you're focused on what you're doing; it's a very positive feeling." According to the author, that optimal balance of challenge and experience gives knitters the same endorphin rush felt by musicians, by runners—by anyone whose passion puts them "in the zone."

In knitting, she believes, it is easy to modulate the challenges we set for ourselves and even to have different projects for different days, different activities, and especially for different levels of concentration. "We get that positive feeling from knitting whenever we're truly 'in the moment.' Dinner could be boiling over on the stove, and the phone could be ringing, but you don't care about any of that—you just want to work on your knitting."

WORKING ALL THE ANGLES BLANKET

by Kristi Porter

This blanket is composed of four triangular pieces worked separately and then joined using the three-needle bind-off. This construction means that the pieces never become outrageously cumbersome to knit and the finishing is neat and tidy.

While a large blanket may seem like an ambitious project, the knitting is straightforward and well within the grasp of the adventurous beginner. The play of lines and textures on the finished piece is dynamic and eye-catching. With so many interesting colorways to choose from, you'll surely find a combination that speaks to you.

Difficulty: Easy

SIZE

60 x 60"

MATERIALS

- [Yarn A] Schaefer Yarn Company Nancy (95% Merino, 5% nylon; 600yd per 225g), color: Elena Piscopia, 1 skein

- [Yarn B] Schaefer Yarn Company Little Danya (78% mohair, 13% wool, 9% nylon; 240yd per 113g), color: Margo Jones, 3 skeins

- [Yarn C] Schaefer Yarn Company Miss Priss (100% Merino; 280yd per 113g), color: Julia Child, 2 skeins

- [Yarn D] Schaefer Yarn Company Miss Priss (100% Merino; 280yd per 113g), color: Margo Jones, 2 skeins

- 36" US 13 (9mm) circular needles, or size needed to obtain gauge

- Spare circular needle for three-needle bind-off

- Tapestry needle

GAUGE

12 sts and 16 rows = 4" in St st

DIRECTIONS

Each section of the blanket is a triangle that starts at the base and grows outward in a series of stockinette and reverse stockinette stripes in alternating colors. This shaping will be familiar to shawl knitters! Spines of stockinette stitch at the outside edges and down the center create a contrast to the chevron shaping and will create a subtly rolled border when the piece is complete.

As you complete the sections, you will join them using the three-needle bind-off.

COLOR SEQUENCES:

Section 1: D, A, B, C, A, B, D, A, B, C, A, B

Section 2: C, B, A, D, B, A, C, B, A, D, B, A

Section 3: C, A, B, D, A, B, C, A, B, D, A, B

Section 4: D, B, A, C, B, A, D, B, A, C, B, A

Begin with Section 1. With the yarn specified, CO 8 sts.

Row 1 and following WS rows: Purl.

Row 2 (RS): K2, M1, k4, M1, k2—10 sts.

Row 4 (RS): K2, M1, k1, M1, k4, M1, k1, M1, k2—14 sts.

Row 6 (RS): K4, pm, M1, k1, M1, pm, k4, pm, M1, k1, M1, pm, k4—18 sts.

Row 8 (RS): K4, sm, M1, k to next marker, M1, sm, k4, sl marker, M1, work to last marker, M1, sm, k4—4 sts increased.

REVERSE STOCKINETTE STRIPE:

Change yarns.

Row 1 (WS): P4, sm, k to next marker, sm, p4, sm, k to last marker, sm, p4.

Row 2 (RS): K4, sm, M1, p to next marker, M1, k4, sm, M1, p to last marker, M1, k4.

Rep these 2 rows 3 times more—8 rows total.

STOCKINETTE STRIPE:

Change yarns.

Row 1 (WS): Purl, slipping markers as you come to them.

Row 2 (RS): K4, sm, M1, k to next marker, M1, sm, k4, sm, M1, k to last marker, M1, sm, k4.

Rep these 2 rows 3 times more—8 rows total.

Cont alternating between the Reverse Stockinette Stripe and the Stockinette Stripe, while at the same time following the color sequence for the section. When the 12 stripes are complete, there are 198 sts on the needle.

Slip sts to spare needle.

Make Section 2. Do not BO.

Joining Sections

Hold Section 1 and Section 2 with RS together. Working from the outside edge to the center, use the three-needle bind-off over the first 99 sts. The triangles will be attached on one edge. Keep the rem 99 sts from Section 1 and the rem 99 sts from Section 2 on a spare needle.

Make Section 3. Do not BO. Join one side of Section 3 to the rem 99 sts from Section 2, using the three-needle bind-off as above. Keep rem 99 sts from Section 3 on a spare needle.

Make Section 4. Do not BO. Join one side of Section 4 to rem sts of Section 3 with the three-needle bind-off. Join the rem sts of Section 4 to the held sts from Section 1.

FINISHING

Weave in ends. Close up center hole if needed. Block the piece as desired. Allow outside edges to roll to WS.

Sean Riley, personalknitter.com

For more than 2 years, native Bostonian Sean Riley was the owner of the established Cambridge yarn shop Woolcott & Co., and it was one of the most satisfying periods of his life. To assume ownership of Woolcott & Co., he left a long-term corporate career where, he readily admits, "The only person I made happy was the company CEO." If it wasn't exactly destiny that compelled him to assume ownership of the shop, he credits the timing and his career frustrations as major motivators. But timing isn't everything, as he ruefully admits. "I loved it, even though it was the most difficult job I've ever had."

Growing up with 26 first cousins who lived in his immediate neighborhood, he was the only member of the family taught to knit as a young teenager by his grandmother "as a way to keep me out of trouble." As an adult, his knitting hobby was a source of after-hours relaxation after long days spent in the office. At first, he was persuaded by Woolcott & Co.'s original owner to fill in at the shop part-time. When she fell seriously ill some months later, he accepted her offer to become the shop's manager. "I figured, I hated my job, I was going to get laid off anyway, so let me help someone. Let me try. So I quit my job." When the shop's owner eventually died from her illness, her family approached him with a plan: Woolcott & Co. was all they had left of her, and she had insisted that Sean was the one to keep it going. They made it possible for him to buy the business; and with that, his new life began.

Despite heroic efforts, the economic downturn of 2009 forced him, with great sadness, to close the shop. In his sadness, he thought he'd take a break from knitting altogether, but he found himself unable to ignore the lure of needles and yarn. Even such a painful setback could not dampen either his passion for knitting or for entrepreneurship.

The shop's eventual closure notwithstanding, his business model included useful lessons for owners of brick and mortar yarn shops who are struggling to mobilize the Internet and to adapt to the changes in today's knitting marketplace. During his time at the helm of Woolcott & Co., Sean made sure that an Internet newsletter was sent to all regular customers to announce the arrival of new inventory, sales, and class schedules. Recognizing a dramatic upswing in the popularity of hand-knit socks, he ordered enough sock yarn to fill an entire section of the shop. He offered classes in a range of techniques, but streamlined them when he recognized that private lessons were the most requested. Understanding that a male yarn shop owner is still an anomaly in the industry, he made sure to hire a diverse staff so that every customer would feel comfortable coming into the shop to seek assistance.

In the end, his experiences taught him tremendous respect for those who run profitable yarn shops. He realized that his own involvement with the industry would be more satisfying as a designer and teacher than as a retail proprietor. In the last days that the shop remained open, most heartbreaking to Sean was that, ". . . people kept asking me where they could find help" once Woolcott & Co. closed its doors.

Following a much-needed break, he seized upon this void in the marketplace to launch a new Web-based business, www.personalknitter.com. As he states on the new site, "I figured there are personal trainers, personal chefs, why not a personal knitting coach?" Offering a variety of knitting services—from one-on-one to group lessons and shopping excursions to find the perfect project for the yarn-challenged, to finishing services for those who would rather be knitting than seaming—personalknitter.com has brought a steady stream of work to this entrepreneur.

Similar to his role as the former owner of a convivial shop where knitters gathered around a center table to knit, ask questions, and share information, this new venture plays to his strengths. "I'm really enjoying helping empower people about their knitting. I am still surprised at how much of my 'job' is simply encouraging them along the path they suspect they should be taking and giving them confidence that what they're doing is correct. People just need a little encouragement."

Economic downturns require greater marketing creativity than ever, but Sean has learned firsthand that ". . . even in this terrible economy, people are not giving up their simple pleasures. They still need something [to feel good about]. In the end, that $20 you spent on yarn will take you a lot further than a dinner out. It gives you more than $20 worth of pleasure when you have something to keep and wear, above and beyond all the hours you spent on the pure enjoyment of making it."

The Internet definitely makes his job easier. He regularly reads several knitting blogs as well as Ravelry to see what kinds of yarns and patterns knitters are looking for. He has grown adept at employing the Internet ". . . as a tool to see what's out there [and] to see 'What are people wanting to knit?'"

At any one time, Sean has as many as five projects in progress; some at home, some at work, and one for traveling. But he wasn't always a designer. He cites Elizabeth Zimmermann's books as the biggest inspiration behind his independent design efforts; her writing opened his eyes to the possibility of creating his own projects. "She gives you the tools to branch out on your own, and she made me think, 'What else is in my head?'" Early original patterns include the Cabled Skull Cap he designed for the inaugural (Fall 2005) issue of online magazine *MenKnit*, followed by the iPod Mittens that appeared in the same publication (Winter 2006) and the Harvard Square Cap that was featured in *Interweave Knits* (Winter 2008).

"[Design opportunities] find me. A light turns on and I have to follow it. I like to make more challenging things because they hold my interest." But, he admits, the biggest challenge of all is to find the time to design. He has been a regular attendee at the annual Men's Spring Knitting Retreat held in upstate New York, where ". . . to be surrounded by only men who are knitting and enjoy the same interest in fibers and knitting as you do is a wonderful experience and, I think, helps fuel one's spirit." Even today, he finds, men knitters are often "looked at a bit askew," so he relishes the opportunity to meet with these kindred souls.

The year 2010 got off to an exciting start with an invitation from self-publishing guru Cat Bordhi to join her "Men's Visionary Knitting Retreat." In addition to his design work, he is convinced he has a book inside him with a unique perspective on what knitters want, and he plans to see it come to fruition this year. He will have more original designs published in a variety of knitting publications this year as well, such as a sweater vest for Universal Yarns. He misses Woolcott & Co. and the pleasures of being a small-business owner, particularly being among the first to know what's going on in the industry regarding books and new yarns. In fact, when he ventures into another LYS, Sean invariably winds up helping another customer; it seems to be in his blood.

HELIX SOCKS
by Sean Riley

A fun and simple sock that uses just one pattern stitch to create a lovely swirl effect down the leg and across the top of the foot.

Difficulty: Easy
Skills Used: Knitting socks on two circular needles, Kitchener stitch

SIZE

Women's medium/large
Note: *To alter the socks for a custom fit, follow instructions for varying the length of the foot or leg of the sock.*

Finished Measurements
Cuff to bottom of heel: 9½"
Foot (from back of heel to toe): 8½"

MATERIALS

- Blue Moon Fiber Arts Socks That Rock Heavyweight (100% superwash Merino; 350yd per 198g); color: Sand; 1 skein (2 skeins for sizes larger than size 10 foot)

- 2 24" US 3 (4.25mm) circular needles, or size needed to obtain gauge

- Tapestry needle

GAUGE

24 sts and 32 rows = 4" in St st

28 sts and 28 rows = 4" in patt st, unblocked

PATTERN NOTES

The stitches for the sock will be divided between two 24" circular needles. When knitting, only one of the needles is used at a time while the other needle "rests." When using the first needle (referred to as Needle 1), move all of the stitches on that needle toward the needle tip in the left hand and work across all the stitches on that needle, then move the stitches to the cord to rest and pick up Needle 2. Move the stitches of Needle 2 toward the needle tip in the left hand and work across the stitches on Needle 2. One round is complete. Continue alternating between the needles, remembering to always work the stitches on a given needle with the tips of that same needle.

Due to the nature of the pattern, there will be times when you will have to move stitches from one needle to the other. To do this, simply slip the stitches purlwise off of one needle and onto the other. This is the only time when you will be using ends of two different needles.

SPECIAL STITCHES

LT: Left Twist: Insert the right-hand needle into the back of the second st on the left-hand needle and knit it. Do not remove the st from the needle. Knit the first st on the left-hand needle through the front loop, and slip both sts off of the needle.

DIRECTIONS
Sock Cuff

Using a 30" tail and Needle 1, CO 54 sts. Transfer 27 sts to Needle 2. Join in the rnd, being careful not to twist.

Work in k1, p1 rib for 1½".

Set-up rnd: K to last 2 sts on Needle 1, k2tog, k 27 sts on Needle 2—53 sts.

BEGIN HELIX PATTERN:

Note: *Because the twist sts swirl around the sock, when necessary move 1 st to the next needle in order to work the left twist.*

Rnd 1: (LT, k4) 8 times, LT, k3.

Rnd 2: K1, (LT, k4) 8 times, LT, k2.

Rnd 3: K2, (LT, k4) 8 times, LT, k1.

Rnd 4: K3, (LT, k4) 8 times, LT.

Rnd 5: K4, (LT, k4) 8 times, slip last st to other needle unworked, beginning of round shifts 1 stitch.

Rep Rnds 1–5 for 37 rnds. Work more or fewer rnds to alter the length of the sock, ending with Rnd 2.

Next rnd: Work Rnd 3 to the last st. Sl the last st to Needle 1.

Work Heel

With Needle 1, K14, m1, k14, moving sts if necessary. These 29 sts are the heel sts. Leave the 25 sts on Needle 2 on hold.

Cont working back and forth on the 29 heel sts on Needle 1 only.

Row 1 (WS): Sl 1 knitwise wyif, p28, turn.

Row 2 (RS): Sl 1 knitwise wyif; *k1, sl 1 purlwise wyif, rep from * to end of row, turn.

Rep Rows 1 and 2 14 more times—30 rows for heel.

Turn Heel

Next Row (WS): P16, p2tog, p1, turn.

Next Row (RS): Sl 1, k5, ssk, k1, turn.

Next Row (WS): Sl 1, p6, p2tog, p1, turn.

Cont in this manner, working to 1 st before the gap left from turning in the previous row; end ssk, k1 on RS rows and p2tog, p1 on WS rows. Cont until you reach the ends of the rows and 16 sts rem, ending with a RS row.

Pick Up Heel Flap Stitches

Cont with Needle 1, pick up and k16 sts along the left side of the heel flap. PM, (LT, k4) twice, then, using Needle 2 (LT, k4) twice, k1, pm, pick up and k16 stitches from right side of heel flap. K8 sts from Needle 1 using Needle 2. Both needles now contain sts from each side of the sock. Rename needles so that the next needle is Needle 1 and has 36 sts; Needle 2 has 37 sts.

Work Gusset

Rnd 1: K24, sm, k1, (LT, k4) 4 times, sm, k24.

Rnd 2: K22, k2tog, sm, k2, (LT, k4) 3 times, LT, k3, sm, ssk, k22.

Rnd 3: K23, sm, k3, (LT, k4) 3 times, LT, k2, sm, k23.

Rnd 4: K21, k2tog, sm, k4, (LT, k4) 3 times, LT, k1, sm, ssk, k21.

Rnd 5: K22, sm, k5, (LT, k4) 3 times, LT, sm, k22.

Rnd 6: K20, k2tog, sm, (LT, k4) 3 times, LT, k5, sm, ssk, k20.

Rnd 7: K21, sm, k1, (LT, k4) 4 times, sm, k21.

Rnd 8: K19, k2tog, sm, k2, (LT, k4) 3 times, LT, k3, sm, ssk, k19.

Rnd 9: K20, sm, k3, (LT, k4) 3 times, LT, k2, sm, k20.

Rnd 10: K18, k2tog, sm, k4, (LT, k4) 3 times, LT, k1, sm, ssk, k18.

Rnd 11: K19, sm, k5, (LT, k4) 3 times, LT, sm, k19.

Rnd 12: K17, k2tog, sm, (LT, k4) 3 times, LT, k5, sm, ssk, k17.

Rnd 13: K18, sm, k1, (LT, k4) 4 times, sm, k18.

Rnd 14: K16, k2tog, sm, k2, (LT, k4) 3 times, LT, k3, sm, ssk, k16.

Rnd 15: K17, sm, k3, (LT, k4) 3 times, k2, sm, k17.

Rnd 16: K15, k2tog, sm, k4, (LT, k4) 3 times, LT, k1, sm, ssk, k15.

Rnd 17: K16, sm, k5, (LT, k4) 3 times, LT, sm, k16.

Rnd 18: K14, k2tog, sm, (LT, k4) 4 times, k1, sm, ssk, k14.

Rnd 19: K15, sm, k1, (LT, k4) 3 times, LT, k4, sm, k15.

Rnd 20: K15, sm, k2 (LT, k4) 3 times, LT, k3, sm, ssk, k13.

Rearrange sts on needles so that the 25 sts for the top of the foot are on Needle 1 and 29 sole sts are on Needle 2, k to end of Needle 2.

Foot

Rnd 1: K3, (LT, k4) 3 times, LT, k2, k to end of rnd.

Rnd 2: K4, (LT, k4) 3 times, LT, k1, k to end of rnd.

Rnd 3: K5, (LT, k4) 3 times, LT, k to end of rnd.

Rnd 4: (LT, k4) 3 times, LT, k5, k to end of rnd.

Rnd 5: K1, (LT, k4) 3 times, LT, k to end of rnd.

Rnd 6: K2, (LT, k4) 3 times, LT, k to end of rnd.

Rep Rnds 1–6 until sock is 2" short of desired foot length. Rearrange sts on needles once more so there are 27 sts on each needle.

Rnd 1: Knit.

Rnd 2: *K1, ssk, k to last 3 sts on needle, k2tog, k1, rep from *.

Rep Rnds 1 and 2 until 13 sts rem on each needle.

Rep Rnd 2 until 7 sts rem on each needle.

FINISHING

Kitchener stitch the toe closed. Weave in ends. Wash and block.

Knitters' Guide to Essential Blogging Terminology

Frog—verb: to "rip it, rip it, rip it" when deconstructing one's knitting far enough back to correct a mistake.

Ysolda Teague, Ysolda.com

When Ysolda self-published her first pattern collection, *Whimsical Little Knits*, in 2009, she left her home in Edinburgh, Scotland, crossed the Atlantic Ocean, and hit the road to promote it. In so doing, she became the poster child for the power of social media to connect far-flung members of the twenty-first century knitting community. Documenting her travels on her blog, she spent the next 2½ months criss-crossing the United States, sleeping at the homes of knit-blogger acquaintances with whom she'd previously communicated only online. She was the guest of honor at well-attended book signings in local yarn shops up and down the east coast and all around the Midwest. In addition, careful scheduling made it possible for her to promote her book at both TNNA and the Maryland Sheep and Wool Festival. "I got to hang out with all these designers I'd met on the Internet but not in person. All these people are now real friends."

Not bad for a recent college graduate who had promised her mother that if she couldn't earn the equivalent of minimum wage within 6 months of starting her knitting design business, she'd go out and find a "real" job. Also not bad for a designer who has submitted only one unsolicited pattern to a knitting publication (*Knitty.com*). Several more of her patterns have been published in *Twist Collective* and others have appeared in print magazines, but those were by invitation from the editors. Just 3 years out of college, she has created two collections of more than 40 fresh-as-a-breeze patterns that are available through her site and on Ravelry.

Although she learned the basics of knitting as a child, her relationship with yarn and needles was more contentious than companionable for many years. "I was stubborn and arrogant, and my knitting would have been a lot better without the arrogance." Only in high school did she begin knitting in earnest and selling her hat designs to friends, using the proceeds to buy—what else?—more yarn. Mostly self-taught, there were times when her trial-and-error knitting experiments seemed destined to languish in a drawer labeled "Insurmountable Frustration."

But then she was inspired to design a lace wrap cardigan, and her natural tenacity finally prevailed. Around the same time, she discovered *Knitty.com* and on a whim submitted that first design. "I just thought, 'This looks cool. I'm going to submit a pattern there.' I thought it was just some little magazine that no one looked at." When she came to the designer bio line on the submission form, there was a space for her blog link. "I thought, 'Maybe I need a blog.' So I started the blog in order to have something to put in that box." To her surprise, the cardigan, called Arisaig, was accepted for publication in *Knitty*.

In June 2005, a few of her friends were the only readers of the new blog. Unable to find existing patterns she wanted to make, she was already working up more of her own garment designs. "I started reading other designers' patterns so that I could [learn how to] write my own." And as a creative spirit who had always made things for herself, she was active on Craftster.org as well as her blog. "Then [Arisaig] came out in *Knitty* while I was in my third year at university, and suddenly I had traffic." This is an understatement. In fact, her design was featured on the cover of the Fall 2005 issue, resulting in a dramatic spike in her blog traffic. Fans of the Arisaig lace cardigan immediately wanted patterns for more of her designs, which she just happened to have ready.

"I always wanted to do something creative, but I didn't plan on designing knitwear. I was always good at making stuff, but I was also really academic. It was hard to reconcile those; I thought I had to be either arty or academic, but not both. This is a way to combine a lot of the things I love: I get to write the blog, I get to do math, and I get to be creative."

Given her self-described "tendency to daydream about literary characters" (whose names are often pressed into service for her designs) and her minimal interest in fashion trends, Ysolda is enviably prolific. "A lot of people ask me where I get my inspiration, [but] inspiration isn't the problem. The time to actually execute the ideas, that's the problem. It goes in cycles; some days I have a thousand ideas, and others there's nothing. Sometimes the garment itself evokes a particular feeling." But the bottom line is always that she has to be excited about whatever she's working on. "I'm not a process knitter. If it's not something I'd want to wear myself, it will never get finished."

Never a fan of knitting socks, her recent fascination with shawlettes evolved from her quest for the perfect not-a-sock traveling project, and her realization that a lot of knitters collect sock yarn without ever intending to knit socks from it. "Shawlette projects don't take up much room, don't need a lot of yarn, and the lace is easy and fast to knit." Her intuition has proven dead-on; her growing collection of shawlette projects is among her most popular. On Ravelry, her Ishbel design (part of the *Whimsical Little Knits* collection) has either already been made or is on the needles of more than 5,700 knitters.

One of her greatest pleasures is to see all those knitters making endlessly interesting yarn substitutions and sizing choices. "One of the things I love about Ravelry is that it's so easy to see what people are doing with my patterns . . . what yarns they use, what variations they do. For example, somebody did a baby vest version of my Little Birds (*Twist Collective*, Fall 2008) sweater pattern, and it's adorable."

Whimsical Little Knits started out as a pattern subscription series that expanded into book format. By happy coincidence, all the projects were knitted up in a similar color palette, and once they were assembled into a group it was clear that they belonged together. But in a non-traditional business decision that is gathering steam in the publishing world, Ysolda made the patterns available for sale both individually and as part of the book collection. "People might buy one pattern to start, like it, and then they buy the whole book. Or they like several patterns in the book and decide to buy it outright rather than the individual ones."

As a part of the generation that has grown up with the Internet thoroughly integrated into her life, she is well aware of social media's impact on the knitting subculture. "If you learned to knit more than 10 years ago, and you taught yourself from a book, it might take years to become good at it. While the Internet doesn't make people smarter, people learn from it a lot faster. It's such a teaching resource, and people are able to share their experiences so easily. They have someone to ask questions, and there are so many video tutorials. There's always a way to find something out. What's interesting about this resurgence in knitting's popularity is that a lot of what's keeping people interested is the social aspect, the feedback you get instantly when you post a finished project online. You're constantly reinspired to keep going with it, and the Internet . . . facilitates it; there are so many groups that would not exist without it. The Internet actually leads to more real-life social interaction among knitters."

Although she was recently the subject of a complimentary feature article in the *London Times* newspaper, she insists that very few people in Scotland know about her Stateside celebrity and that even her family is mystified by her success. Knitting itself does not seem to enjoy the same level of popularity in Scotland as it does in the United States, allowing her to keep a low profile at home. But working at home can be isolating even for a designer who is "somewhat introverted," an irony that doesn't escape her. "Knitting has always been sociable. [It's] always been a craft you could do with other people. But there's also the fact that some people are more comfortable and open to talking if they're doing something with their hands. They don't have to make constant eye contact. When people are knitting, they're often willing to share more."

New pattern collections are in store for Ysolda's fans (*Whimsical Little Knits II* was published in 2010), and they should be easier to find in U.S. yarn shops going forward. Last year's promotional tour around the country, coupled with her commitment to supporting small businesses, meant that she spent a lot of time getting to know yarn shop owners around the country. "It was great touring and connecting with [shop] owners and getting my patterns into stores. Consistently they all wanted to be able to sell my patterns, and I really want knitters to support their local yarn stores. It works out well for everyone."

THE ORCHID THIEF SHAWLETTE
by Ysolda Teague

Extravagant botanical borders are reminiscent of hothouse orchid blooms, and the sultry, mysterious yarn color ensures that the lace will be the real stand-out here. This shawlette will keep the shoulders warm and the romantic soul even warmer.

Difficulty: Advanced
Skills Used: Working from charts, lace knitting

SIZE

Finished Measurements
Width: 40"
Length: 20"

MATERIALS

- Malabrigo Yarn Sock (100% superwash Merino wool; 440yd per 100g); color: #811, Eggplant; 1 skein*

- 24" US 6 (4mm) circular needle, or size needed to obtain gauge

  ***Note:** The sample shawlette used nearly the whole skein. Cautious knitters should consider buying a second skein of the same dye lot.*

GAUGE

20 sts and 32 rows = 4" in St st

PATTERN NOTES

Only RS rows are shown on the charts. All WS rows are purled with a 3-st garter edging on both sides.

DIRECTIONS

CO 3 sts.

K 10 rows.

Without turning, pick up and k 5 sts along one side edge of strip then 3 sts across the CO edge—11 sts.

Row 1 and all following WS rows: K3, p to last 3 sts, k3.

Beg lace patt as follows: k3, work Row 2 of Chart 1, k3.

Maintain 3 st garter edging throughout.

Work through Row 30 of Chart 1 once—67 sts.

Work the 6 rows of Chart 2 once—91 sts.

Work the 12 rows of Chart 3 four times—283 sts.

Work the 30 rows of Chart 4 once—403 sts.

Next row (WS): BO loosely as follows: With the WS facing, BO loosely: *P2tog, sl st on right needle back to left, rep from * to end.

Note: *Stitch key and chart on page 220.*

FINISHING

Weave in ends and block, arranging the two columns of double yarnovers in a horizontal line and pinning out scallops between petals.

Knitters' Guide to Essential Blogging Terminology

LYS—noun: "Local Yarn Shop"—the place in your hometown where you go to knit, chat, learn, and visit with a community of like-minded knitters.

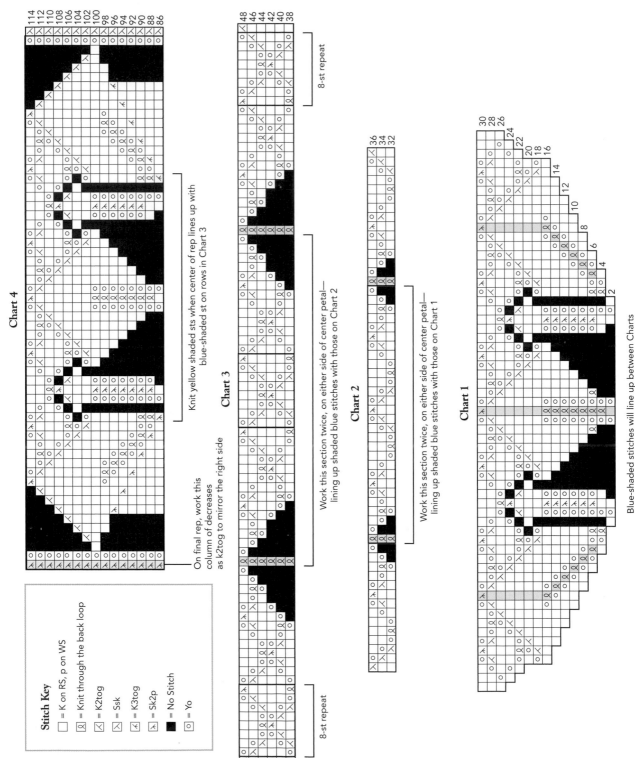

Chart 4

Chart 3

Chart 2

Chart 1

Stitch Key

☐ = K on RS, p on WS

⊠ = Knit through the back loop

╱ = K2tog

╲ = Ssk

⊼ = K3tog

⅄ = Sk2p

■ = No Stitch

○ = Yo

Knit yellow shaded sts when center of rep lines up with
blue-shaded st on rows in Chart 3

On final rep, work this
column of decreases
as k2tog to mirror the right side

Work this section twice, on either side of center petal—
lining up shaded blue stitches with those on Chart 2

Work this section twice, on either side of center petal—
lining up shaded blue stitches with those on Chart 1

Blue-shaded stitches will line up between Charts

8-st repeat

8-st repeat

Kathy Veeza, Grumperina

"**G**rumperina" is the nom de plume of a brilliantly focused and wryly unassuming lab manager at a New England cancer genetics lab. But unlike her colleagues, she's the only one at the lab with a wardrobe of gorgeous handknitted socks and complex lace scarves, and the only one who applies her methodical, highly scientific mind to a popular knitting blog as well as to her science career. In both arenas her willingness to experiment combines spectacularly with her attention to detail, yielding consistently impressive results. Veeza, the pseudonym that separates her professional identity as a scientist from her growing reputation in the knitting universe, was chosen because "*Visat* in Russian means 'to knit,'" and Kathy is originally from Ukraine.

Although she has no memory of who taught her the basics, she comes from a long line of expert knitters. After many years devoted to hard science and with little time for hobbies, she became interested in knitting again in 2004, but "I had to teach myself from scratch. I remembered how to hold the yarn and needles, but . . . I didn't know how to bind off . . . and I kept twisting my stitches." The learning curve was steep but swift for this knitting perfectionist, who speaks thoughtfully and articulates those thoughts in complete sentences.

She picked up the craft again through one of those happy accidents that later seem like destiny. While attending a friend's baby shower, she noted that one of the other guests brought a hand-crocheted baby blanket as a gift for the mother-to-be. "I was amazed at how personal it was to give someone such a gift. I went straight to the bookstore from the baby shower and picked up Pam Allen's *Knitting for Dummies*; I remembered so little that I thought the baby blanket I had seen was knitting." It proved to be a fortuitous mistake.

She relearned the basics that summer, and this time the craft took firm root in her imagination. The curiosity and persistence she applies to science blossomed into genuine passion for knitting as she mastered ever more challenging techniques. Six months later she started the blog as a vehicle to keep track of her projects online. Even before the blog, she had started to photograph her finished projects. And, of course, "There were not so many bloggers then; there was no Ravelry. There was Yarn Harlot (Stephanie Pearl-McPhee) and Wendy Knits (Wendy D. Johnson), so I came across them right away. But there was no getting lost in the blogs at that point."

Inspired by a specific post on Yarn Harlot's blog, in which she wrote hilariously about making two left mittens with afterthought thumbs, Kathy decided to document her own knitting. "I had the same kinds of thoughts in my head, and I wished I could tell [them to] somebody." Her blog quickly gained a following because once she had studied other popular blogs, she threw herself into making her own successful; from the outset she was a conscientious and involved member of the online knitters' community. "I participated in swaps, and I commented on other peoples' blogs; I was not blogging in isolation. I really put myself out there, investing time and making connections. People reciprocated right away. It's hard to make connections on the Internet if you're not an active participant yourself."

The decision to write a blog evolved at a watershed moment, during an unhappy period in her life when she was dissatisfied with everything and everyone. "I was grumpy at work, grumpy while knitting, and grumpy while blogging. I was always a very grumpy child," but in those days, "Grumpy was my middle *and* last name." Casting about for a blog name, in another nod to her Ukrainian roots she combined her given name, Yekaterina, with Grumpy, and settled on Grumperina. The name stuck, and in a measure of her blog's success, she is often recognized in public by other knitters who greet her warmly by the sobriquet. But she remains unfazed by her celebrity. "A friend once told me, 'It's not important to be a generally well-known person. It means more to be well-known within your own community.'"

Just as when she was a grad student writing neurophysics papers, even now she methodically thinks through her blog posts and organizes her thoughts before writing them down—although she admits that with knitting that thought process is much more fun. "Blogging is an entity for me. I think about what I want to say and how I want to say it; I think, this is what I'm going to say first; this is what each paragraph is going to be like. The links go *here,* and there should be a picture right *there*." While her approach may be similar to that of writing up a scientific paper, her blog is engaging to read and conversational in tone, making it hard to believe that she doesn't create the entries spontaneously. Still, she says, "I don't just sit down and write unless I have an idea of what I want to write about."

Although it has been only 5 years since she resumed knitting after that 20-year hiatus, she has progressed rapidly from beginner to sought-after designer. Her patterns have appeared in the online magazine *Knitty.com*, in *KnitScene* (Art Deco Beret, Fall 2007) and *Interweave Knits* (Roza's Socks, Spring 2007), and many others are available for sale on her blog. In addition to her own projects, she finds the time to do sample and test knitting for several other designers, all of whom admire her precision and speed. Not wanting to spread herself too thin, she distributes most of her designs through Grumperina.com and only a few on Ravelry, where her Odessa hat has been made by more than 3,000 Ravelers, her Jaywalker socks by more than 7,000, and her Shifting Sands Scarf by nearly 800. That said, she appreciates Ravelry for many things and marvels at how quickly the site has become intertwined with the knitting community.

When she creates her own designs, her greatest desire is for them to "flow organically from beginning to end." For example, edge stitches must act as natural extensions of the main pattern. No abrupt transitions are allowed. "The pattern has to be just so, otherwise I'm not satisfied." A remarkably intuitive designer, she can visualize what the stitches will do and what the overall effect will be even as she maps out each new stitch combination. She does not usually plan out her designs on paper but prefers to swatch until she is satisfied with the results. Then she determines whether to turn her creation into a hat or a scarf, or perhaps a pair of socks. On the rare occasion that she does take notes, "it's scary to go back and look at them after I've put them aside for a while! It's like, what was I thinking? They make no sense if I come back to them later. I can't always figure out what I intended to do."

Sometimes, she imagines a project as a gift for a specific person. For example, "I've designed three hats for my little cousin, Sarit. She's adorable but she loses hats on a yearly basis, which is why I've made her so many." With her recipient in mind, Kathy works out the shape and style, and then considers how best to design it to suit the wearer. At other times, it is the yarn itself that suggests a design, such as the Lubov stole here. Both the yarn's feminine color and the resulting delicate lace project suggested this Russian woman's name, which means "love" in Russian.

There will be no comfortable rut for this designer-blogger; she recently completed a shawl using detailed Japanese knitting charts, and on her list of yet-to-be-conquered skills Kathy includes steeking, cable-intensive Aran sweater design, and crochet. In addition, she has earned a reputation as an excellent test knitter of other designers' patterns, and those requests come to her often. Her living room contains a bookcase that is packed with binders of knitting patterns, stitch dictionaries, and other craft books. "I never sit in front of the bookshelf and say there's nothing here that inspires me. The day will never come when I can say I've done everything."

It is fortunate that she knits fast, because her knitting for hire includes several intricate lace projects. She can typically complete a lace scarf in just a couple of days, so her productivity seems mind-boggling to the average knitter. "Just when I think that's it—I have twelve things lined up and I can't take on any more, that's when number thirteen comes along." With a full-time job, she knits at night and on weekends. She remembers her graduate school days fondly, at least in terms of knitting. "When I was a grad student, I'd wake up and knit. Now, I wake up and go to work, then I come home exhausted—but I have to knit anyway."

LUBOV SCARF
by Kathy Veeza

The ardent color of the yarn and the scarf's softness and warm embrace all contribute to its name, Lubov, which means "love" in Russian. The scarf begins and ends with airy borders, which are connected by a series of diamond motifs. The diamonds are solid in the center of the scarf, to keep the neck warm and protected, and gradually transition to a more ornate and delicate version toward the ends of the scarf, where the airy borders organically emerge. As a cost-effective project, Lubov makes a single skein of this luxurious yarn go a long way.

Difficulty: Intermediate
Skills used: Basic increasing and decreasing, basic lace, following a chart

SIZE

Finished Measurements
12½" wide and 74" long

MATERIALS

- Sundara Yarn Fingering Silky Merino (50% silk, 50% Merino; 500yd per 150g); color: Flaming Flamingo; 1 skein

- US 5 (3.75mm) needles, or size needed to obtain gauge

- US 7 (4.5mm) needles

- Tapestry needle

GAUGE

24 sts and 28 rows = 4" in St st on smaller needles

20 sts and 27 rows = 4" in patt st on smaller needles

PATTERN NOTES

Following the chart instructions as written will produce gradual transitions in your scarf—from airy to solid and back to airy again. However, you may choose to mix and match the charts for a different effect. For example, leaving the borders as is but using Chart E throughout will result in a more solid, substantial scarf.

DIRECTIONS

Using larger needles, loosely CO 67 sts. Switch to smaller needles and work the body of the scarf as follows:

Work Chart A 36 times—72 rows completed.

Work Chart B 1 time—74 rows completed.

Work Chart C 4 times—138 rows completed.

Work Chart D 4 times—202 rows completed.

Work Chart E 5 times—282 rows completed.

Work Rows 1–8 of Chart E 1 time—290 rows completed.

Work Rows 9–16 of Chart D 1 time—298 rows completed.

Work Chart D 3 times—346 rows completed.

Work Rows 1–8 of Chart D 1 time—354 rows completed.

Work Rows 9–16 of Chart C 1 time—362 rows completed.

Work Chart C 3 times—410 rows completed.

Work Rows 1–10 of Chart C 1 time—420 rows completed.

Work Chart F 1 time—422 rows completed.

Work Chart A 36 times—494 rows completed.

BO using larger needles. Weave in all ends. Soak thoroughly, then stretch and pin to shape and allow to dry.

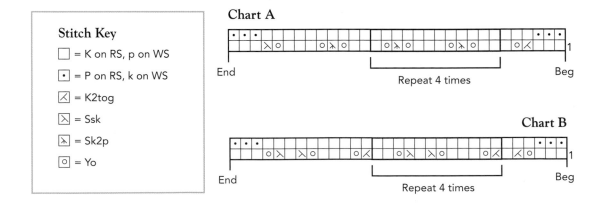

Stitch Key

☐ = K on RS, p on WS

· = P on RS, k on WS

⟋ = K2tog

⟍ = Ssk

⅄ = Sk2p

○ = Yo

Chart A

End / Repeat 4 times / Beg / 1

Chart B

End / Repeat 4 times / Beg / 1

Chart C

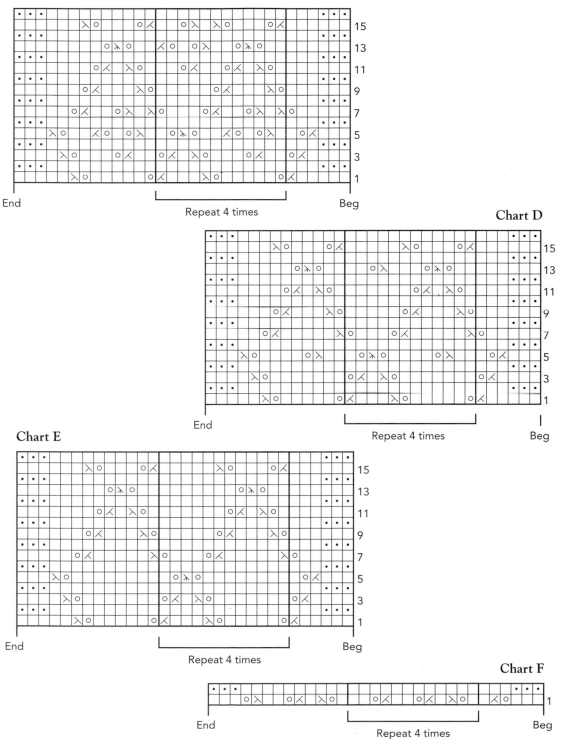

End

Repeat 4 times

Beg

Chart D

End

Repeat 4 times

Beg

Chart E

End

Repeat 4 times

Beg

Chart F

End

Repeat 4 times

Beg

STANDARD KNITTING ABBREVIATIONS

[ ]	work instructions within brackets as many times as directed		p	purl
* *	repeat instructions between asterisks as directed		patt	pattern
"	inch(es)		pm	place marker
alt	alternating (every other)		p2tog	purl 2 stitches together
beg	begin/beginning		psso	pass slipped stitch over
BO	bind off		pwise	purlwise
C1	color 1, color 2, etc. (for colorwork)		rem	remain/remaining
CC	contrasting color		rep	repeat/repeating
cn	cable needle		rev St st	reverse stockinette stitch
CO	cast on		RH	right hand
cont	continue/continuing		rnd(s)	round(s)
dec	decrease/decreasing		RS	right side
dpn(s)	double-pointed needle(s)		skp	slip 1, knit 1, pass slipped stitch over
foll	follows/following		sk2p	slip 1, k2tog, psso
g	gram		s2kp	slip 2, knit 1, psso
inc	increase/increasing		sl 1	slip 1 stitch (purlwise)
k	knit		sl 1 kwise	slip 1 knitwise
k2tog	knit 2 stitches together		ssk	slip 2 stitches as if to knit, then knit those two together through the back loops
kwise	knitwise		st(s)	stitch(es)
LH	left hand		St st	stockinette stitch
m	meter		tbl	through the back loop
M1	make 1		tog	together
M1L	make 1 left		WS	wrong side
M1R	make 1 right		wyib	with yarn in back
M1p	make 1 purl		wyif	with yarn in front
MC	main color		yd	yard(s)
mm	millimeter		yo	yarn over
oz	ounce			

SPECIAL TECHNIQUES

Backward Loop Cast-On: *Create a loop with the working yarn and place it on the needle backward so it cannot unwind. Repeat from * for the required number of stitches.

Buttonhole: A simple two-stitch buttonhole (as specified in Joan McGowan-Michael's Kimberly cardigan pattern, page 57) is worked as follows: After measuring the place where you want the buttonhole, k2tog, yo. On the return row, purl the stitch created by the yarnover. Continue to work these small buttonholes at evenly spaced intervals along the garment's buttonband.

Cable Cast-On: Make a slipknot and place it on the left needle. Insert the right needle into that stitch as if to knit, wrap the working yarn around the needle, and pull the loop through the stitch toward you. Place that stitch back on the left needle, twisting the stitch so that the left side of that second loop sits on the back side of the left needle.

Next, insert the right needle between the two stitches on the left needle. Wrap the working yarn around the right needle as if to knit, and pull the yarn through to make a new stitch. Twisting slightly, place the new stitch back on the left needle. Continue for desired number of stitches, always inserting the right needle between the last two stitches on the left needle.

I-Cord: Using a short circular needle or two double-pointed needles, cast on the number of stitches specified in the pattern. Knit one row. Do not turn. Slide the stitches to the other end of the needle. Pull the working yarn tightly across the back of the knitted stitches, and knit them again. Repeat until the I-cord has reached the desired length.

Joining New Yarn: Although there are many methods to join a new ball of yarn, my favorite is simply to work to the end of a row, leaving a tail of the finished skein. Start the new ball at the beginning of the next row, pulling up on the tail end of the old skein to maintain proper tension. This avoids unsightly double thicknesses, knots in the middle of a row, and the possibility of splitting in spliced yarns.

If the working yarn is not bulky, I sometimes knit both the tail end of the old skein and the beginning of the new skein together for extra security in the first few stitches, then weave in the remaining tails when the knitting is complete.

Grafting & Kitchener Stitch: This technique is most commonly used for grafting sock toes so that the seam is invisible, appearing to be a continuous row of stockinette stitch. It has other uses as well, such as the underarm seams of sweaters knitted in the round. My favorite mini-tutorial on Kitchener stitch is in Nancy Bush's *Knitting Vintage Socks* (Interweave Press, 2005). It is paraphrased here:

Place the stitches to be seamed on two separate knitting needles held together with the tips pointing to the right. Cut the working yarn to a length of about 12"–18", and thread this tail onto a tapestry needle. Working back and forth between the two rows of stitches on the knitting needles, maneuver the tapestry needle as follows:

Step 1: As if to purl, bring the threaded needle through the first stitch on the front needle. Leave this stitch on the needle.

Step 2: As if to knit, bring the threaded needle through the first stitch on the back needle. Leave this stitch on the needle.

Step 3: As if to knit, bring the threaded needle through the first stitch on the front needle again (same stitch), and slip this stitch off the needle. As if to purl, bring the threaded needle through the next stitch on the front needle (which has moved into the first position). Leave this stitch on the needle.

Step 4: As if to purl, bring the threaded needle through the first stitch on the back needle again (same stitch), and slip this stitch off the needle. As if to knit, bring the threaded needle through the next stitch on the rear needle (which has moved into the first position). Leave this stitch on the needle.

Repeat Steps 3 and 4 until no stitches remain on the needles.

Long-Tail Cast-On: With a length of yarn (estimate up to 1" for each stitch to be cast on), make a slip-knot and place it on the right needle (this cast-on method uses one needle only). Place the thumb and index finger of the left hand through the ends of the yarn so that the working yarn is around the index finger and the tail is around the thumb. Hold the yarn in place with your other fingers and turn your hand palmside up, making a "V" of yarn. *Bring the needle up through the loop on the thumb, pick up the first strand around the index finger with the needle, and drop back down through the loop on the thumb. Drop the loop off the thumb, and, placing the thumb back into the "V" position, tighten the resulting stitch on the needle. Repeat from * for the desired number of stitches.

Pick Up and Knit: This technique is used to pick up stitches from the edge of a garment in order to add a button band or collar. It is standard to pick up the required number of stitches on the appropriate section of the garment, adjusting count as necessary to ensure that pieces match up evenly, and knit the row of picked-up stitches separately.

For the traditional method along a shaped edge such as a neckline, work from the right side and from right to left. Insert the tip of the needle between the last and the second-to-last stitches, wrap yarn around the needle, and draw it through. Pick up and knit roughly three stitches for every four rows of the work. Make adjustments to the stitch count as necessary to ensure that the picked-up edge will lie flat.

To pick up stitches along a bound-off edge, work from the right side and from right to left. Insert the tip of the needle into the center of the stitch just below the bind-off edge, wrap working yarn around the needle, and draw it through. Pick up one stitch for every bound-off stitch to match stitch count.

Provisional Cast-On (Open or Invisible): This temporary cast-on method uses waste yarn and is ideal when you will need to access the bottom loops of your cast-on row later in the project, such as when you will add an edging or border to a lace shawl. I'm a fan of

Vicki Square's excellent instructions in *The Knitter's Companion* (Interweave Press).

Start by knotting a length (a yard or so) of waste yarn to your working yarn. Ideally, the waste yarn will be the same weight as your main yarn, but in a contrasting color. With a knitting needle in your right hand, hold the knot against the needle with your right thumb. Hold both yarns in your left hand, main yarn over the needle and waste yarn over your thumb. As in the long-tail cast on method, insert the right needle up into the waste yarn on your thumb, around the main yarn on your index finger, and back down through the waste yarn loop on your thumb. Slide your thumb out of the loop and pull the needle to firm the tension. Repeat until you have cast on the correct number of stitches. When the time comes to pick up the open stitches, clip the waste yarn out of each stitch using fine, sharp scissors. Place each resulting open stitch on a needle.

The Crochet Chain Stitch method used in Jared Flood's Woodsmoke Scarf project is another provisional cast-on technique worth mentioning here. For this method, use an appropriately sized crochet hook and a length of waste yarn to work a length of loose chain stitch. Then, using the project needles and the working yarn, pick up and knit one stitch through the underside bump (the back loop) of each chain until the correct number of stitches has been worked. When you are ready to work the project's edging or border, release the crocheted chain and pick up the resulting "live" knitted stitches onto a needle.

Reading Charts: Read charts from right to left. Lace motif and colorwork repeats are customarily bordered in a contrasting color on the chart for ease. Unless otherwise indicated, wrong side rows are not specified in charts.

Short-Row Shaping/Wrap and Turn (W&T): Used to create shaping in garment pieces such as collars, short-row shaping is accomplished as follows: On the knit side of the work, bring the working yarn to the front as if to purl. Slip the next stitch onto the right needle, bring the working yarn to the back as if to knit, and slip the stitch back onto the left needle. Turn the work. On wrong side rows, reverse the wrapping directions of the working yarn.

Three-Needle Bind-Off: Often used to give a neat and virtually invisible join to shoulder seams, this method requires a third needle in the size of those used to knit the garment. Place the live stitches that will form both sides of the shoulder seam onto two separate needles. Hold the garment pieces right sides together. Using a third needle, place the tip through the first stitch on both the front and back needles, and knit them together. Knit the next stitch in the same manner, and pass the first knitted stitch over the second. Continue until all stitches have been bound off.

YARN AND NOTION RESOURCES

YARN RESOURCES

ALCHEMY YARNS OF TRANSFORMATION
www.alchemyyarns.com
Featured in Foxgloves and Silke Jacket

BERROCO, Inc.
www.berroco.com
www.Info@berroco.com
*Featured in Johnny Rotten Jacket and
    Sprouting Cloche*

BEAVERSLIDE DRY GOODS
www.beaverslide.com
*Featured in Global Cable Coat and
    Woodsmoke Scarf*

BLUE MOON FIBER ARTS
866-802-9687
www.bluemoonfiberarts.com
Featured in Helix Socks

BLUE SKY ALPACAS
888-460-8862
www.blueskyalpacas.com
*Featured in Delysia Camisole and
    Milk Maiden Pullover*

CASCADE YARNS
www.cascadeyarns.com
*Featured in Lace Flower Pin and Kimberly
    Cardigan*

CLASSIC ELITE YARNS
www.classiceliteyarns.com
*Featured in Krookus Cardigan and
    Tulip Peasant Blouse*

FEARLESS FIBERS
fearlessfibers@comcast.net
www.fearlessfibers.com
Featured in Sockstravaganza

HANDMAIDEN FINE YARNS
www.handmaiden.ca
Featured in Origami Shrug and Seaweed Vest

LORNA'S LACES
www.lornaslaces.net
*Featured in (It Comes in) Waves Pullover and
    Textured Tam and Mitts*

MALABRIGO YARN
www.malabrigoyarn.com
*Featured in Lenina Cap and The Orchid
    Thief Shawlette*

PATONS
888-368-8401
www.patonsyarns.com
Featured in Lace Flower Pin

ROWAN YARN
Distributed by Westminster Fibers
800-445-9276
www.knitrowan.com
www.westminsterfibers.com
*Featured in Koukla Cardigan and
    Lace Flower Pin*

SCHAEFER YARN COMPANY
800-367-9276
www.schaeferyarn.com
Featured in *Working All the Angles Blanket*

SUBLIME YARNS
Distributed by Knitting Fever, Inc.
www.knittingfever.com
Featured in Button Tunic

SUNDARA YARN
www.sundarayarn.com
*Featured in Chutes and Ladders Socks
    and Lubov Scarf*

WOOLEN RABBIT
www.thewoolenrabbit.com
Featured in Hydrangea Neckwarmer

BUTTON RESOURCES

Global Cable Coat: Buttons from Jay Beesmer of Wooden Treasures (www.woodentreasures. etsy.com)

Button Tunic: Machine-washable resin buttons by Gail Hughes, and available for this project through the cocoknits website (www.cocoknits.com)

Koukla Cardigan: Buttons from Britex Fabrics in San Francisco, CA (www.shopbritexnotions.com)

Krookus Cardigan: Buttons from designer's personal collection

Johnny Rotten Jacket: Buttons from Windsor Button in Boston, MA (www.windsorbutton. com)

Textured Tam and Mitts: Buttons from designer's personal collection

Knitting bags (shown above) available from
Jordana Paige (www.jordanapaige.com)

DESIGNER CONTACT INFORMATION

Wendy Bernard
Knit and Tonic
knitandtonic.net

Connie Chang Chinchio
Physicsknits
www.conniechangchinchio.com

Kat Coyle
Coiled
www.katcoyle.com

Jared Flood
Brooklyn Tweed
www.brooklyntweed.net

Chrissy Gardiner
Knittin' Mom
http://knittinmom.blogspot.com/

Norah Gaughan
Berroco Design Studio
http://blog.berroco.com/

Teresa Gregorio
CanaryKnits
http://canaryknits.blogspot.com/

Jennifer Hagan
Figknits
http://www.jenhagan.com/

Angela Hahn
Knititude
http://knititude.com/

Anne Hanson
Knitspot
http://knitspot.com/

Stefanie Japel
Glampyre Knits
www.StefanieJapel.com

Kirsten Kapur
Through the Loops
http://throughtheloops.typepad.com/

Jessica Marshall Forbes and Casey Forbes
Ravelry site
www.Ravelry.com

Joan McGowan-Michael
White Lies Designs
http://whiteliesknits.wordpress.com/

Mari Muinonen
Madebymyself
http://madebymyself.blogspot.com/

Shannon Okey
Knitgrrl
http://www.knitgrrl.com/

Ruth P.
Woolly Wormhead
http://woollywormhead.squarespace.com/

Jordana Paige
http://jordanapaige.com/

Clara Parkes
Knitter's Review
http://www.knittersreview.com/

Kristi Porter
The Domestic Sphere
www.domesticsphere.com

Sean Riley
http://personalknitter.com/

Hilary Smith Callis
The Yarniad
http://www.theyarniad.blogspot.com/

Ysolda Teague
Ysolda Knits
http://ysolda.com/wordpress/

Kathy Veeza
Grumperina
http://www.grumperina.com/knitblog/

Ann Weaver
Weaverknits
http://weaverknits.blogspot.com/

Melissa Wehrle
Neoknits
http://www.neoknits.com/

Julie Weisenberger
Cocoknits
http://www.cocoknits.com/

ACKNOWLEDGMENTS

No book is truly a one-person project, and *Brave New Knits* is no exception. This book would not exist but for the creative talents and unrivaled generosity of the contributing designers whose blogging exploits inspire and inform knitters everywhere. I am grateful to all of you for "getting" why this book needed to be written. Thank you for sharing your blogging and designing experiences with me, and most of all for the garments and accessories of exceptional beauty that you created for these pages. Special thanks must go to Jess Marshall Forbes and Casey Forbes, the brilliantly creative founders of Ravelry.com, for giving knitters worldwide a home on the Web.

Meredith Hays recognized the value of this book to the knitting community, and Karen Bolesta and Chris Gaugler at Rodale Inc. had the vision and enthusiasm to make it happen. For their confidence in me and excitement about knitwear design and blogging personalities, I thank them. Kristi Porter ensured the technical accuracy of the book's patterns, responding to all questions with calm assurance. Erin Slonaker, Lois Hazel, and Peggy Greig dotted all the editorial Is and crossed all the charting and schematic Ts, striving for error-free perfection in both prose and patterns. Jared Flood's stunning photography lends a cohesive style to the diverse projects in these pages, revealing the common ground among 26 highly individual designers. And special thanks to Ursula Krogermeier for last-minute knitting of the Chutes and Ladders Socks. It has been a pleasure to work with all of you.

The book's wide variety of projects was made possible by the generosity of more than a dozen yarn companies. I thank them for donating such splendid yarns and for suggesting the perfect fibers to do each project justice.

Tony and Rachel have always believed that there was a book in me, and they encourage me to keep knitting even when my obsession with yarn and needles threatens to take over every spare corner of our home. I love you both up to the sky and back again.

Author Julie Turjoman and photographer Jared Flood

ABOUT THE AUTHOR

In search of a new hobby many years ago, Julie Turjoman wandered into a yarn shop. There, after admiring some particularly gorgeous hand-dyed yarn and fantasizing about the sweater it could become, she persuaded the owner to teach her the basics. More than 20 years and hundreds of skeins later, Julie writes, designs knitwear, and blogs at www.julieturjoman.com. Her designs have been published in *Interweave Knits* and *Twist Collective*, and in the book *Vampire Knits* (Potter Craft, 2010), and will appear in *Knitting in the Sun for Kids* (Wiley, 2011). She lives in the San Francisco Bay area.

STANDARD YARN WEIGHT SYSTEM

Categories of yarn, gauge ranges, and recommended needle and hook sizes

Source: Craft Yarn Council of America

www.YarnStandards.com

Yarn Weight Symbol & Category Names	0 Lace	1 Super Fine	2 Fine	3 Light	4 Medium	5 Bulky	6 Super Bulky
Types of Yarns in Category	Fingering 10-count crochet thread	Sock, Fingering, Baby	Sport, Baby	DK, Light Worsted	Worsted, Afghan, Aran	Chunky, Craft, Rug	Bulky, Roving
Knit Gauge Range* in Stockinette Stitch to 4 inches	33–40** sts	27–32 sts	23–26 sts	21–24 sts	16–20 sts	12–15 sts	6–11 sts
Recommended Needle in Metric Size Range	1.5–2.25 mm	2.25–3.25 mm	3.25–3.75 mm	3.75–4.5 mm	4.5–5.5 mm	5.5–8 mm	8 mm and larger
Recommended Needle in U.S. Size Range	000–1	1 to 3	3 to 5	5 to 7	7 to 9	9 to 11	11 and larger
Crochet Gauge* Ranges in Single Crochet to 4 inch	32–42 double crochets**	21–32 sts	16–20 sts	12–17 sts	11–14 sts	8–11 sts	5–9 sts
Recommended Hook in Metric Size Range	Steel*** 1.6–1.4 mm	2.25–3.5 mm	3.5–4.5 mm	4.5–5.5 mm	5.5–6.5 mm	6.5–9 mm	9 mm and larger
Recommended Hook U.S. Size Range	Steel*** 6,7,8 Regular hook B–1	B–1 to E–4	E–4 to 7	7 to I–9	I–9 to K–10½	K–10½ to M–13	M–13 and larger

* GUIDELINES ONLY: The above reflects the most commonly used gauges and needle or hook sizes for specific yarn categories.

** Lace weight yarns are usually knitted or crocheted on larger needles and hooks to create lacy, openwork patterns. Accordingly, a gauge range is difficult to determine. Always follow the gauge stated in your pattern.

*** Steel crochet hooks are sized differently from regular hooks—the higher the number, the smaller the hook, which is the reverse of regular hook sizing.

INDEX

Underscored page references indicate boxed text. **Boldface** references indicate photographs.